OBJECTIFYING MOTIF

ADVANCES IN OBJECT TECHNOLOGY SERIES

Dr. Richard S. Wiener
Series Editor

Editor
Journal of Object-Oriented Programming
Report on Object Analysis and Design
SIGS Publications, Inc.
New York, New York

and

Department of Computer Science
University of Colorado
Colorado Springs, Colorado

Additional Volumes in Preparation

OBJECTIFYING MOTIF

CHARLES F. BOWMAN

SoftWright Solutions, Inc.
Suffern, New York

SIGS
BOOKS

New York

Library of Congress Cataloging-in-Publication Data

Bowman, Charles F.
   Objectifying Motif / Charles F. Bowman.
      p.   cm. — (Advances in object technology ; 10)
   Includes bibliographical references and index.
   ISBN 1-884842-13-5 (pbk. : alk. paper)
   1. Object-oriented programming (Computer science) 2. C++
(Computer program language) 3. Motif (Computer file) I. Title.
II. Series.
QA76.64.B69 1995
005.13'3—dc20   95-22142
                                                      CIP

PUBLISHED BY
SIGS Books
71 W. 23rd Street, Third Floor
New York, New York 10010

Design and composition by Kevin Callahan
Cover design by Jean Cohn
Printed on acid-free paper.

SIGS Books ISBN 1-884842-13-5
Prentice Hall ISBN 0–13–234436-x

Printed in the United States of America
99 98 97 96 95   10 9 8 7 6 5 4 3 2 1
First Printing August 1995

TO MY CHILDREN
Charles, Michael, and Nicole

You can do anything if you try

ABOUT THE AUTHOR

CHARLES F. BOWMAN is a principal of SoftWright Solutions, Inc., a consulting and training firm specializing in relational, GUI, object-oriented, and client/server technologies.

Mr. Bowman has had over 16 years' experience developing software systems and applications. As an independent consultant, he has designed and developed numerous GUI applications in both the procedural and object-oriented paradigms. In addition, as part of his consulting practice, he develops courseware and training materials in a wide-range of subject matter for both public and on-site delivery.

Mr. Bowman is a popular speaker who has lectured throughout the United States and Canada, as well as the United Kingdom, France, and Germany. His lecture topics include Creating New Widgets, Objectifying Motif, Object-Oriented Analysis and Design, Client/Server Design and Development, and Multiparadigm Development. He was also selected as a featured speaker for Borland's nationwide Client/Server Tour that took place throughout January of 1995.

As an Adjunct Lecturer for both St. John's University and the City University of New York, he has taught at both the undergraduate and graduate levels. Mr.Bowman has published a wide range of articles for many prestigious journals and magazines. He is a regular columnist for both *The X Journal* and *Client/Server Developer.* In addition, he is editor-in-chief of *The X Journal* and series editor for the Managing Object Technologies series of SIGS Books. Mr. Bowman's first book was *Algorithms and Data Structures: An Approach in C* (Harcourt Brace, 1995). His third book is due to be published by SIGS Books in the fall of 1995.

A graduate of New York's prestigious Brooklyn Technical High School, Mr. Bowman holds a B.S. degree in computer science from St. John's University and an M.S. degree in computer science from New York University.

FOREWORD

OUR HOPE FOR SOLVING the software crises in the next decade centers around the object-oriented paradigm, human-oriented user interfaces, and computer-aided software engineering (CASE). The basic idea underlying the CASE technology is the use of tools to provide automated assistance in performing software development and maintenance tasks. With the use of CASE tools, software development can be speeded up and software quality can be improved.

Although CASE tools are being used to increase productivity by automating many activities—especially many of the labor-intensive, clerical-type software tasks—they are far from addressing and automating the entire system life-cycle process. System development tasks are made more complex by the need to apply information technology to model "real world" business and organizational problems. This requires that information systems professionals and users be able to work together in solving identifying problems and modeling the environment.

The trend for the next decade is for system developers to spend more of their time defining the business or organizational system environment and for CASE tools to take over more of the implementation function. This means that analysis techniques will become more important and must grow and change to be able to specify complex applications.

The future of computing is a battle with complexity. While the complexity of business and organizational environment is constantly growing, no place has this battle been more apparent than in the development of user communication, or the user interface, with the system. Graphical user interfaces (GUI) have radically changed the way people interact with computer systems. The development of user interfaces was almost totally ignored by researchers of traditional and structured paradigms. Object-oriented development methods provided a unique opportunity to view the user interface as a class of standard objects that could be reused by application developers. Developing user interfaces using the object-oriented paradigm holds the promise of reducing the difficulty of coding user interfaces, aiding in managing complexity, minimizing maintenance, simplifying customization, and encouraging reuse.

Two approaches—one evolutionary and the other revolutionary—are being taken toward the implementation of the object-oriented paradigm. The evolutionary approach attempts to integrate object-oriented constructs with traditional methods; the revolutionary approach contends that these methods cannot be reconciled and that traditional and structured approaches should be thrown out. The evolutionary approach reduces the learning curve and is the fundamental approach of this book.

The author of this book discusses new, powerful analysis techniques based on the object-oriented behavior paradigm. User interface models (specifically, X-based and Motif) complement and extend traditional (legacy), structured, and object-oriented paradigms, and they offer a method to better capture and meet user requirements.

To use these sophisticated new GUI tools, system developers need a firm grounding in the set of principles, derived from the object-oriented paradigm and C++ language (extensions to C), that serve as the foundation for this new development environment. *Objectifying Motif* provides this foundation. Its unique approach to describing the object-oriented paradigm, extensions to the C programming language for C++, and in-depth discussions of X-Windows and Motif provide a unique and valuable service to the system's developer. This, coupled with extensive examples and a full-featured application framework (Motif Windows Library), provide the developer or student with a complete foundation for present and future development needs.

The examples found in *Objectifying Motif* are based on the author's expertise and extensive work background, giving the book a practical as well as a theoretical grounding. This allows the reader to immediately apply the material presented to either a development exercise or an academic exercise

Systems developers in the next decade will be challenged more than ever to sharpen their problem-solving skills. Understanding the real world in which systems are used and developing abstract models that can be implemented by object-oriented paradigm is the best way to build the right system for the user.

—Fred Strauss
Assistant Professor, Dowling College

PREFACE

THE ADVENT OF GUIS

Graphical user interfaces (GUIs) have revolutionized the way people interact with computers. GUIs have brought computers to the mainstream by creating the perception that computers are the tools, not the problem. One of the more popular GUI packages is the X Window System. Originally developed as part of Project Athena at the Massachusetts Institute of Technology, X is a device-independent software system that allows programmers to design and implement GUI-based applications on a variety of platforms. It has gained a large following in recent years due to its portability and performance.

However, for all their benefits, GUIs have one drawback: they are tedious, if not outright difficult, to code. Programmers must deal with a myriad of details to complete even the simplest of interfaces. To compound the problem, when they complete the interface, developers realize that they have done just that: completed the interface. They must still develop the rest of the application.

One of the ways to minimize the complexity of any system is to increase the level of abstraction. We can achieve this in the X environment through the use of the Xt toolkit and widgets sets. Widgets are self-contained screen components such as push buttons, scroll bars, menus, etc. One of the more popular widgets sets is called Motif. We can use Motif widgets in combination to create custom GUIs. This reduces the amount of interface code programmers must develop.

THE PROMISE OF OBJECTS

Despite their advantages, toolkits and widgets sets merely reduce the magnitude of the problem, they do not overcome it. Moreover, interfaces are only one facet of a complete program. As noted above, programmers must also write the application behind the GUI. This, too, has become more complex. Due mostly to technological advances in hardware, we are now solving problems that we would not have even attempted just a few years ago. As a result, what we really need is an all-encompassing tool that will address application complexity in its entirety. That is, both the GUI and the back-end.

Enter Object-oriented (OO) methodologies. OO programming techniques fundamentally alter the way we develop systems. Rather than concentrate on procedures, we focus on objects and abstractions. Objects encapsulate complex programming elements in simple-to-use components. These components can then serve as building blocks to construct large-scale applications more efficiently and accurately. Used correctly, the OO paradigm holds the promise of managing complexity, minimizing maintenance, simplifying customization, and encouraging code reuse.

One of the more popular object-oriented programming languages is C++. C++ is a powerful, multiparadigm tool that provides a complete and efficient implementation of the OO model. Moreover, because of its lineage, it can combine easily with libraries developed in C (such as X, Xt, and MOTIF).

OBJECTIFYING MOTIF

Object-oriented programming is a powerful weapon in our development arsenal. However, as with any tool, we must learn how to harness it. Enter *Objectifying Motif*. In this text, we demonstrate powerful techniques through which we can encapsulate Motif widgets and features in C++ classes. We show you, step-by-step, how to create class hierarchies that combine the best features of both paradigms. Moreover, we will show you how to develop a complete, fully-featured *Application Framework* that we call MWL (Motif Windows Library). This framework can serve as a foundation for all present and future development needs. More importantly, you can apply the ideas and concepts presented in this book to other object-oriented languages and graphical environments as well.

The ideas and techniques contained in this book are based on work performed by the author for several clients. Although scaled down for pedagogical reasons, the book contains a complete implementation of the MWL library. It also contains many practical examples based on the author's experience in this field.

STRUCTURE

The book is divided into three sections. Section I is appropriately entitled *Beginnings.* It provides overviews of all the tools we will use throughout the remainder of the text.

Section II, *Introduction to Object-Oriented Analysis and Design,* describes a hybrid and practical approach to OO design and development. It introduces an example program (a calculator) to highlight the techniques contained in the section. We will return to the example several times throughout the remainder of the text.

Section III, *The MWL Library,* uses the knowledge gleaned from Sections I and II to create a complete, functioning applications framework. It describes how we can realize all the benefits of OO development in a Motif environment.

CODING EXAMPLES

There are many practical coding examples presented throughout the text. This includes both the MWL library and examples of its use. All classes are fully-functional and may be used as written. In addition, the book contains two appendices. Appendix A is a complete listing of the MWL library. Appendix B contains the source listing for a complete, functioning calculator constructed using MWL. It serves as an excellent and practical example of the programming techniques demonstrated herein.

ACKNOWLEDGMENTS

ALTHOUGH ONLY ONE NAME appears on the cover, many people have graciously assisted me with this project. I gratefully acknowledge all the efforts of the following people: Peter Arnold, Deirdre Auton (nee Griese), Michael Blum, Kevin Callahan, Sarah Hamilton, and Karen Tongish.

This project has benefited greatly from all of their assistance. Nonetheless, the author assumes full responsibility for any oversights or omissions contained in the text.

I would also like to thank my family. Yes, I know that almost all authors thank their families. However, I can honestly state that, in my case, this is not pro forma—they really deserve it. My three wonderful children Charles, Michael, and Nicole are a constant source of joy and inspiration. I love them dearly. And Florence, my wife, is more than just a spouse. She is my friend and confidant, critic and agent, colleague and conscience. She does more for me than I have a right to ask. A mere 'thank you' seems so inadequate—the fact is, I would be lost without her—Thanks Kid!

Charles F. Bowman
Suffern, NY
March 1995

CONTENTS

PART 2
INTRODUCTION TO OBJECT-ORIENTED ANALYSIS AND DESIGN

Chapter 7—An Introduction to OO Analysis and Design   115

Chapter 8—Redesigning the Calculator   131

PART *1*

BEGINNINGS

P ART 1 LAYS THE FOUNDATION for the goal of this text: *Objectifying Motif.* Though necessarily brief, this section acquaints the reader with the important concepts covered later in the text. The topics we cover include introductions to X, Xt, Motif, C++, and object-oriented programming. In addition, we describe the basic mechanics involved with combining the GUI and OO paradigms. Readers familiar with one or more of the subject areas should feel free to omit appropriate chapters.

1

INTRODUCTION

1.1 THE ADVENT OF GUIS

During the lifetimes of most readers of this book, there have been a number of significant technological advances in the computer industry. Among the most important has been the advent of the graphical user interface (GUI).

As its name implies, a GUI is a user interface based on graphics and icons, rather than the line-oriented styles of traditional terminals. Ironically, GUIs did not become popular because of their aesthetic marvel or technical wizardry, but because of their more humble qualities: GUIs made computer systems accessible to the masses. GUIs increase productivity and facilitate the transfer of information. As a result, people view computers as problem-solving tools that assist, rather than hinder, their efforts.

However, as with most things in life, these benefits do not come without a cost. Although easy to use, GUI-based applications are not easy to develop. Programmers spend a disproportionately large percentage of their time coding interfaces for GUI applications. Moreover, the very design of GUI-based applications differs from that of traditional models. Historically, application interfaces have been program driven. That is, users respond to program prompts.

By contrast, GUI-based applications are user-driven. Armed with the mighty mouse, users can select any program option at any time. This places an additional burden on application developers in that they must responded to user requests in an order determined by the user, rather than the programmer.

1.2 The X Window System

One of the more popular GUI interfaces is the X Window System. X is a device-independent software system that allows programmers to design and implement portable GUI-based applications. Since its initial release, X has grown substantially in popularity and use and has become the de facto standard GUI for the mini-computer environment.

1.3 OSF/Motif

Unfortunately, X-based applications are tedious, if not outright difficult, to implement. To simplify matters, a programmer's toolkit was developed that supports the creation of self-contained screen components called *widgets*. As we will see in Chapter 2, programmers can use widgets as building blocks to design and implement GUI interfaces in the X environment. This greatly reduces the effort programmers must expend developing the interface.

Motif is one of the more popular widget sets. Developed by the Open Software Foundation (OSF), Motif provides a set of reusable screen components that are easy to use and that maintain a consistent look-and-feel across applications. Motif has become the de facto standard widget set for the X environment.

1.4 The Advent of Object Technology

Traditional development techniques have become overburdened by the complexity of today's applications. As an industry, we are addressing (and solving!) problems that we would never have attempted just a few years ago. Applications have become so complex that one individual can no longer understand all design and implementation subtleties.

As a result, business and software development companies have become mired in maintenance. In an effort to manage complexity, many companies are discovering (or should we say *rediscovering*) the power of object-oriented (OO) development techniques. OO methodologies provide many advantages over their traditional counterparts. We will discuss the OO model in great detail in Chapter 3, but here are just a few of the reasons this paradigm is finding favor in so many environments:

- OO methodologies allow humans to think in a very natural way. That is, the object-oriented paradigm more closely reflects the we solve problems in the real world.

- The object model supports a modularized approach to system development.

- Object-oriented development techniques achieve a greater degree of code reuse (as compared with traditional methodologies).

1.5 C++

As previously mentioned, object-oriented technologies are not new. Yet, despite their obvious advantages, their use is just now becoming wide-spread. There are many reasons why the OO revolution has been slow in coming. One of the most important is the inertia caused by existing technology. Companies have a large investment is what we now call *legacy systems*. Naturally, they are reluctant to rewrite all of their existing applications with each new technological achievement. Some of their concerns include:

- The cost of rewriting the world (or at least their portion of it).

- The cost of maintaining two different technologies (if they do not chose to rewrite all existing applications).

- The cost of hiring new people and/or retraining the existing employee pool.

- Existing products and tools are both known and stable.

- Existing technologies come replete with well-defined analysis and development techniques and the tools to support them. OO is a comparatively young methodology and the tool base is meager.

What our industry needed was a tool that would allow organizations to migrate to the OO world in a more pedestrian manner. Enter C++. C++ enjoys a lineage from C, a very popular third-generation programming language (3GL). In fact, C++ is essentially a superset of ANSI C. Thus, C shops could purchase an OO compiler (C++) and not make any changes to existing applications. In effect, they merely have to change compilers. Thus, companies are afforded a relatively safe migration path: buy a C++ compiler and begin using C++ constructs as opportunity permits.

C++ also benefits from its C lineage in another way. It can handle all the "low-level" tasks that C handled so well. Thus, system designers could use the more advanced features of the grammar and still rely on low-level capabilities being available when needed. In addition, C++ developers can draw upon the vast number of C-based libraries available today. In particular, we can link C++ programs with the X/Xt/Motif libraries used throughout this text. (Refer to Chapter 5 for details.) However, this in not to say that C++ is not a complete OO programming language. On the contrary, it supports all the constructs associated with OO development (refer to Chapter 4 for an overview). It just enjoys the benefits of being a multiparadigm tool.

1.6 GOALS OF THIS BOOK

Stated simply, the goals of this book are two-fold. First, we will show you how to combine two powerful development <$iparadigms>: GUI and OO. We would like to demonstrate that, if used correctly, the tools described in this book can create a whole that is greater than the sum of its parts. Second, and just as important, we will show ways to develop a so-called application framework that can serve as the basis for developing complex and sophisticated user interfaces.

1.7 PEDAGOGICAL TREATMENT

Unfortunately, this text cannot serve as a complete tutorial on X, Motif, object-oriented analysis and design, and C++ programming. The resulting tome would become prohibitively large. Yet to derive the maximum benefit from the material discussed in this book, you do need to understand all of these technologies. This begs the obvious question: how can we possibly reconcile these conflicting positions?

The answer is simple: We have divided the text into three distinct sections. Section I contains introductions and overviews of the important prerequisite topics: X Windows, Motif, the object-oriented model, and the C++ programming language. Although necessarily brief, these chapters are fairly comprehensive and provide an adequate foundation for the material that follows.

Section II describes a synthesized approach to object-oriented analysis and design. It is a complete tutorial that describes each engineering activity and its associated deliverables. It includes a complete example—a functioning calculator—that demonstrates all of the design techniques.

Section III describes how we can *Objectify Motif;* that is, it describes the design and implementation of an OO-based application framework called the Motif Windows Library (MWL). MWL is a complete class library that encapsulates X/Motif. Our discussion begins by describing the implementation of a set of foundation classes. We then describe how to build on those classes to create a complete, functioning application framework. Section III culminates with a reimplementation of the calculator program introduced in Section II.

The text also includes two appendices. Appendix A contains the complete source listing for the MWL classes. Appendix B contains a complete listing of the example calculator program implemented using MWL.

1.8 WHERE TO BEGIN?

If you feel comfortable with the basics of X/Motif and C++ development, feel free to skip one or more of the chapters in Section I. However, we recommend that everyone read Chapters 5 and 6, which contain basic information used throughout Sections II and III.

2

OVERVIEW OF X/MOTIF

2.1 GRAPHICAL USER INTERFACES

Graphical user interfaces (GUIs) are based on graphics and icons, rather than the line-oriented approach of traditional CRTs (cathode ray tubes). It is somewhat of an understatement to note that GUIs are fast becoming the standard for user-oriented applications. Users prefer GUIs for many reasons, including:

- Program interfaces are more consistent across applications.

- GUIs are attractive and promote a pleasant work environment.

- Visual control elements (such as icons) provide users with the perception that they control program features directly.

- GUI-based programs are user-driven (rather than the other way around).

- People find GUI-based applications easier to learn and use.

2.2 THE X WINDOW SYSTEM: THE NICKEL TOUR

2.2.1 A Brief History

One of the more popular GUIs is the X Window System (X for short.) Originally developed as part of MIT's Project Athena in 1984, X is a device-independent software system that allows programmers to design and implement portable GUI-based applications. Since its initial release, X has grow substantially in popularity and use, and is now supported by a consortium of industry manufacturers.

2.2.2 Client-Server Architecture

The architecture of X is based on the *client-server* model. Under this model, we divide applications into separate program components. Each component either provide services to or draws upon the services of other components. If a component provides a service, it is called, surprisingly enough, a *server; clients* are components that use one or more services. Typically, a server may service more than one client; similarly, clients can draw upon the services of more than one server.

Because clients and servers are separate processes, they require some formal communication method. Typically, this is referred to as an application programming interface (API). The API formalizes the types of requests and responses cooperating processes may exchange. Cooperating programs exchange messages through some communication medium, which can range from message queues, if both processes coexist on the same processor, to a full-fledged network protocol, if the processes reside on different processors (e.g., TCP/IP).

As depicted in Figure 2.1, one common implementation of the client-server architecture involves databases. In this model, the database "engine" functions as the server. Client applications interact with the server to access and update tables, query records, etc.

There are several misconceptions regarding the client-server architecture. First and foremost, servers are not limited to database engines. The services that servers can provide are as diverse as the applications that use them. Examples include communication, print, multimedia—to name a few.

Another misconception is that *server* implies hardware. On the contrary, most servers are software-based and often run on a variety of platforms.

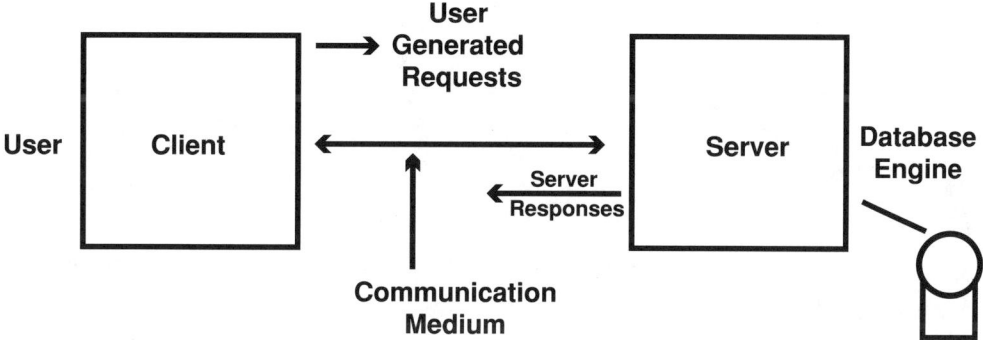

FIGURE 2.1. The client-server architecture.

The client-server architecture embodies several unique advantages including:

- A wide range of clients that have access to the same set of services. For example, Figure 2.2 depicts a LAN wherein several types of hardware platforms share resources provided by a server running atop a UNIX-based platform. This implies that character-, MS Windows-, PM-, and X-based applications can all access the same resources.

- We can upgrade and enhance servers without affecting client programs (so long as the API remains unchanged).

- Clients can draw upon the services of several servers to complete an application task.

- We can tune client and server processes to maximize individual potential.

As mentioned previously, X applications are based on the client-server architecture. As depicted in Figure 2.3, a single user seated at an X-station can execute several applications on multiple machines. Each client process is associated with one or more windows appearing on the screen. Under the X model, users interact with a server running at their workstation. The server informs client processes of events that have taken place in their windows through a standard set of messages called, oddly enough, *events*. (We discuss this in more detail later in the chapter.)

As an aside, don't worry if the X-based client-server model appears backwards; it's not you. The user *does* interact directly with the server, not the client.

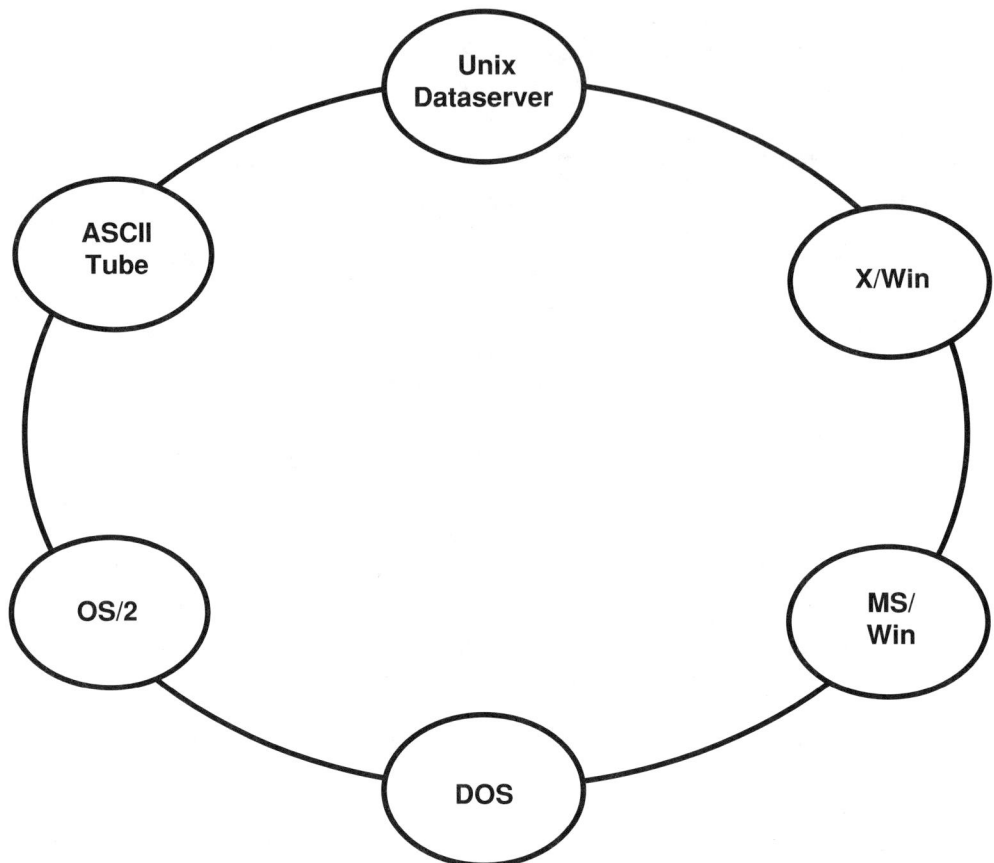

FIGURE 2.2. Sharable resources.

2.3 X PROGRAM DEVELOPMENT

2.3.1 *Window and Resource Management*

All application programs run as clients under the X model. One of the jobs of the server is managing display resources, including windows, cursors, fonts, etc. As a rule, clients request the creation of a given resource and, if successful, the server returns its XID (an X resource identifier). Clients use the identifier in all subsequent requests involving that resource. For example, when a client creates a window, the server returns a window ID. The client references

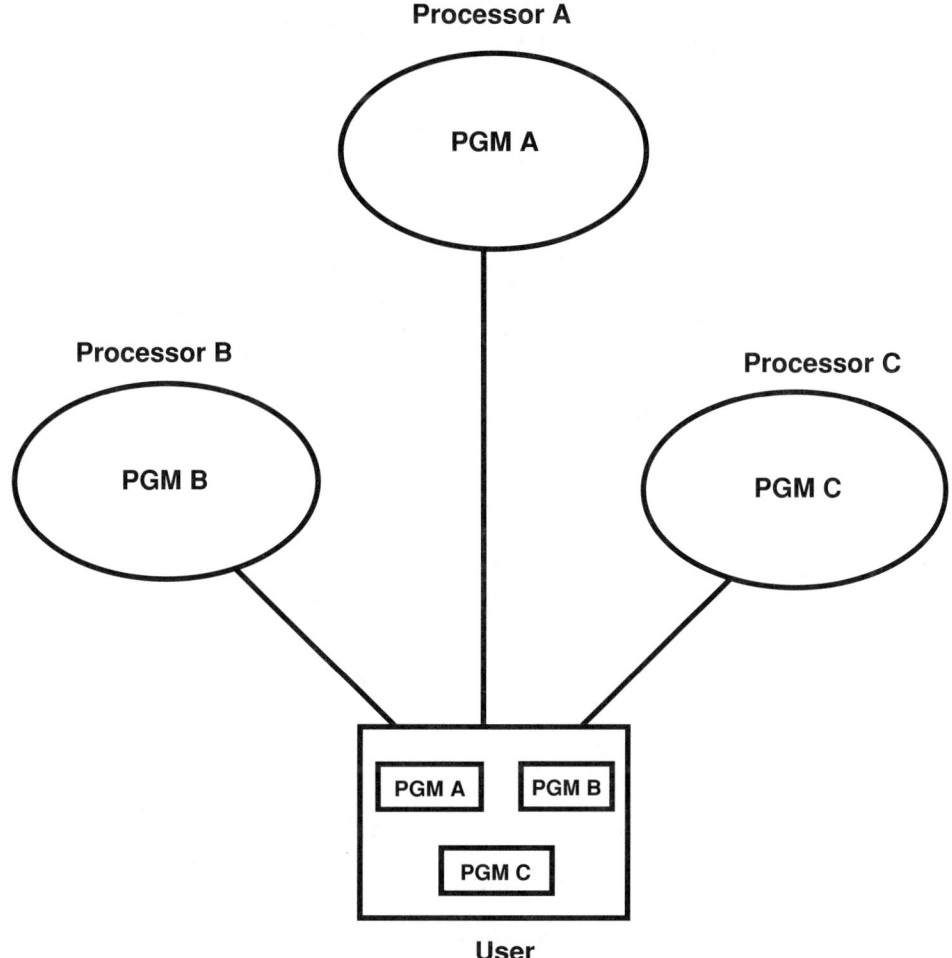

FIGURE 2.3. X-Based client-server model.

the ID whenever it needs to perform any action on that window (e.g., drawing). The following sections introduce and describe some important server-managed resources.

2.3.1.1 *Windows*

A *window* is a rectangular screen region that functions like, well, a window into an application. An X client will typically use many windows to construct

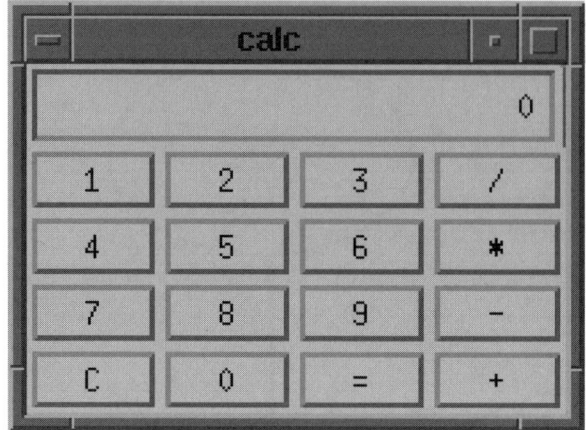

FIGURE 2.4. A Motif calculator.

its GUI. Indeed, one can think of a graphical interface as an appliqué of windows. As an example, please refer to the calculator program depicted in Figure 2.4. Each one of the screen components (buttons, display, etc.) is a window. Other examples of some not-so-obvious windows include scrollbars, title bars, menu buttons, and labels.

Windows share a number of common characteristics, including:

- Every window has a *parent*. That is, every window is created as a child of some other window. There is one exception: the *root window*. The root window has no parent; it is created by the server and fills the entire screen. We refer a window's lineage as its *instance hierarchy*.

- Windows have defined boundaries. This implies the following:

  - A child window must be completely contained within its parent's window.

  - Programs cannot draw outside window boundaries.

  - Windows cannot receive input (from the keyboard or the pointer) unless the pointer is positioned within its boundaries. (There is one exception to this last point—a *grab*—that we will ignore for the moment.)

- Windows have *geometry attributes*. A window's *origin* is its top, left-hand corner; by definition it has a coordinate value of $(0, 0)$. All other coordinates are integral values that represent the center of *pixels* (picture elements). The x coordinate increases toward the right (from the origin); the y coordinate increases toward the bottom. All measurements within windows, including height and width, are relative to the origin. A window's *position*—that is, the coordinate of its origin—is relative to its parent's origin.

- Windows may have borders. Borders are measured in pixels; a width of 0 indicates an invisible border.

- Windows have *depth*. This attribute is somewhat of a misnomer. Depth, in this case, does not measure the "thickness" of the window; rather, it indicates the number of bits available to display color (or shades of gray). The greater the depth, the larger the pallet.

- Windows have *input attributes*. That is, for each window, clients inform the server as to what events are of interest. The server will send a message to the client whenever a selected event occurs within a window.

- Windows are either *mapped* or *unmapped*. A map request instructs the server to make the window visible; an unmap request removes the window from the screen. Applications need not display all windows all the time. As an example, consider a popup menu. Although typically created by clients during program invocation, popup menu windows are usually only visible (mapped) when needed.

2.3.1.2 *Other Resources*
A number of other resources are managed by the server. They include:

PIXMAPS Pixmaps are another drawable resource available to X programs. Like a window, a pixmap is an array of pixels. However, unlike a window, servers cannot map pixmaps. That is, pixmaps are never visible. Rather, X clients use pixmaps as off-screen repositories for graphical images. When required, clients can copy a pixmap image directly into a window.

GRAPHICS CONTEXTS To implement a drawing request, the server requires quite a bit of information. For example, consider drawing a simple line. How thick should the line be? Should it be solid or dashed? What color should it be? Should the ends be round or square? Imagine how much information your program would have to send to the server with each drawing request.

To simplify matters, X servers create and manage a resource called a *graphics context* (GC). A GC contains all the information the server needs to render a drawing. Clients may create as many different GCs as required; then, when they want to draw, they need only pass to the server the ID of the GC they want it to use.

FONTS A *font* describes the size, shape, and style of a collection of (displayable) characters. Quite a number of fonts are available to X programmers. Most display text, but some display images (e.g., *cursors*).

COLORMAPS One of the most attractive elements of most X stations is color. Each pixel on a color X station displays the three primary colors—red, green, and blue (RGB for short)—in combination. Displays create distinct colors by varying the intensity of each RGB signal (e.g., from 0 to 256). For example, X stations create 'white' by using equal portions of all three primary colors. We call the set of all possible colors an X station can display its *gamut*. Thus, for RGB intensities ranging from 0 to 255, the gamut is 256^3 or 16,777,216 colors. However, many workstations limit the number of colors they can display at any one time. This constraint is based on the size of a resource called a *colormap*. Each index in the colormap contains values for each of the primary colors. For example, slot 10 could be 'Bisque' (red=255, green=228 blue=181), slot 25 could be 'Papaya Whip' (red=255, green=239, blue=213).

2.3.2 *Event-Driven Programming*

The design and development of an X window application differs from typical programming environments. Traditionally, programs drive users. That is, a program prompts the user for data, responses, etc., and will not proceed to the next processing step until the current one completes. However, in a windowing environment, users drive programs. Empowered by the mighty mouse, users can click anywhere on the screen. As a result, we cannot develop X clients using traditional methods. Rather, we must design and construct X clients that are responsive to user demands. This begs the question: How do programs "know" which button or screen element the user selected?

The server keeps clients informed by means of *events*, which are message packets that contain information regarding user actions. There are a number of different events for which the server can provide notification. Most are generated as a result of some direct user action (e.g., pressing a key or a mouse button). However, clients can also receive events from other clients (e.g., the window manager), or as a result of some indirect user action. For example, when the user moves one window and uncovers another, the server sends the newly visible window an *expose* event.

The preceding example underscores one of the basic tenets of the X environment: Clients are responsible for the contents of their windows. As a rule, servers do not take "snapshots" of windows when they become obscured. Thus, when exposed, clients must either recreate or restore the window's image.

2.3.3 The X Library

Figure 2.5 depicts a somewhat simplified view of the X programming environment. Clients make calls to Xlib functions. Xlib routines convert client requests into protocol packets, which they send to the server. The server interprets the requests and converts them into the specific tasks required to implement them on a particular display. Thus, to be proficient, programmers must understand all the calls provided as part of Xlib.

2.3.3.1 Sample X-Windows Program

To give you a feel for structure of X clients, Listing 2.1 contains the X version of the now traditional "Hello World" program. Figure 2.6 depicts its output.

```
1    /*
2    *         FILE:      hellox.c
3    *
4    *         FUNCTION:  Display a "Hello World" Message in X
5    */
```

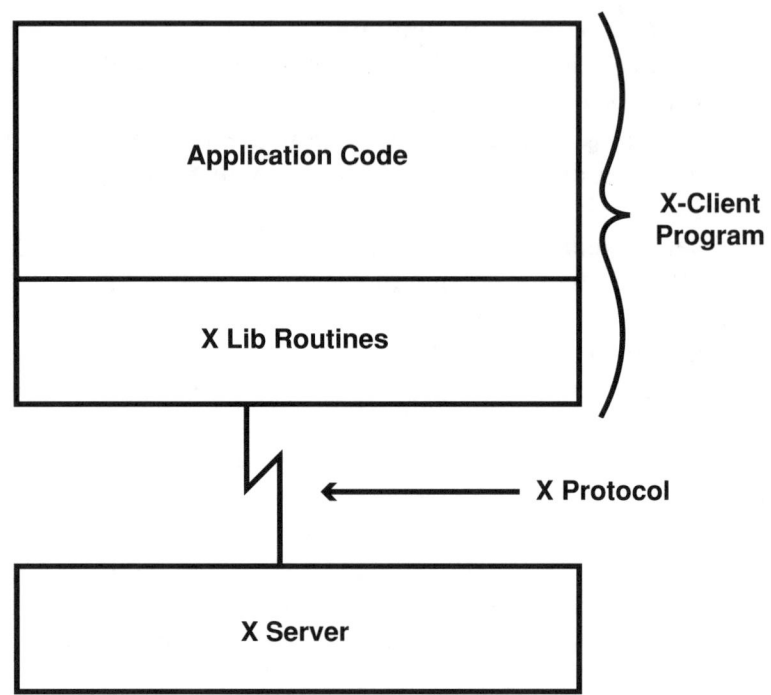

FIGURE 2.5. X programming environment.

```
 6
 7    #include <X11/Xlib.h>
 8    #include <X11/Xutil.h>
 9    #include <X11/Xresource.h>
10
11    int main( int argc,   char** argv )
12    {
13    char*        message = "Hello World";   /* Display Str    */
14
15    GC           gc;                /* A Graphics Context    */
16    int          screen;           /* The  Screen           */
17    Display*     display;          /* The  Display          */
18    Window       window;           /* The  Window           */
19    XEvent       event;            /* X Event Structure     */
```

```
20
21     XWMHints          wm_hint;          /* WM Hints              */
22     XSizeHints        size_hint;        /* Size Hints           */
23     XTextProperty     iconName;         /* Icon Name            */
24     XTextProperty     windowName;       /* Window Name          */
25
26     int               x = 50;           /* Geometry Values      */
27     int               y = 50;           /*           "          */
28     unsigned int      width = 250;      /*           "          */
29     unsigned int      height = 150;     /*           "          */
30     unsigned int      border = 10;      /*           "          */
31
32     unsigned long     blackpixel;       /* Black Pixel Value    */
33     unsigned long     whitepixel;       /* White Pixel Value    */
34
35     /*
36      *      Open the Display
37      */
38     display = XOpenDisplay( "" );  /* Use $(DISPLAY)            */
39
40     /*
41      *      Get the Default Screen
42      */
43     screen = DefaultScreen( display );
44
45     /*
46      *      Get Basic Pixel Values
47      */
48     whitepixel = WhitePixel( display, screen );
49     blackpixel = BlackPixel( display, screen );
50
51     /*
52               * Set Size Hints
53               */
54     size_hint.min_width = 250;
55     size_hint.min_height = 150;
```

```
56    size_hint.flags = PPosition | PSize | PMinSize;
57
58    /*
59                * Set WM Hints
60                */
61    wm_hint.flags = StateHint;
62    wm_hint.initial_state = NormalState;
63
64    /*
65     *    Create a Window
66     */
67    window = XCreateSimpleWindow( display, DefaultRootWindow(display),
68     x, y, width, height, border, blackpixel, whitepixel );
69
70    /*
71     *    Create & Set Name Properties
72     */
73    XStringListToTextProperty( &message, 1, &iconName );
74    XStringListToTextProperty( &message, 1, &windowName );
75    XSetWMProperties( display, window, &windowName, &iconName,
76            argv, argc, &size_hint, &wm_hint, NULL );
77
78    /*
79     *    Create a Graphic Context to Draw
80     */
81    gc = XCreateGC( display, window, 0, 0 );
82    XSetBackground( display, gc, whitepixel );
83    XSetForeground( display, gc, blackpixel );
84
85    /*
86     *    Select Input Events
87     */
88    XSelectInput( display, window, ButtonPressMask|ExposureMask );
89
90
91    /*
92     *    Map the Window
```

```
93     */
94     XMapWindow( display, window );
95
96     /*
97      *      Enter Event Loop & Process Events
98      */
99     while( 1 )
100          {
101          /*
102           *      Read the Next Event
103           */
104          XNextEvent( display, &event );
105
106          /*
107           *      Process the Event
108           */
109          switch( event.type ) {
110
111          case Expose:
112
113              /*
114               *      Draw the Message String
115               */
116              if( event.xexpose.count == 0 )
117                  XDrawImageString( display, window, gc,
118                          90, height/2,
119                          message, strlen(message) );
120              break;
121
122          case ButtonPress:
123
124              /*
125               *      Cleanup
126               */
127              XFreeGC( display, gc );
128              XDestroyWindow( display, window );
129              XCloseDisplay( display );
```

```
130
131                  /*
132                   *     Exit on any Button Press
133                   */
134              exit(0);
135          }
136      }
137  }
```

LISTING 2.1. "Hello World"—X style.

2.4 MOTIF AND WIDGETS

Although popular with users, programmers typically find X-based applications tedious (if not outright difficult) to construct. Indeed, some studies have
estimated that as much as 80% of the total programming effort required to
develop a GUI-based application is expended constructing the user interface.
Obviously, it would be in our own best interests to develop techniques to simplify this process. In the X world, the use of so-called widget sets has eliminated
some of the tedium.

FIGURE 2.6. Output of Listing 2.1.

2.4.1 The Intrinsics Toolkit

The Intrinsics Toolkit (Xt for short) is a set of programming tools that simplify the construction of GUI applications. Its goal is to alleviate much of the tedium associated with developing graphics-based programs. The easiest way to accomplish this is to prepackage common screen components such as scrollbars, push buttons, menus, dialog boxes, etc. Thus, client programmers can develop applications by selecting and grouping various components together to form an interface, rather than create and draw all of the components themselves.

Each prepackaged screen component is called a *widget*. (Yes, we've finally found a real use for the product used in all college economics classes.) We refer to a complete collection of screen components as a *widget set*. Xt forms the foundation for the construction and run-time support of widgets. However, in keeping with the stated philosophy of not defining policy, Xt does not provide any (displayable) widgets. Rather, it provides the mechanism to create reusable components.

2.4.2 The Motif Widget Set

The Motif widget set was designed and developed by the Open Software Foundation (OSF), a not-for-profit consortium that includes such notable companies as IBM, Hewlett-Packard, and Digital Equipment. Figure 2.7 contains examples of several Motif widgets.

The Motif design specification divides along two major sectors:

- A definition of the visible attributes of widgets (e.g., shapes, 3D effects. etc.)
- The style and interface of the input model (e.g., how users interact with screen elements.)

2.4.3 Example Motif Program

Listing 2.2 contains a Motif version of the "Hello World" program. Contrast it in terms of style and content with Listing 2.1. Figure 2.8 depicts the program's output.

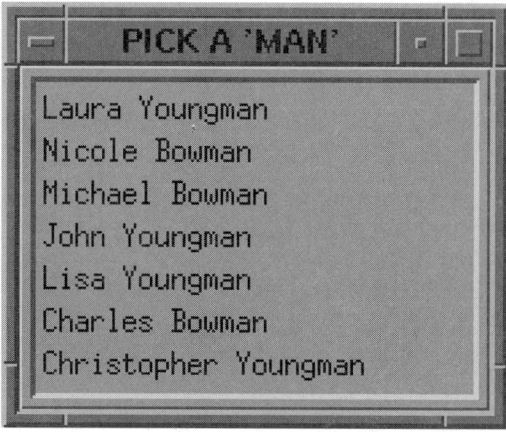

FIGURE 2.7. Motif widgets.

```
1     /*
2      *          FILE:      hellom.c
3      *
4      *      FUNCTION:     Display a "Hello World" Message in MOTIF
5      */
6
7     #include <stdio.h>
8     #include <stdlib.h>
9
10    #include <Xm/Xm.h>            /* Main Motif Header     */
11    #include <Xm/PushB.h>         /* XmPushButton Widget   */
12
13    /*
14     *      Define a Callback Routine
15     */
16    void exitCB( Widget w, XtPointer clientData,
                  XtPointer callData )
17    {
18    printf( "Good By World!\n" );
19    exit( 0 );
20    }
21
22    int main( int argc, char* argv[] )
23    {
24        Widget        pb;        /* Push Button Widget       */
25        Widget        top;       /* Top Level Shell Widget */
26        XtAppContext  app;       /* Application Context      */
27
28        int           i;         /* Count Num of Resources */
29        Arg           args[20];/* Resource Arg Array       */
30
31        XmString      pblabel;   /* Label for Push Button    */
32
33
34    /*
35     *      Initialize the X Toolkit
36     */
```

```
37    i = 0;
38    top = XtAppInitialize(
39          &app,                          /* App Context           */
40          "Hellom",                      /* Program Class         */
41          (XrmOptionDescList)NULL,       /* Program Options       */
42          0,                             /* Number of Options     */
43          (Cardinal*)&argc,              /* Number of Cmd Line Opts */
44          argv,                          /* Command Line Opts     */
45          (String*)NULL,                 /* Fallback Resources    */
46          args,                          /* Resource Arg Array    */
47          0                              /* Number of Resources   */
48    );
49
50    /*
51     *    Create Label for Push Button
52     */
53    pblabel = XmStringCreateSimple( "HELLO WORLD" );
54
55    /*
56     *    Create a PushButton Widget
57     */
58    i = 0;
59    XtSetArg( args[i], XmNheight, 50 ); i++;
60    XtSetArg( args[i], XmNwidth, 100 ); i++;
61    XtSetArg( args[i], XmNlabelString, pblabel ); i++;
62    pb = XmCreatePushButton( top, "pb", args, i );
63    XtAddCallback( pb, XmNactivateCallback, exitCB, NULL );
64    XtManageChild( pb );
65
66    /*
67     *    Realize Widgets
68     */
69    XtRealizeWidget( top );
70
71    /*
72     *    Enter Main Loop
```

```
73      */
74      XtAppMainLoop( app );
75      }
```

LISTING 2.2. "Hello World"—the Motif version.

As you peruse Listing 2.2, you will see how much simpler this version was to write. However, the question is, is it simple enough? We will answer that question throughout this book.

2.5 SUMMARY

GUIs are here to stay. They are favored by users and developers alike. In the open systems world, the X Window System has become a standard. Based on the client-server architecture, X allows users to execute an eclectic set of applications on their workstations. The down-side of GUI applications is that they are difficult to design and develop.

To overcome that difficulty, the X Consortium has developed widget sets. Widgets provide X developers with a reusable set of screen components that they can combine to form user-friendly interfaces. One of the most popular widget sets is Motif. Developed by the Open Software Foundation, it has become the de facto standard widget set for the X environment.

FIGURE 2.8. Output of Listing 2.2.

As we will see, however, the productivity gained by using widget sets is not enough. The complexity of modern-day applications is testing the limits of existing development methodologies. In the next chapter, we will begin to explore a more powerful development methodology based on the object model.

3

INTRODUCTION TO THE OBJECT-ORIENTED PARADIGM

3.1 SOFTWARE COMPLEXITY

The frenetic pace at which hardware technology has improved has stretched the limits of current software development methodologies. There are several reasons for this:

- Software systems are becoming more and more complex. We now have the processing power to address—and solve—problems that we would have considered too difficult just a few years ago. Examples include multimedia, high-resolution graphics, CAD/CAM, and full-motion video. The list is growing.

- As an industry, we have no objective metric for measuring complexity. That is, we have no method by which we can determine and quantify software complexity. Most organizations have found that program size (i.e., the number of lines of source code) is not a suitable metric. As a result, we as an industry do not have an accurate, deterministic technique to estimate development effort.

- Software applications must often satisfy conflicting requirements. A typical example is the trade-off between speed and size. Programs that store critical data in memory—as opposed to a secondary storage medium such as a disk drive—are usually faster, but the price you must pay is increased program size.

- Applications, even small ones, evolve over time. This not only adds to their complexity, it increases the difficulty of making additional modifications in the future. More importantly, without an accurate metric for complexity, we have no way to measure the "ripple" effect of program changes.

We can underscore the last point with the following example. Civil engineers would think you were crazy if you even considered modifying the support structure of a bridge once it was built. Yet, data processing professionals routinely do that to software architectures without so much as a second thought!

To summarize, software systems are becoming arbitrarily complex, to the point where one person cannot understand all design complexities and component interaction. Thus, if we do not get a handle on complexity, the software maintenance effort will overwhelm us.

This type of growth is not new. Consider that during the early days of telephony, switching engineers were concerned that the growth rate of the network could not keep pace with burgeoning demand. They predicted that at the projected rate of growth, they would need every person in the country to serve as operators to handle the anticipated call volumes. Ironically, they solved the problem rather ingeniously by doing precisely that. By allowing the user to dial numbers directly, they indeed made everyone an operator. In a similar manner, our industry must also find ways to place computing power in the hands of the people who need it.

3.2 COMPLEXITY MANAGEMENT

As alluded to above, complexity management is the one of the driving forces behind the science. If we want to solve ever-more complex problems, we must develop ways to manage complexity. Before we address complexity management from a software developer's point of view, we should examine the techniques by which humans handle complexity in general: abstraction, decomposition and hierarchy.

3.2.1 Abstraction

According to the dictionary, an *abstraction* is a thought or model apart from any particular instance or material object. Thus, in essence, an abstraction is a *view*. It defines the way we wish to think about an object or concept. All human thought is an abstraction of the real world in that we think in language, and in that sense, language shapes out thoughts. Yet language is an imperfect tool. It cannot accurately describe every facet of the real world.

Humans create abstractions at every conceptual level. For example, consider a simplified model of our industry:

- Chemical engineers create molecular models to grow silicon crystals.
- Electrical engineers create models of electron behavior to etch circuits on silicon.
- System designers combine circuit boards to build computer systems.
- Software designers create models of system architectures to develop software.
- Users view the application as a tool.

This example highlights an important point regarding the abstractions we create: they must have a *focus*. An effective abstraction includes only those features and attributes of specific importance to our model. It excludes all other nonessential elements. For example, an aircraft manufacturer might create several different models of its aircraft: one for wind-tunnel tests, one for safety features, one for passenger comfort, and so on. Each model will only include features specific to its purpose.

To further clarify our understanding, we can classify abstractions into three major groups:

> ENTITY An entity abstraction is a model of an object. We can create entity abstractions for tangible objects such as *car* and *flower* as well as for intangible concepts such as *account* and *order*.

RELATIONSHIP We can also create abstractions for the relationships that objects share. For example, a supervisor *manages* employees and a bank teller *works at* a branch.

ACTION We can also create abstractions for the actions or operations entities undertake. For example, employees are *transferred*, cars *accelerate*, and planes *land*.

Obviously, the use of abstraction in software development is not new. One very common example is a *stack*. However, the object-oriented paradigm allows us to more fully harness the power of abstraction. As we will see in Part II, object-oriented development techniques focus on the identification, design, and implementation of efficient, intuitive abstractions.

3.2.2 *Decomposition*

Decomposition is the process by which we divide large problems into smaller ones. This is often referred to as the *divide-and-conquer* approach. Decomposition allows us to partition a problem into manageable pieces. These pieces, in turn, can also be sub-divided into even smaller pieces. For example, consider writing an operating system. Viewed as a whole, such a program appears rather daunting. However, if we divide the program into its logical components—process management, device interfaces, memory management, etc.—the problem becomes more manageable. Figure 3.1 provides an example.

3.2.3 *Hierarchy*

Abstractions often share common attributes. For example, consider a *stack* and a *linked list*. A stack is essentially a restricted form of a linked list wherein insertions and deletions occur at only one end (called the *top*.) In effect, we can say that a stack is linked list with restricted insertions and deletions. Thus, to simplify development efforts, we could create the stack abstraction as an extension of the linked list abstraction.

In general, these two abstractions share a relationship that we term *is-a* or *kind-of*. For example, a rose *is a* flower; a jet *is a kind of* aircraft. In a typical application, we might find a number of abstractions that are related in this manner and form hierarchies. Figure 3.2 illustrates one example. Note that as we move down the tree the abstractions become more specific; as we move up, they become more general, less tangible.

3.3 COMPLEXITY MANAGEMENT IN SOFTWARE

Computer scientists take a more formal view of complexity management through *paradigms*. Paradigms are structures or models by which we attempt to organize, define, and solve problems. An effective software paradigm must include three major features: analysis techniques, design techniques, and implementation languages.

> **ANALYSIS TECHNIQUES** Paradigms must provide methods to analyze and define a problem. This is the conceptual framework upon which we will construct a solution.

> **DESIGN TECHNIQUES** Design techniques allow us to formulate a solution for the problem in terms of the paradigm.

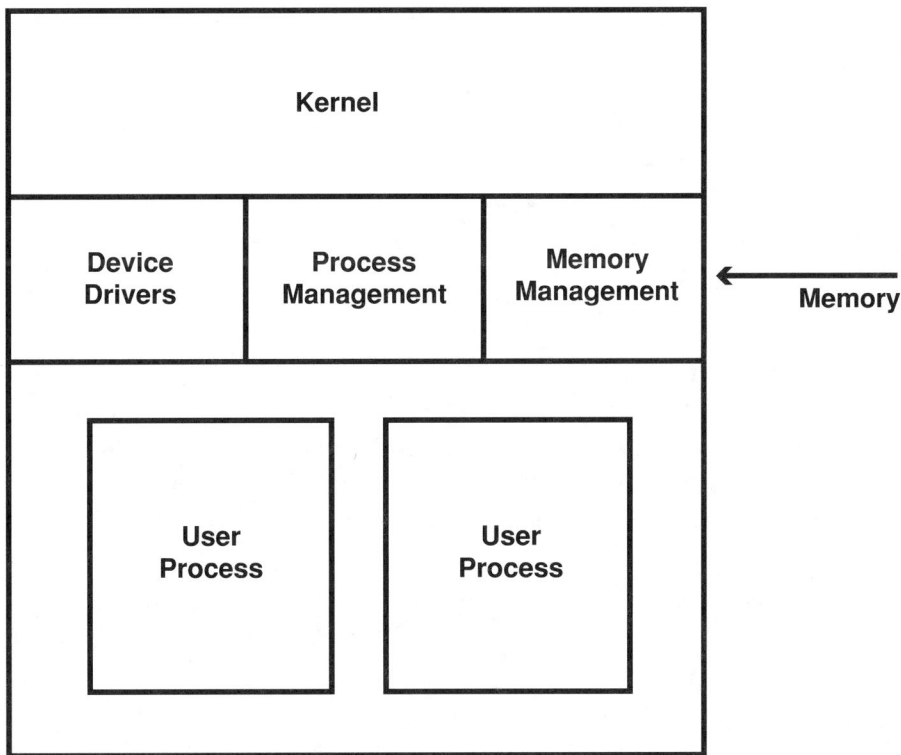

FIGURE 3.1. Operating system components.

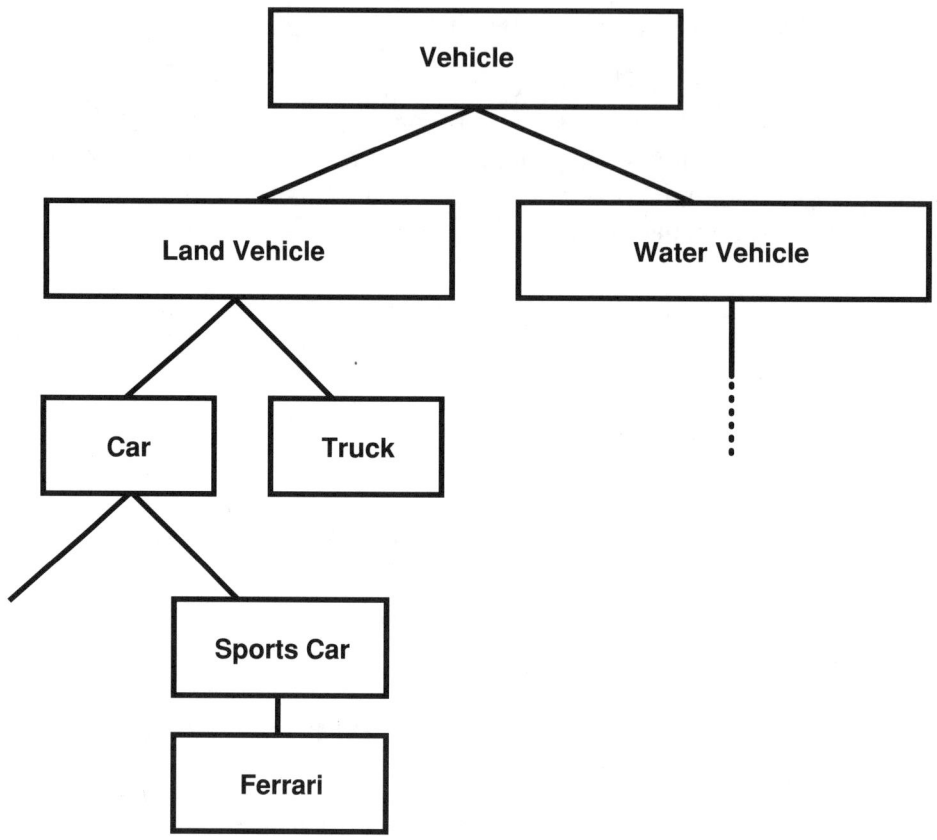

FIGURE 3.2. Example abstraction hierarchy.

LANGUAGES A paradigm must provide or support implementation languages. That is, we must have a way to implement the solution created in the design phase.

A number of paradigms are in use today. Examples include:

- Functional (LISP)
- Procedural (e.g., PL/1, C, ADA)
- Rule oriented (e.g., PROLOG)
- Object oriented (e.g., Smalltalk, C++, Eiffel)

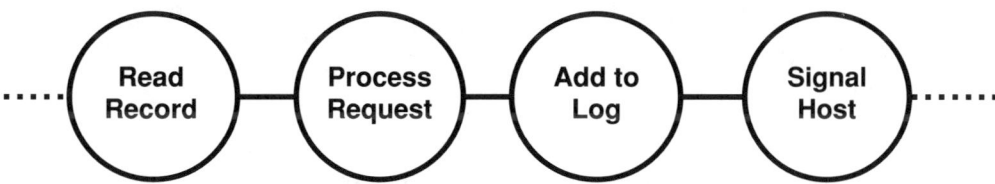

FIGURE 3.3. Process Flow Diagram.

Obviously, the main focus of this text will be the object-oriented paradigm. However, to gain clearer insight into the benefits of the OO paradigm, let's begin our discussions with the procedural paradigm.

3.3.1 *Procedural Paradigm*

As its name implies, the procedural paradigm focuses on the procedure. That is, when working within this model, our goal is the development of algorithms. As a result, when we review a set of system requirements, our focus is drawn to verbs (i.e., actions.) Thus, the subroutine becomes the level of abstraction. Figure 3.3 depicts a typical example.

The basic design approach for the procedural paradigm is *functional decomposition*. Using this methodology, we view problems as a set of actions that can be decomposed into subroutines. As a result, we tend to design top-down (i.e., divide and conquer) and develop bottom-up (as a check for proper design).

The procedural paradigm has a number of advantages:

- It encourages modularity.
- It is mature and is understood by a large number of developers.
- A large number of languages support it.
- Its design techniques are well understood.

However, it also suffers some disadvantages, including:

- Design emphasis is placed on procedure, not data. In reality, information (i.e., processed data) is more important than process.

- The solution set is not "well bounded." Give 100 programmers the same application specification, and you will likely receive 100 unique solutions.

- It is difficult to ascertain with any degree of accuracy the costs associated with any system modification (however modest).

As a result, many people question whether we have reached the limit of this model. In other words, many believe that the procedural paradigm cannot support the level of complexity attainable with future technologies.

3.3.2 Object-Oriented Paradigm

In the object-oriented model, the level of abstraction is, oddly enough, the *object*. When using OO methodologies, we concentrate our efforts on modeling real-world objects. Thus, we tend to concentrate our design efforts on "nouns" rather than verbs.

An object is a self-contained unit that contains both data and procedure. It interacts with other objects by sending messages to them. If a receiving object recognizes a message, it can "react" to it by invoking a *method*—more on this later. This is very much akin to the way objects behave in the real world. For example, humans are objects that send messages to each other (via speech, prose, visual stimuli, etc.) We respond to some, ignore others. An object's response to messages may vary with its state. For example, our response to a joke will vary with time or mood. A well-constructed object-oriented program is essentially a palette upon which objects interact naturally. Figure 3.4 depicts the anatomy of an object.

As we will see, the OO paradigm has many distinct advantages over its counterparts.

3.4 OBJECT-ORIENTED PROGRAMMING

It has been stated that objected-oriented programming merely enforces coding practices that we should otherwise adhere to in traditional development environments. Although that statement is essentially true, it does not tell the whole story. In fact, OO design, programming, and data management does provide many advantages over traditional development methodologies.

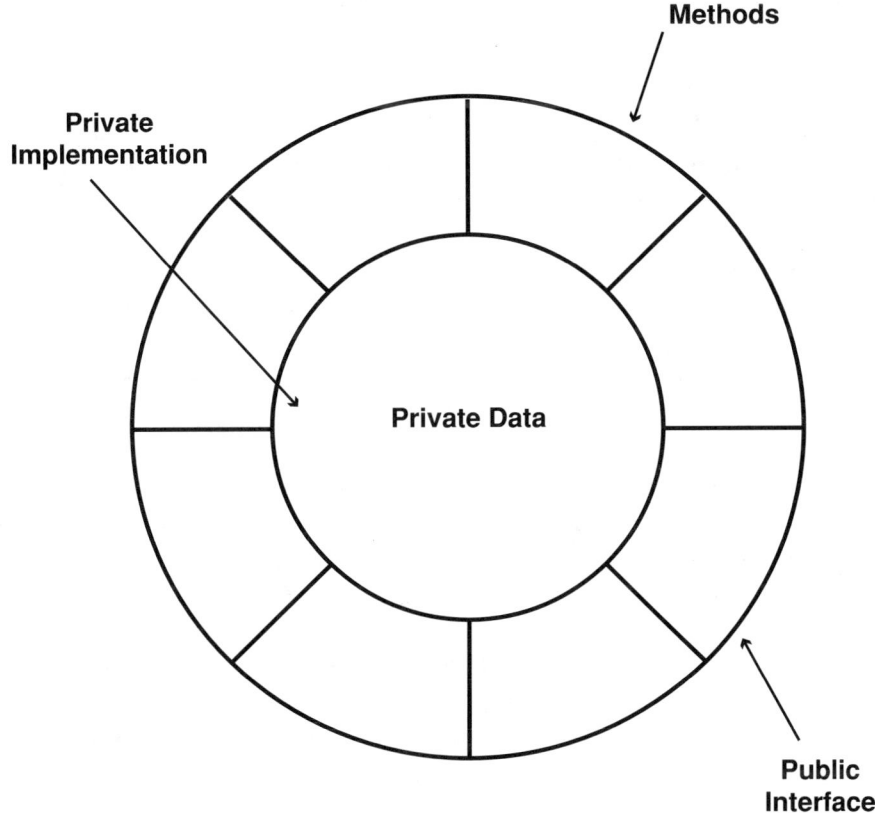

FIGURE 3.4. Anatomy of an Object.

3.4.1 *What Is Object Orientation?*

Using object-oriented methodologies, we attain solutions by modeling real world entities. In essence, the problem domain is viewed as an interacting set of objects. Using this paradigm, we develop solutions as follows:

- Identify the entities (objects) we wish to model.
- Describe the behavior of entities. As we will see, this means developing *classes*.
- Finally, we write programs that allow objects to interact naturally.

Before we can delve too deeply into OO development techniques, we must understand some of the important aspects of the model.

3.4.2 *Components of the Object Model*

Three major features distinguish the OO paradigm from its counterparts: *class, inheritance,* and *polymorphism.* If a programming language does not contain all three features, it is not object oriented. The following sections discuss these and several other aspects of the OO paradigm.

3.4.2.1 *Data Abstraction*

As mentioned previously, an abstraction is a thought or model apart from any particular instance or material object. In computer science, we apply this concept when we create abstract data types (ADTs). An ADT models real world objects and concepts. It denotes the essential characteristics of an object that make it unique (at least in terms of the particular application.) For example, it is not enough to say that we want to "model a car." Rather, we must determine the perspective from which we want to create our abstraction: aerodynamics, ergonomics, performance, etc. Furthermore, programmers should not have to make assumptions or allowances for the implementation or internal representation of the ADTs they use. That is, if we have achieved our goal, programmers should be able to think in terms of the abstraction, rather than the implementation of the abstraction. Obviously, if programmers must concern themselves with implementation details, they've lost the illusion created by the abstraction. In essence, the role of abstraction is to separate behavior from implementation.

3.4.2.2 *Class*

In traditional programming languages, compilers "know" how to construct the basic (i.e., built-in) data types. For example, when we code:

```
int i;
```

the compiler can construct i because it knows its structure. What if we wanted to declare an instance of a programmer-developed ADT such as a *car?* Obviously, to build such an object, the compiler must also understand its structure. That's where the concept of *class* comes into play. A class is a formal description of an abstraction. Classes describe every aspect of an abstraction that we wish to model in terms of some host programming language. Class is akin to the notion of *data type* in traditional programming languages. However, there is one important difference: classes contain code (i.e, behavior).

3.4.2.3 *Object*

An object is a specific instance of a particular class. It is the embodiment of an abstraction and contains both methods (procedures) and data. We call the process of creating an object *instantiation*. Each instance of an object is unique. That is, although objects of the same class share the same attributes, their state data is unique. For example, assume we have declared two integer variables i and j. If we were to assign i=6;, we would not affect the value of j. The same holds true for objects: If we change the state of object A, we do not affect object B.

Much as it is in the real world, it is the interaction of objects that solves problems in object-oriented programs. Loosely speaking, we can partition object-oriented programs into two sections. In section one, the program instantiates all required objects; in section two the objects interact naturally.

Note the symbiotic relationship the concepts of class and object share. We really cannot consider an object without regard to its class; nor can we define classes without regard to the objects they will represent.

3.4.2.4 *An Example*

As an example of these concepts, consider the abstraction "humankind." Assuming that Nature holds the formal class description, we are all instantiations of the class *Homo sapiens*. We humans share similar attributes that distinguish us from all other forms of life. Yet we are all unique and distinguishable from each other. Each of us contains our own state data embodied in our DNA and brain tissue.

3.4.3 *Message/Method*

As alluded to above, the goal of an object-oriented program is to allow objects to interact naturally. This is accomplished through the *message/method* paradigm. When object A wants object B to do something, A sends B a message. Messages can be of any type, and communicating objects need not be of the same class. If a receiving object recognizes a message, it may invoke a *method* in response. Methods are the behind-the-scenes procedures that manipulate an object's state.

Most classes provide a so-called public signature that defines the full range of messages to which objects of that type will respond. The public interface is extremely important: it defines the abstraction to *clients* (users of the class.) We can group methods into four types: constructors, destructors, accessors, and transformers.

3.4.3.1 *Constructors*

Constructors are methods invoked automatically whenever an object is created. They ensure that objects come to life in a "sane" state (i.e., all state variables are initialized and all required resources are available.) Typically, classes have several constructors; this provides clients with a choice of initial states for individual objects.

3.4.3.2 *Destructors*

The compiler invokes destructor functions automatically whenever an object goes out of scope. Destructors ensure that objects relinquish all allocated resources.

3.4.3.3 *Transformers (Mutators)*

Transformer methods change an object's state. As an example, consider implementing the classic stack in an OO environment. The typical *push* and *pop* operations would be two examples of potential transformer methods.

3.4.3.4 *Accessors*

Accessor functions report on the internal state of an object in a implementation-independent manner. For example, our stack class might include an accessor function that returns the value of the top element (without popping it.)

3.4.4 *Encapsulation*

Encapsulation (or information hiding) is the process through which we hide the implementation details from clients. As a result, clients can remain blissfully unaware of any "nasties" and can think solely in terms of the abstraction.

3.4.5 *Relationships*

Classes do not usually exist in isolation. Classes within a given problem domain are usually related in some way. We can categorize relationships into several types. (We will discuss only two here.) The first is a *has-a* or *part-of* association. This is an aggregation relationship that implies containment or inclusion. For example, a flower *has a* petal, a car *has an* engine, and a plane *has a* wing. In programming environments, we employ this type of relationship when we include one object inside another. For example, consider a record that contains a field which, in turn, contains sub-fields. As another example, Figure 3.5 depicts an employee object that contains several date objects.

The second type of relationship is termed *kind of* or *is a*. For example, a rose *is a* flower, a car *is a kind of* vehicle, a plane *is an* aircraft. This type of association is rather uniquely expressed in OO environments through a feature called *inheritance*. Inheritance defines a relationship wherein one class can acquire the structure and behavior of another class. For example, Figure 3.6 depicts a class hierarchy for employees in a typical company.

In OO terminology, "Employee" is a base or super class; "Management," "Technical," and "Hourly" are all derived (or sub-) classes; they all inherit behavior from a common base class. Thus, the features common to all employees reside in the "Employee" class; features unique to specific types of employees appear in individual derived classes. Inheritance trees can evolve. We can extend them at will and derive new classes from any existing class. For example, we could add an "Executive" class that is derived from "Management."

Figure 3.6 contains examples of *single inheritance*. That is, derived classes inherit from only one parent class. However, we might need to create a "Consultant"

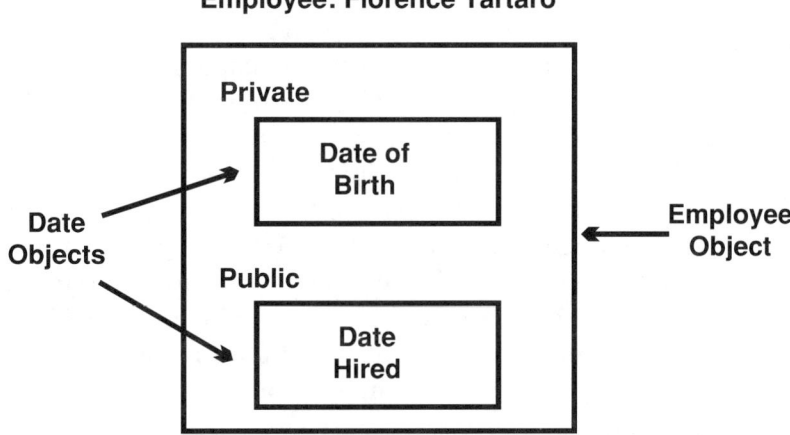

FIGURE 3.5. Example of a containment relationship.

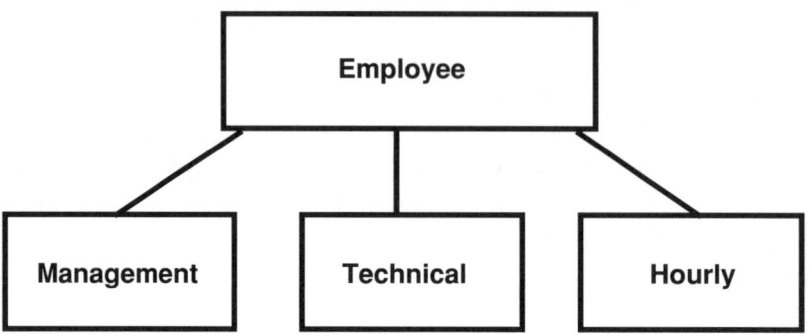

FIGURE 3.6. Example of an *is a* relationship.

class that could benefit from features contained in both the "Technical" and "Hourly" classes. Some OO environments provide *multiple inheritance*, which allows classes to inherit behavior from more than one parent class. If this functionality exists, we can construct lattice-like class hierarchies.

An important point to note is that inheritance does not imply that we can circumvent encapsulation. Base classes can deny derived classes access to private data. However, it does imply that objects are built from the ground up. For example, if D is derived from B, and we create an instance of D, constructors for both B and D will execute (in that order.)

3.4.6 Polymorphism

Polymorphism is a Greek term that literally means "many forms." Before we describe polymorphism in programming, let's discuss an example from the real world. Consider a manager in a development shop that has two types of employees, full-timers and consultants. The full-time employees use blue timesheets; consultants use red timesheets. Moreover, it's Friday and, as usual, everyone has forgotten to submit a timesheet. Polymorphism occurs when the manager walks up to an employee—any employee—and says, "Fill out your timesheet." The manager does not have to change the message for each different employee type. He or she just says, "Fill out your timesheet." On the other hand, each object should respond to the message uniquely. That is, employees know their "type," and each will select the appropriate timesheet.

This example highlights the two facets of polymorphism: the sender does not need to know the data type of the object to which it is sending a message; and receivers can respond uniquely to a given message. Conceptually, this is how objects interact in an OO-developed program. Sending objects can send messages to receiving objects without regard to data type, and receiving objects can respond to messages in ways specific to their type. In Chapter 4, we will see how C++ implements polymorphism using a technique called *dynamic binding*.

3.4.7 *Advantages of the OO Model*

The benefits of the object-oriented paradigm are numerous:

- The paradigm is well-suited to the human mind. It mimics the way we think. If we get the model right, clients can think in terms of the abstraction, not its implementation.

- The paradigm focuses on data (objects). Cooperating objects form solutions.

- We can more easily manage programming complexities that arise in today's systems.

- The paradigm fosters modularity and data hiding. This minimizes the negative effects of maintenance and feature expansion.

- Using inheritance and containment we can realize a greater degree of code reuse. In addition, class relationships provide a mechanism by which we can accurately model real-world behavior and associations.

- We can prototype classes and change (tune) their implementation later.

- Application programs tend to be smaller (most of the code is contained within classes).

- We can extend the capabilities of classes without affecting existing programs (so long as we do not modify the public signature).

3.5 SUMMARY

As an industry, we want to address and solve ever-more complicated problems. As a result, complexity is a driving force behind the science. From a hardware perspective, we have begun to achieve that goal. The price/performance ratio afforded by today's systems has allowed us to address problems that we might not have even considered just a few years ago.

Yet there is a major concern confronting us. From a software perspective, we must address the ways in which we can manage the complexity of large-scale system development. The current design and development methodologies do not seem up to the task. Object-oriented methodologies offer many solutions to today's problems and will likely be a driving force into the next century.

In closing, we should note that, traditional and object-oriented methodologies are not wholly incompatible. In fact, they come together quite nicely in the C++ programming language. In addition to its OO constructs, C++ also supports the procedural paradigm. Thus, it can serve as a migration tool for many organizations, especially those with experience in C. In the next chapter, we will introduce C++ and its implementation of the object-oriented model.

4

OVERVIEW OF C++

Despite a slow start, object-oriented development techniques are beginning to gain wide acceptance in the industry. This is no accident. Many development organizations have discovered that, although far from perfect, object-oriented development methodologies provide many distinct advantages over their traditional counterparts. Obviously, the intent of this text is to demonstrate how we can harness the power of the object-oriented paradigm to develop sophisticated GUI interfaces. To achieve this goal, we need a powerful, widely available OO language.

C++ was introduced in the early 1980s by Bjarne Stroustrup of AT&T Bell Laboratories. Developed as an extension of C, C++ is a complete object-oriented programming language. (C is retained as a subset of the C++ grammar.) In fact, its very name, C++, reinforces its evolutionary extension of the C grammar.

C++ supports all the major features found in OO languages, including classes, objects, encapsulation, and polymorphism. (Refer to Chapter 3 for a discussion of these terms.) In addition, because it is based on C, C++ supports traditional procedural programming constructs. As a result, it can serve as a powerful tool that supports multiparadigm development. Indeed, the current popularity of object-oriented methodologies may be due largely to the hybrid approach embodied within the C++ grammar. Most development organizations are reluctant to migrate new environments. The primary reason is cost. To do the job right, an organization must either absorb the expense of a complete rewrite of all existing code or assume the inherent costs associated with maintaining two (or more) separate development environments. A multiparadigm tool such as C++ can minimize the pain and effort associated with paradigm shifts.

The sections that follow describe the C++ programming language in some detail. Although far from complete, the discussions provide a more-than-adequate foundation for the needs of this text. (Refer to the bibliography for more complete references on C++.) We will begin our tutorial by describing the C++ features that make it a better C. We will follow that discussion with a description of the object-oriented features of the grammar.

4.1 A Better C

Before we address its support for the object-oriented paradigm, we would like to describe some C++ features that we can view as extensions to the C grammar. Although added to support the object-oriented paradigm, many of these language constructs, in and of themselves, are not object-oriented in nature. Viewed independently, they make C++ a better C.

To simplify our discussions, Listing 4.1 contains a simple C++ program that demonstrates many of these features. The program's output appears in Listing 4.2.

```
 1    #include <iostream.h>
 2
 3    //
 4    //         C++ Features: A Better C
 5    //
 6
 7    //
 8    //         Function Declarations
 9    //
10    void print( int );
11    void print( double );
```

```
12    void set_variable( int& );
13    void print_one_or_two( char *one, char *two = "DEFAULT" );
14
15    int main()
16    {
17        int i = 0;
18        double f = 3.14159;
19        const int k = 1024;    // Example of a const Variable
20
21        cout << "Program Begins\n\n";
22
23        //
24        //        Example of Stream I/O
25        //
26        cout << "\n    Example of Stream I/O\n";
27        cout << "\tFloat: " << 123.45 << "  Int: "    << 123
28             << "  Char: " << 'C'    << "  String: " << "A String"
29             << "\n";
30
31        //
32        //        Example of Default Function Arguments
33        //
34        cout << "\n    Example of Default Arguments\n";
35        print_one_or_two( "111" );
36        print_one_or_two( "111", "222" );
37
38        //
39        //        Example of Call by Reference
40        //
41        cout << "\n    Call by Reference\n";
42        cout << "\ti: Before: " << i << "\n";
43        set_variable( i );
44        cout << "\ti:  After: " << i << "\n";
45
46        //
47        //        Example of Function Name Overloading
48        //
```

```
49          cout << "\n     Function Name Overloading\n";
50          print( k );
51          print( f );
52
53          //
54          //        Example of Dynamic Memory Allocation
55          //
56          cout << "\n     Dynamic Memory Allocation\n";
57          int *iptr;
58          iptr = new int;                  // Allocate Storage
59          *iptr = 10;
60          cout << "\t*iptr = " << *iptr << "\n";
61          delete iptr;                     // Relinquish Storage
62
63          cout << "\nProgram Ends\n";
64          return( 0 );
65      }
66
67  //
68  //          Call by Reference
69  //
70  void set_variable( int &call_by_value )
71  {
72              call_by_value = 100;
73  }
74
75  //
76  //          Function Name Overloading
77  //
78  void print( int val )
79  {
80              cout << "\tInteger value is: " << val << "\n";
81  }
82
83  void print( double val )
84  {
85              cout << "\tDouble value is: " << val << "\n";
```

```
86    }
87
88    //
89    //        Default Function Arguments
90    //
91    void print_one_or_two( char *one, char *two )
92    {
93            cout << "\tFunction print_one_or_two():"
94                    << "\n\t\tOne:  " << one
95                    << "\n\t\tTwo:  " << two
96                    << "\n";
97    }
```

LISTING 4.1. C++ As a Better C.

```
1     Program Begins
2
3
4         Example of Stream I/O
5             Float: 123.45   Int: 123   Char: C   String: A String
6
7         Example of Default Arguments
8             Function print_one_or_two():
9                     One: 111
10                    Two: DEFAULT
11            Function print_one_or_two():
12                    One: 111
13                    Two: 222
14
15        Call by Reference
16            i: Before: 0
17            i:  After: 100
18
19        Function Name Overloading
20            Integer value is: 1024
21            Double value is: 3.14159
22
```

```
23          Dynamic Memory Allocation
24                *iptr = 10
25
26      Program Ends
```

LISTING 4.2. Output of Listing 4.1.

4.1.1 Stream I/O

Like C, C++ has no integral I/O capability. However, rather than using procedural libraries, C++ introduces `iostream` classes.* Note the differences as compared to classic C I/O. First, instead of `stdio.h`, the program includes `iostream.h`. Also, rather than using traditional function calls, the program uses something called `cout` and the left bitshift (`<<`) operators. The variable `cout` is a pre-instantiated object (of class `ostream`) that supports C++'s basic I/O capability. It is analogous to the standard output stream in C. As a result, you may redirect its destination in the usual manner.

You *insert* output into the `cout` stream using the `<<` operator. This operator, sometimes referred to as the *stream insertion operator,* accepts any integral values. For example:

```
float f;
int   i = 10;
char  *str = "Hello, World!\n";

cout << i;
cout << f;
cout << str;
```

Stream operators allow you combine multiple requests into a single statement. For example, the following code fragment

```
float f;
int   i = 10;
char  *str = "Hello, World!\n";

cout << i << f << str;
```

---

* Note that C++ programs can link to any function written in C. This includes the standard C library.

produces output identical to that of the previous example.

There are two other basic streams that you should know about. The first, `cerr` is used for diagnostic output and is analogous to `stderr`. The second, `cin`, is used for reading and is equivalent to `stdin`. You can use these streams as follows:

```
int    age;

cout << "Please enter your age:  ";
cin age;
if( age < 0  ||  age >> 200 )
{
        cerr << "You've got to be kidding!\n";
}
```

4.1.2 *Constants*

In addition to symbolic constants (e.g., `#define`), C++ supports a `const` type qualifier. When you include this qualifier as part of a variable declaration, the identifier becomes a "read-only" quantity. The following is a typical example:

```
const int max_windows = 15;
```

Note that because a `const` variable cannot change, you must supply an initial value (the compiler enforces this requirement). The compiler treats `const` variables as constant expressions. As such you may use them any where a constant expression may be used. The following code fragment contains an example.

```
const int max_buttons = 15;
          .

          .

          .

Widget    bottom_row[ max_buttons ];   // Permissible in C++
```

4.1.3 *Default Function Arguments*

C++ allows you to declare function arguments with default values. That is, when you invoke a function, you may omit arguments, and the compiler will supply default values. For example, consider the program given in Listing 4.3:

```
1    #include          <iostream.h>
2
3    void      some_function( int  j  =  10,    float  f  =  15.7  );
4
5    int  main()
6    {
7       cout  <<  "\n\nCalled  as  some_function():\n";
8       some_function();                   // No  args
9
10      cout  <<  "\n\nCalled  as  some_function(  20  ):\n";
11      some_function(  20  );               // 1  arg
12
13      cout  <<  "\n\nCalled  as  some_function(  20,  3.14159  ):\n";
14      some_function(  20,  3.14159  );   // 2  args
15
16      return(  0  );
17   }
18
19
20   void      some_function(  int  k,    float  g  )
21   {
22           cout  <<  "\tK  =  "  <<  k  <<  "\n";
23           cout  <<  "\tG  =  "  <<  g  <<  "\n";
24   }
```

LISTING 4.3. Default Function Arguments.

The program produces the output depicted in Listing 4.4.

```
1
2
3    Called  as  some_function():
4            K  =  10
5            G  =  15.7
6
7
8    Called  as  some_function(  20  ):
```

```
 9              K = 20
10              G = 15.7
11
12
13   Called as some_function( 20, 3.14159 ):
14              K = 20
15              G = 3.14159
```

Listing 4.4. Output of Listing 4.3

Note that in the first two calls to some_function(), we omitted some arguments and the compiler inserted default values as provided in the declaration (line 3). At first blush, this seems contrary to the stricter type checking provided by ANSI C (and C++) compilers. However, I assure you it's not a bug—it's a feature! (Where have I heard that before?) Default function arguments allow you to write and provide generic functionality, so programmers can omit detail when appropriate.

There are some restrictions and observations we must address. First, note that you specify default argument values in the function's declaration (line 3), not its definition (line 20). Technically, this allows you to specify different defaults in different modules, but this is not considered good programming practice. Default values, if any, should reside in one, and only one, header file. Second, during function invocation, you may omit arguments only from the right—and only if they have default values. That is, you cannot omit the first argument and provide the second and third.

Thus, given the following function declaration,

```
void another_function( int i = 10, int j = 11, int k = 12 );
```

all the following are valid invocations:

```
another_function( 1, 2, 3 );        // Valid
another_function( 1, 2 );           // Valid
another_function( 1 );              // Valid
another_function();                 // Valid
```

All of the following references are invalid:

```
another_function(  ,  2,  3 );       // Invalid
another_function(  ,    ,  3 );       // Invalid
another_function( 1,    ,  3 );       // Invalid
```

4.1.4 *Inline Functions*

In any language, function calls can place a processing burden on systems. This is due to the overhead required by the operating environment to save/restore the machine state before/after each function invocation. Ironically, this can be especially burdensome in OO languages.

In an effort to minimize processing overhead, C++ compilers allow you to define `inline` functions. This declaration directs the compiler to replace each call with a copy of the function's code. That is, rather than normal function call semantics (e.g., save state, jump to subroutine, return to caller, restore state) the compiler inserts the actual body of the function into your executable at every point of invocation. Note that, although we do reclaim some CPU cycles, it is at the expense of larger executables. (Alas, there are no free lunches.) Listing 4.5 provides an example.

```
 1    #include <iostream.h>
 2
 3    inline void print_string( char *string )
 4    {
 5            cout << string << "\n";
 6    }
 7
 8    int main()
 9    {
10            print_string( "Hello" );
11            print_string( "World" );
12
13            return( 0 );
14    }
```

LISTING 4.5. Defining an Inline Function.

We need to point out two features of `inline` functions. First, you must define an `inline` function before you can invoke it. Obviously, the compiler

would had to have seen—and translated—the function's code before it was
able to insert it. As a result, for any `inline` functions that you will invoke from
several modules, you must place the function's definition in a header file. Second, the `inline` declaration is only a request. The compiler ultimately
decides whether a function is suitable for inlining.

On the plus side, inline functions are better than macros. They provide real
function-call semantics at the source-code level. Thus, we need no longer be
wary of preprocessor abuses such as the following:

```
#define MAX(a, b)  ( (a) > (b) ? (a) : (b) )
x = MAX( y++, z++ );    // Oops - 3 increments will occur!!
```

4.1.5 Call by Reference

In addition to the call-by-value, C++ provides *call-by-reference* argument passing. Thus, functions can modify the values of parameters. For example, we
could write a swap() function as follows:

```
swap( int& a, int& b )
{
        int tmp;

        tmp = a;
        a = b;
        b = a;
}
```

Note that you indicate reference parameters with a ('&'). You call the function
in the normal manner:

```
main()
{
        int i = 10;
        int j = 20;

        swap( i, j );         // Note: i and j Change Values!
}
```

Note that the actual variables (those in the call) are subject to modification.
There is one potential drawback with this feature. Note that we identify reference arguments in the function's declaration, not during it invocation. As a
result, clients might unwittingly pass an argument and *not* know that the variable is subject to modification. This would not be possible in the old days with
C. Using pointers, clients must typically add an ('&') operator in the call.

4.1.6 *Function Name Overloading*

Traditionally, if we wanted to provide generic functionality embodied in a sub-
function, we would have provide a unique version of the function for each
data type we wanted to support. For example, let's return to our max() function. If we wanted to implement this functionality, we would probably need to
provide several versions:

```
int iMax( int, int );
float fMax( float, float );
```

However, C++ has a better solution. We can provide multiple, *overloaded* definitions of a function and let the compiler determine which one to call based
on the invocation signature. For example, we could define the following versions of max():

```
int max( int i, int j )
{
     return( i > j ? i : j );
}

float max( float i, float j )
{
     return( i > j ? i : j );
}
```

Based on the data type of the arguments, the compiler decides which version
to call. Thus, given the call:

```
int i, j, k;
i = max( j, k );
```

the compiler would select the first version. If the call were made as follows:

```
float i, j, k;
i = max( j, k );
```

the compiler would select the second version.

This idea is not as radical as it might first appear. We humans perform the same trick with alarming regularity. For example, what word is this: *read*? It can be pronounced as either "reed" or "red". You can only infer its meaning by context. A C++ compiler does the same with `max(arg1, arg2)`.

Keep the following points in mind when using overloaded functions.

- The compiler uses only the function's name and argument signature for its selection process; that is, the function's return type plays no role whatsoever.

- If the compiler cannot locate an exact match, it will apply standard conversions (casts) followed by user-defined conversions, in that order. For example, if we were to invoke our sample function as:

```
char a, b, c;
a = max( b, c );
```

the compiler would not be able to locate an exact match. It would need to cast the `chars` into `ints`.

- One, and only one matching signature may be found. Any call that yields zero or more than one match is considered an error.

4.1.7 *Dynamic Memory Allocation*

Anyone who has experienced any difficulty in using `malloc()` and `free()` will be happy to note that C++ includes a set of built-in memory allocation operators. They are called new and `delete`. The best way to demonstrate their use is by example. The following code fragment allocates, uses, and then deallocates an int.

```
int* p;              // Used to point to allocated memory
p = new int;         // Allocate a new int
*p = 50;             // Use it
cout << *p;          // Use it
delete p;            // Free it
```

Note that you do not need a cast. Because new is a built-in operator, the compiler implicitly converts the address to the proper data type. However, new is not a candy store. Just like `malloc()`, new can return a NULL pointer if it cannot satisfy the request. As such, you should always test the result of any new operation. In addition, it is strongly recommended that you use only new and `delete` in C++ programs; that is, do not use `malloc()` and `free()`.

4.2 OBJECT-ORIENTED FEATURES OF C++

As mentioned previously, three major features distinguish the OO paradigm: *class*, *inheritance*, and *polymorphism*. This section describes their implementation and use in C++.

4.2.1 Classes

In C++, a class is defined as follows:

```
class ClassName {

private:
    int data_element;

public:
    int getValue() { return(data_element); }
};
```

A class definition begins with the keyword `class`, followed by a programmer-provided *tag* name, and is delineated by curly braces. The `public` and `private` keywords are access specifiers. They determine which parts of a class are visible to clients. In keeping with the object-oriented paradigm, a `class` may contain both data and functional members. (Function members are the *methods* that

provide the *behavior.*) As a rule, all data elements should be declared `private`.
    We instantiate objects as follows:

```
ClassName objectName;
```

We reference members using the (.) operator as in:

```
int j;

j = objectName.getValue();
```

There is a third access qualifier: `protected`. Members defined with this qualifier are private to clients, but visible to derived classes. This level of access fosters code reuse by encouraging inheritance.

4.2.2 Constructors

I'm sure every reader of this book has been burned by uninitialized variables. C++ addresses this problem through special member functions called *constructors,* which support automatic initialization of objects. That is, they are invoked automatically by the compiler whenever it instantiates an object.
    A constructor takes as its name the tag name of the class. Like other member functions, you may overload its signature. This allows clients to select from among a set of initial states. The following code provides an example of a class with two constructors.

```
class MyClass {


private:
        int dataItem;

public:
        MyClass() { dataItem = 0; }
        MyClass( int d ) { dataItem = d; }
    };
```

The compiler invokes first constructor when an `MyClass` object is instantiated, but not initialized, as in:

```
MyClass myObject1;
```

The compiler invokes the second signature if the an object is instantiated as follows:

```
MyClass myObject2 = 10;
        - or -
MyClass myObject3( 10 );
```

4.2.3 Destructors

Destructors are the complement to constructors. They are automatically invoked by the compiler whenever an object goes out of scope. Their job is to relinquish any resources claimed by objects during their lifetime. Destructors take as a name the tag name of the class prepended with a tilde ('~'). Destructors do not takes arguments and, as a result, may not be overloaded. For example, consider the following class outline:

```
class AnotherClass {

private:
        char* charData;

public:
        AnotherClass()
        {
                charData = new char[ 256 ];
                // ...
        }
        ~AnotherClass()
        {
                delete charData;
        }
};
```

The destructor automatically deletes storage allocated in the constructor.

4.2.4 static *Members*

Classes may declare members (both data and procedure) static. This allows all objects of a particular class to share the same members—without resorting to external (i.e., global) storage.

4.2.4.1 static *Data Members*

There is only a single instance of static data members that all objects share. static data members share the same scope as the class itself. For example, consider the following class outline:

```
class YetAnotherClass {

private:
        static int sharedData;
        // ...
};
```

The variable sharedData becomes static by prefacing the declaration with the keyword. You also must explicitly define static data members as in:

```
int YetAnotherClass::sharedData = 15;
```

4.2.4.2 static *Functional Members*

Member functions declared static are not associated with objects; rather, they are associated with the class. As a result, they do not expect, and are not passed, a this pointer. We will use static members as *bridge* functions later in the text.

4.2.5 *Inheritance*

Inheritance allows us to successively refine class behavior. For example, given a class Car, we can create a SportsCar class as a refinement of a Car, rather than creating the new class from scratch. In C++, the syntax is as follows:

```
class Car {                         // Base Class
private:
```

```
        // Not Shown
public:

        // Not Shown
};


class SportsCar : public Car {   // Point of derivation

private:

        // Not Shown

public:

        // Not Shown
};
```

This example demonstrates how we can create a new class `SportsCar` as a refinement of a `Car`. You can pronounce the colon operator "is a"; thus `SportsCar` *is a* Car and inherits every feature of Car. Moreover, we can provide the additional behavior that makes a Car a `SportsCar`.

4.2.6 Polymorphism

C++ implements polymorphism using `virtual` functions. The easiest way to describe a `virtual` function is by way of example. Assume the following class definitions:

```
        class Base {

        private:

                // Not Shown

        public:

                int func() { ... } // A member function

        };
```

```
class Derived : Base {

private:

    // Not Shown

public:
        int func() { ... } // Derived class also has one
};
```

Let's create a some objects and a Base pointer:

```
Base*       ptr;
Base        b_obj;
Derived     d_obj;
```

If we set ptr to point at b_obj,

```
ptr = &b_obj;
```

when we send the following message:

```
ptr->func();
```

we expect Base::func() to execute (and it does). However, if we set ptr to point at d_obj,

```
ptr = &b_obj;
```

and send the same message,

```
ptr->func();
```

the function Base::func() still executes (i.e., instead of the function Derived::func()). Why? Because the compiler assumes that if ptr is a Base*, we must be pointing at a Base object. As a rule, the compiler decides which function to call based on the type of pointer, not the type of object at which it's pointing.

To achieve the intuitive behavior we would expect, we need to declare `func()` `virtual` in `Base`, as in:

```
class Base {

private:

        // Not Shown

public:
        virtual int func() { ... }

};

class Derived : Base {

private:

        // Not Shown

public:

        int func() { ... }

};
```

Now, when we send the message to the d_obj,

```
ptr->func();
```

the function `Derived::func()` executes.

4.3 PROGRAMMING EXAMPLE

We have highlighted several C++ features in this chapter. It's now time for an example. The following listings contain an implementation of a simple string class. This is an excellent pedagogical vehicle for several reasons:

- C does not support a string data type. In C, "string" is synonymous with "null-terminated character array".

- A robust implementation of a string class will exercise most of the important C++ language constructs.

- It is not too tedious to write.

- It really works!

Listing 4.6 presents the class definition for `String` as it appears in `string.h`. Listing 4.7 presents the implementation file `string.cxx`, which contains definitions for several class members. Finally, Listing 4.8 depicts a sample test program. I urge all readers new to this grammar to develop their own version of a string class before proceeding to subsequent chapters.

```
1    //
2    // FILE:      string.h
3    //
4    //      DESCRIPTION:    Definition of a simple string class
5    //
6
7    #ifndef _STRING_H_
8    #define _STRING_H_
9
10   #include         <stdlib.h>
11   #include         <string.h>
12   #include         <iostream.h>
13
14   class String {
15
16   private:
17
18           //
19           //      Pointer to the String
20           //
21           char    *theString;
22
23   public:
```

```
24
25              //
26              //         Default Constructor w/ defaulted argument
27              //
28              String( char *s = "" )
29              {
30                      theString = new char[ strlen(s)+1 ];
31                 if( !theString )
32                 {
33                         cerr << "Allocation error" << endl;
34                         exit( 0 );
35                 }
36                      strcpy( theString, s );
37              }
38
39              //
40              // Copy Constructor
41              //
42              String( const String &s )
43              {
44                  theString = new char[ strlen(s.theString)+1 ];
45                 if( !theString )
46                 {
47                         cerr << "Allocation error" << endl;
48                         exit( 0 );
49                 }
50                 strcpy( theString, s.theString );
51              }
52
53              //
54              //         Destructor
55              //
56              ~String()
57              {
58                      delete theString;
59              }
60
61              //
```

```
62                  //          Additional Function Declarations
63                  //
64                  String &operator=( const String &s );
65
66                  friend String operator+(const String &s1, const
                                            String &s2);
67
68                  friend ostream &operator<<( ostream &o, const
                                            String &s );
69
70     };
71
72     #endif
```

LISTING 4.6. string.h.

```
1      //
2      //              FILE:     string.cpp
3      //
4      //          DESCRIPTION:    Function Definitions for String
5      //
6
7      #include "string.h"
8
9      //
10     //          Assignment Operator
11     //
12     String &String::operator=( const String &s )
13     {
14          if( this != &s )
15          {
16               delete theString;
17               theString = new char[strlen(s.theString)+1];
18               if( !theString )
19               {
20                    cerr << "Allocation error" << endl;
21                    exit( 0 );
22               }
```

```
23                    strcpy( theString, s.theString );
24              }
25
26         return( *this );
27    }
28
29    //
30    //        Concatenation Operator
31    //
32    String operator+( const String &s1, const String &s2 )
33    {
34       String t;
35
36       delete t.theString;
37       t.theString=
            new char[strlen(s1.theString)+strlen(s2.theString)+1];
38       if( !t.theString )
39       {
40          cerr << "Memory allocation error" << endl;
41          exit( 0 );
42       }
43       strcpy( t.theString, s1.theString );
44       strcat( t.theString, s2.theString );
45
46       return( t );
47    }
48
49    //
50    //        Stream Insertion Operator
51    //
52    ostream &operator<<( ostream &o, const String &s )
53    {
54            return( o << s.theString );
55    }
```

LISTING 4.7. string.cpp.

```
1      #include            <stdlib.h>
2      #include            <iostream.h>
3
4      #include            "string.h"
5
6      int main()
7      {
8              String s2 = "foo";       // String(char*)
9              String s1 = s2;          // String(String&)
10             s2 = "bar";              // String(char*), operator=()
11
12             cout << "S1: " << s1 << "\n";
13             cout << "S2: " << s2 << "\n";
14
15             String s3;               // String(char*="")
16             s3 = s1 + s2;            // operator+(), operator=()
17
18             cout << "S3: " << s3 << "\n";
19
20             return( 0 );
21     }
```

LISTING 4.8. main.cpp.

4.4 SUMMARY

In this chapter, we highlighted many C++ programming constructs. We demonstrated its extensions to C as well as its support for the object-oriented paradigm. We will use all of the features we discussed throughout the remainder of the text.

However, please keep in mind that C++ is a powerful language, and this has been but a brief overview. Please refer to the bibliography for several excellent language references.

CHAPTER **5**

COMBINING CLASSES AND WIDGETS

5.1 CLASSES AND WIDGETS

5.1.1 Widget Creation

Motif widget classes are an extension of the object-oriented architecture defined in the toolkit. As a result, each widget we create is an instantiation of a widget *class*. For example, let's consider a simple push button. The Motif class name for this widget is XmPushButton, and its class hierarchy is

Core $\rightarrow$ XmPrimative $\rightarrow$ XmLabel $\rightarrow$ XmPushButton

However, unlike a true object-oriented development environment—X, Xt, and Motif are written in C—we must use functions to *instantiate* widgets. For example, Listing 5.1 contains a program that creates an XmPushButton widget.

```
1    #include <stdlib.h>
2    #include <Xm/Xm.h>
3    #include <Xm/Label.h>
4
```

```
 5    main( int ac, char **av )
 6    {
 7    Widget top, pb;
 8    XtAppContext app;
 9
10    //
11    // Initialize Intrinsics
12    //
13    top = XtAppInitialize( &app, "Pushme", NULL, 0,
14            &ac, av, NULL, NULL, 0 );
15
16    //
17    // Instantiate a Push Button Widget
18    //
19    pb = XtCreateManagedWidget( "pb", xmPushButtonWidgetClass,
20                                      top, NULL, 0 );
21
22    //
23    // Realize Widgets
24    //
25    XtRealizeWidget( top );
26
27    //
28    // Main Event Loop
29    //
30    XtMainLoop();
31    }
```

LISTING 5.1. Sample motif program.

When executed, this code displays a push button on the user's screen. For our purposes, the two most important statements are the calls to XtCreate-ManagedWidget() and XtRealizeWidget(). The former instantiates a push button widget, and the latter asks the server to create a window for it.

5.1.2 Callbacks

Unfortunately, the ability to display widgets is not enough. Programs also need to know when users interact with them. To facilitate this process, most widgets support a feature called *callbacks*. Through callbacks, widgets notify clients programs that some widget-specific event has occurred. They are termed *callbacks* because widgets "call back" to the application code via programmer-defined functions.

Callbacks are easy to use. The programmer only needs to register one or more functions with a widget-specific event. Then, whenever that event occurs, the widget invokes the specified function(s). Most widgets support several types of callbacks. Note that although the types of callbacks widgets support are defined by class, each object (i.e., each instantiated widget) maintains its own, individual callback lists.

Returning to our previous example, the XmPushButtonWidget supports several types of callbacks. One that is commonly used is called XmNactivate-Callback. It is invoked whenever the user presses and releases a mouse button while the sprite (cursor) remains positioned within the button. Let's add this callback to our previous example so that it will cause the program to exit whenever the user presses the button.

To register the callback we add the statement:

```
XtAddCallback( pb, XmNactivateCallback, my_quit_function, NULL );
```

after the we create the widget. The function's first two arguments specify the widget and its callback. The third parameter is a pointer to the actual callback routine. We can use the last argument to pass program-specific data to the callback function. We will return to this point shortly.

When invoked, a callback routine receives three arguments: the widget in which the event took place, a pointer to the client data (NULL in our example), and a pointer to event-specific data. (The contents and use of this last field is beyond the scope of this discussion.) Thus, we can define the callback routine as follows:

```
//
// Exit when the user presses the button
//
void my_quit_function( Widget w, XtPointer client_data,
                          XtPointer call_data )
{
    exit( 0 );
}
```

We add this function to our original program. Thereafter, when the user clicks on the button, the widget will invoke my_quit_function() and the program will exit.

5.2 C++ CLASSES AND WIDGETS

5.2.1 C++ *and Widgets*

Once we understand the basic Motif architecture, the next step is to design the user interface. In particular, when coding in an object-oriented language such as C++, we would like to combine widgets into a set of classes that serve as basic user interface components. (This is the very intent of this text.) With this in mind, our first inclination might be to extend (i.e., inherit from) the Motif widget classes. Unfortunately, the object-oriented architecture of Motif is not compatible with the class hierarchies of C++. (Remember, Motif is implemented in C.) As a result, we cannot create new C++ classes that are derived from Motif widget classes. We can, however, create C++ *wrappers.*

As an example, let's design a C++ class that creates and manages a Motif dialog box. A feature common to most dialog boxes is a 'cancel button'; thus, let's include a push button widget as part of our class. A sample class definition might appear as follows:

```
1     class AppDialog {
2
3     private:
4
5       Widget cancel_button;              // Push Button
6
7       //
8       // Not Shown
9       //
10
11    public:
12
13      AppDialog( Widget, char * );       // Constructor
14
15      void CancelCallBack();             // Member Callback
```

```
16
17     //
18     // Not Shown
19     //
20     };
21
22     AppDialog::AppDialog( Widget parent, char *name )
23     {
24     //
25     // Instantiate the Push Button Widget
26     //
27     pb = XtCreateManagedWidget( name, xmPushButtonWidgetClass,
28                                     parent, NULL, 0 );
29     //
30     // Not Shown
31     //
32     }
```

In the above example, the class AppDialog contains, among other items, a push-button widget to serve as a cancel button. As you might have noticed, we have not yet included any code to register a callback. As implied by the above class definition, we would like the widget to invoke the member function CancelCallBack() whenever the user presses the cancel button, but this presents a problem. In C++, the compiler invokes member functions with a hidden first argument: the this pointer. As a result, we cannot register C++ class members as callback functions. (Motif, written in C, will not invoke class member functions with the expected argument signature.) In general, there are two ways we can address this problem. Both solutions require the overhead of an additional function call.

5.2.2 *Bridge Functions*

One way to solve the above problem is through the use of a *bridge* function. That is, we can register an external (i.e., nonclass member) function as the callback routine and have it, in turn, invoke the appropriate member function on our behalf. However, this solution presents another problem. How does the bridge function know which object should actually receive the callback? Specifically, we may create many AppDialog objects. Which one should be notified of the callback? We can solve this problem by passing the this pointer as client data. For example, we might modify the AppDialog class as follows:

```
1     //
2     //      Bridge Function
3     //
4     void   AppDialogCallBack( Widget, XtPointer, XtPointer );
5
6     //
7     //      Class Definition
8     //
9     class AppDialog {
10
11    private:
12
13        Widget cancel_button;                // Push Button
14
15        //
16        // ...
17        //
18
19    public:
20
21        AppDialog( Widget, char * );         // Constructor
22
23        void CancelCallBack();               // Member Callback
24        //
25        // ...
26        //
27    };
28
29    AppDialog::AppDialog( Widget parent, char *name )
30    {
31            //
32            // Instantiate the Push Button Widget
33            //
34            cancel_button = XtCreateManagedWidget( name,
```

```
35              xmPushButtonWidgetClass, parent, NULL, 0 );
36
37      //
38      // Register the Callback - Pass `this'
39      // pointer as client data
40      //
41      XtAddCallback( cancel_button, XmNactivateCallback,
42                     AppDialogCallBack, (XtPointer)this );
43
44          //
45          // ...
46          //
47      }
48
49      //
50      //      Bridge Function Definition
51      //
52      void  AppDialogCallBack( Widget w, XtPointer client_data,
53                 XtPointer call_data )
54      {
55          // Cast Client Data to Expected Type
56          AppDialog *my_obj = (AppDialog *)client_data;
57
58          // Invoke Appropriate Member Callback Function
59          my_obj->CancelCallBack();
60      }
```

When we register the callback, we pass as client data the address contained in the object's `this` pointer. This value, in turn, is passed to the callback function `AppDialogCallBack()` when it is invoked by the pushbutton widget. Internally, the bridge function simply casts the value contained in `client_data` to the expected type, and invokes the appropriate member function.

5.2.3 `static` *Member Functions*

As simple and direct as the previous solution is, it has one drawback. As written, `AppDialogCallBack()` cannot access the `private` members contained within `AppDialog` objects. (It is not a member of the class.) This is not a concern for this simple example, but in practice, a bridge function might require access to the private members of its associated class. The easiest way to handle this is to grant the bridge function friend status. However, this might expose too much of the class's private implementation. (In effect, we are violating one of the fundamental tenets of object-oriented programming: *encapsulation.*)

A better solution is to use a static member as the bridge function. Although part of a class, static members are not associated with objects—they are a class construct. As a result, they are not passed, and do not expect, a this pointer as a hidden first argument. Specifically, that means that C-based libraries (e.g., Motif) can invoke static member functions directly. As an example of this technique, we can modify our previous class definition as follows:

```
1    //
2    //      Class Definition
3    //
4    class AppDialog {
5
6    private:
7
8    Widget cancel_button;              // Push Button
9
10   //
11   //      Static Bridge Function
12   //
13   static void AppDialogCallBack( Widget, XtPointer, XtPointer );
14
15   //
16   // ...
17   //
18
19   public:
20
21   AppDialog( Widget, char* );        // Constructor
22
23   void CancelCallBack();             // Member Callback
24   //
25   // ...
26   //
```

```
27    };
28
29    //
30    //      Constructor
31    //
32    AppDialog::AppDialog( Widget parent, char *name )
33    {
34      //
35      //   Instantiate the Push Button Widget
36      //
37      cancel_button = XtCreateManagedWidget( name,
38          xmPushButtonWidgetClass, parent, NULL, 0 );
39
40      //
41      //   Register the Callback
42      //
43      XtAddCallback( cancel_button, XmNactivateCallback,
44                  &AppDialog::AppDialogCallBack, (XtPointer)this );
45
46      //
47      // ...
48      //
49    }
50
51    //
52    //      Bridge Function Definition
53    //
54    void  AppDialog::AppDialogCallBack( Widget w,
55    XtPointer client_data, XtPointer call_data )
56    {
57      //
58      //   Cast Client Data to Expected Object Type
59      //
60      AppDialog* my_obj = (AppDialog*)client_data;
61
62      //
63      //   Pass on the Callback
64      //
```

```
65        my_obj->CancelCallBack();
66    }
```

Note that you must reference the address of a `static` member function explicitly (i.e., use the `'&'` operator). In addition, you must explicitly reference the class to which it belongs.

One nice feature of this solution is that it supports polymorphism. Through the use of `virtual` member functions, a bridge function can invoke a method that was inherited from a base class. Alternatively, derived classes can override base class behavior and still use the same basic architecture.

5.3 SUMMARY

In this chapter, we discussed the basic method we will use to support widget callbacks within C++ classes. The basic technique uses a `static` member function to serve as a bridge between the Xt/Motif libraries and C++ classes. This technique is extendible to other, non-GUI programming interfaces as well.

CHAPTER *6*

BRINGING IT ALL TOGETHER

In this chapter, we would like to bring together, by way of example, all of the topics we have discussed thus far. To do this, we will demonstrate how we can construct the simple calculator program depicted in Figure 6.1.

Our task is to meet the physical specification depicted in Figure 6.1 using coding techniques discussed in prior chapters. Most Motif programmers would not find this program difficult to implement. Nevertheless, it will demonstrate the basic techniques we will use throughout the remainder of the text. In later chapters, we will demonstrate other, more sophisticated, implementation techniques.

6.1 IMPLEMENTATION

Let's begin our discussions by examining the widget instance hierarchy used to create the GUI depicted in Figure 6.1. Figure 6.2 depicts the instance tree.

At the top is an `ApplicationShell` widget. It is created during the call to `XtAppInitialize()`. Following that, we create an `XmForm` widget. It manages two children: an `XmTextField` widget that serves as the calculator's display, and another `XmForm` widget that manages all of the buttons.

To facilitate our discussions, we have divided the code for the calculator program into three modules:

main.cxx This is the driving module of the program. It initializes the Xt Toolkit, instantiates a calculator object, realizes widgets, and enters the main event loop.

calc.cxx This module contains the definition of the class Calc. Its associated header file, calc.h, contains the class definition.

utility.cxx This file contains utility functions used by the program.

In the following sections, we discuss the important implementation features of main.cxx and calc.cxx. The complete program listing appears at the end of the chapter. Please familiarize yourself with the listing before continuing on. For your convenience, we have extracted many of the source statements and presented them as part of the discussion.

6.1.1 main.cxx

As usual, program execution begins with the function main(). Lines 12–15 declare all the typical variables required by all toolkit-based programs.

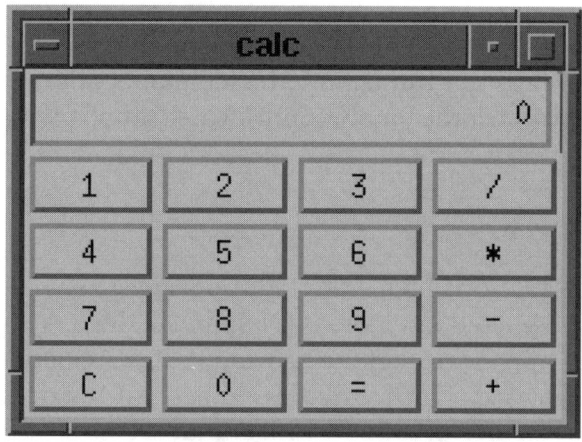

FIGURE 6.1. Calculator program.

```
12              register        i;
13              Arg             args[ 50 ];
14              XtAppContext    app;
15              Widget  top;                    // Toplevel Widget
```

The call to XtAppInitialize() (line 20) initializes the toolkit. The function takes as arguments the address of our application context variable, the class name of our program, and pointers to the command line argument variables. The parameters we have omitted include:

- Arguments 3 and 4 are used to define application-specific command line arguments.

- Argument 7 is used to pass fallback resources for the application.

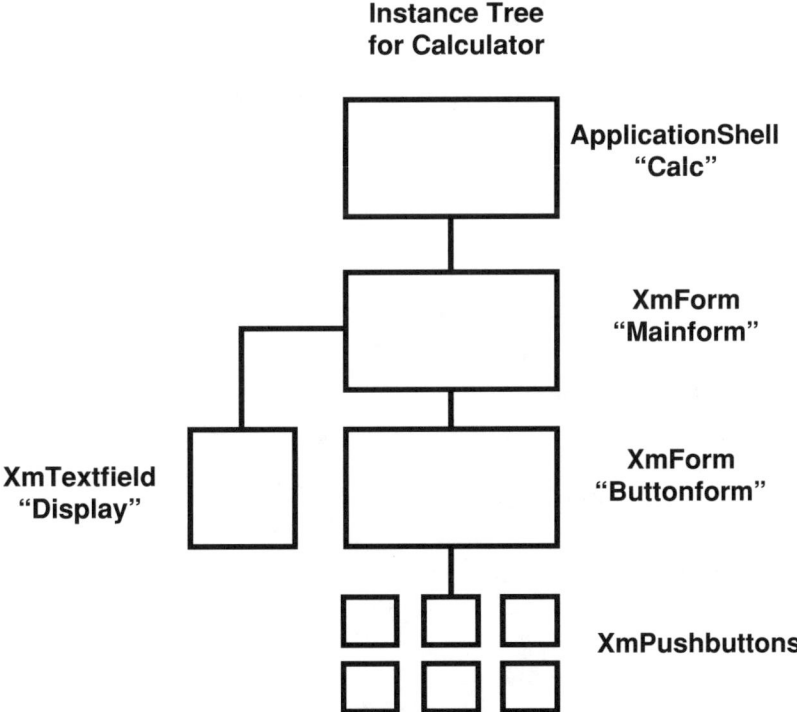

FIGURE 6.2. Widget instance tree for calc program.

- Arguments 8 and 9 are used to pass resources for the shell widget created in the call.

```
17    //
18    //          Initialize Toolkit
19    //
20    top = XtAppInitialize( &app,  "Calc",  NULL,  0,  &ac,  av,
21              NULL,  NULL,  0 );
```

Line 26 contains our first pure C++ statement. Here we instantiate a `Calc` object. Note that we pass the ID of the widget that will serve as parent for all widgets created within the object.

```
22
23              //
24              //          Create Calculator
25              //
26              Calc calc( top );
```

The remaining code in `main()` is also typical of Motif programs. The statement on line 31 realizes all of our widgets; and, with the call to `XtAppMainLoop()`, we enter the main event loop of our program.

```
27
28              //
29              //          Realize Widgets
30              //
31              XtRealizeWidget( top );
32
33              //
34              //          Enter Main Loop
35              //
36              XtAppMainLoop( app );
37    }
```

6.1.2 `calc.h`

The file `calc.h` contains the definition of the class `Calc`. Beginning at line 12, we #include the pertinent Motif header files.

```
12    #include <Xm/Form.h>
13    #include <Xm/Text.h>
14    #include <Xm/TextF.h>
15    #include <Xm/PushB.h>
16    #include <Xm/RowColumn.h>
```

On lines 26 and 27 we define two constants that simplify the arrangement of push buttons.

```
23    //
24    //          Constants
25    //
26    const int max_rows = 4;
27    const int max_cols = 4;
```

Beginning with line 32, we define button_struct. The bridge function will use instances of this struct to facilitate callbacks. We dynamically allocate instances of this structure in the Calc class constructor.

```
29    //
30    //          Button Structure - Serves as Client Data
31    //
32    struct button_struct {
33            char      label;
34            Calc      *object;
35            Widget    widget;
36    };
```

The button_struct structure contains three fields:

label The label field serves as client data in the bridge function. It will also serve as the label for its associated button.

object Nothing prevents the program from instantiating more than one instance of a Calc. The bridge function needs to know to which object it should direct each callback. This field is a pointer to that instance.

widget The bridge function emulates Xt's callback facility. Thus, when processing a callback, it must pass on a the widget ID to the member function.

Line 41 begins the class definition for Calc. It begins by declaring some private data elements. We will discuss all these members in subsequent sections.

```
41    class Calc {
42    private:
43            Widget mainform;        // Main form widget
44            Widget display;         // Calculator Display
45            Widget button_form;     // Form for Buttons
46
47            long     total;         // Calculator Total
48            char     operation;     // Store Operation on Key Press
49            int      clear_flag;    // Clear Display
50
51            button_struct *buttons; // Storage for Callbacks
52
53            //
54            //        Private Member Functions
55            //
56            void Calc::CalcSubTotal();
57            void Calc::AddToDisplay( char c );
58            void Calc::SetCalcDisplay( char *str );
59
60    public:
61            ~Calc();
62            Calc( Widget );
63
64            void Calc::Reset();
65            void Calc::Pushed( Widget, XtPointer, XtPointer );
66            static void Static_Pushed( Widget, XtPointer,
                                        XtPointer );
67    };
```

6.1.3 calc.cxx

The file calc.cxx completes the implementation of the Calc class. A discussion of the member function follows.

6.1.3.1 *Calc::~Calc()*

With line 22 begins the definition of the destructor, Calc::~Calc(). Its only task is to relinquish the dynamic memory allocated in the constructor. Note that the function does not destroy the widgets created within the object. We will return to this point later in the text.

```
22   Calc::~Calc()                          // Destructor
23   {
24           delete buttons;                // Free Dynamic Memory
25   }
```

6.1.3.2 *Calc::Calc()*

The default constructor, Calc::Calc(), begins at line 27. This function is rather long, so let's discuss it in sections. It begins by declaring some local variables used during the construction of its object.

```
27   Calc::Calc( Widget top )               // Constructor
28   {
29
30           Arg            args[ 50 ];
31           int            i, index, row, col;
32           XmString       label;
33
```

Next, the constructor creates the object's widgets. Line 38 contains a call to XmCreateForm().

```
34           //
35           //      Create Parent Form Widget
36           //
37           i = 0;
38           mainform = XmCreateForm( top, "mainform", args, i );
39           XtManageChild( mainform );
```

Following that, on line 44, the constructor creates an xmTextFieldWidget to serve as the calculator's display.

```
41              //
42              //        Create TextField Widget for Calculator Display
43              //
44          display = XtVaCreateManagedWidget( "display",
45
46                  xmTextFieldWidgetClass,       mainform,
47
48                  XmNeditable,                  False,
49                  XmNcursorPositionVisible,     False,
50                  XmNtraversalOn,               False,
51
52          NULL );
```

The next widget created is another form widget to manage the matrix of push buttons. The attachments are set such that the calculator will resize in a reasonable manner. Note that we set XmNfractionBase equal to 4 as a convenient way to position the buttons.

```
55              //
56              //        Create Form to Hold Calculator Buttons
57              //
58          button_form = XtVaCreateManagedWidget( "buttonform",
59                  xmFormWidgetClass, mainform,
60
61                  XmNfractionBase,          4,
62
63                  XmNtopAttachment,         XmATTACH_WIDGET,
64                  XmNtopWidget,             display,
65
66                  XmNleftAttachment,        XmATTACH_FORM,
67                  XmNleftOffset,            0,
68
69                  XmNrightAttachment,       XmATTACH_FORM,
70                  XmNrightOffset,           0,
```

```
71
72                    XmNbottomAttachment,  XmATTACH_FORM,
73                    XmNbottomOffset,      0,
74
75                    XmNlength,            200,
76                    XmNwidth,             200,
77
78                    NULL );
```

The code segment beginning on line 84 constructs all of the buttons. First, the function creates storage for an array of button_struct structures. Following that, it creates all the buttons using a nested loop construct. Again, the attachments are set such that the calculator will resize smoothly. On lines 98 and 99, we assign the appropriate values to members of the buttons[ ] array.

```
84             buttons = new button_struct[ max_rows * max_cols ];
85
86             //
87             //      Create  Calculator  Buttons
88             //
89             for( row = 0;  row < max_rows;  row++ )
90             {
91                     for( col = 0;  col < max_cols;  col++ )
92                     {
93                         index = (row * max_cols) + col;
94
95                         //
96                         // Save  state  info  in  callback  struct
97                         //
98                         buttons[index].object = this;
99                         buttons[index].label = cb[index][0];
100
101                        //
102                        //      Create  Label  String  for  Button
103                        //
104                        label = XmStringCreateSimple( cb[index] );
105
```

```
106                      //
107                      //        Create Button
108                      //
109                      buttons[index].widget=XtVaCreateManaged-
                                          Widget("",

110
111                        xmPushButtonWidgetClass,
                           button_form,
112
113                        XmNlabelString,              label,
114
115                        XmNtopAttachment,
                           XmATTACH_POSITION,
116                        XmNtopPosition,              row,
117
118                        XmNbottomAttachment,
                           XmATTACH_POSITION,
119                        XmNbottomPosition,           row+1,
120
121                        XmNleftAttachment,
                           XmATTACH_POSITION,
122                        XmNleftPosition,             col,
123
124                        XmNrightAttachment,
                           XmATTACH_POSITION,
125                        XmNrightPosition,            col+1,
126
127                      NULL );
```

On line 132 we register the callbacks for each push button. Notice that we have used the `static` member function `Calc::Static_Pushed()`. We register the callback with the `XmNactivateCallback` resource and set the client data to point at the corresponding entry in the button structure.

```
132                      XtAddCallback( buttons[index].widget,
133                          XmNactivateCallback,
134                          (XtCallbackProc)&Calc::Static_Pushed,
135                          (XtPointer)&buttons[index] );
```

Line 140 frees the temporary label string we created for the push buttons. Line 143 invokes the member function Reset() to set the calculator to its initial state. This completes the implementation of the constructor Calc::Calc().

```
136
137                         //
138                         //          Free String
139                         //
140                         XmStringFree( label );     // No Memory Leaks
141                   }
142             }
143             Reset();
144    }
```

6.1.3.3 Calc::SetCalcDisplay()

The next member function defined in calc.cxx is Calc::SetCalcDisplay(). This routine displays a string in the calculator's display. The function ascertains the number of available columns by retrieving the value of the XmNcolumns resource:

```
146    //
147    //          This Function Displays its String Argument
148    //
149    void Calc::SetCalcDisplay( char *str )
150    {
151             register          i;
152             short             cols;
153             Arg               args[ 50 ];
154             char              buf[ 256 ];
155
156             //
157             //          Determine Number of Columns
158             //
159             i = 0;
160             XtSetArg( args[i], XmNcolumns, &cols ); i++;
161             XtGetValues( display, args, i );
```

Following that, on lines 166 and 172, the function formats and displays the
string:

```
162
163                 //
164                 //          Format Buffer
165                 //
166                 sprintf( buf, "%*.*s", cols, cols, str );
167
168                 //
169                 //          Update Display
170                 //
171                 XmTextSetString( display, buf );
172      }
```

6.1.3.4 Calc::AddToDisplay()

The function `Calc::AddToDisplay()` adds a single character to the display. It gets called whenever the user presses one of the calculator's
numeric keys.

```
174     //
175     //          Function to Add a Character to the Display
176     //
177     void Calc::AddToDisplay( char c )
178     {
179             register        i;
180             short           cols;
181             Arg             args[ 50 ];
182             char            *old_str;
183             char            new_str[ 256 ];
184
185             //
186             //          Determine Number of Columns
187             //
188             i = 0;
189             XtSetArg( args[i], XmNcolumns, &cols ); i++;
190             XtGetValues( display, args, i );
191
```

```
192                //
193                //          Get Current Display
194                //
195                old_str = XmTextGetString( display );
196                rtb( old_str );                    // Remove blanks
197                if( strcmp(old_str, "0") == 0 )
198                     *old_str = (char)NULL;
199
200                if( strlen(old_str) < cols )       // Don't Overrun
201                {
202                     sprintf( new_str, "%s%c", old_str, c );
203                     SetCalcDisplay( new_str );
204                }
205
206                XtFree( old_str );                 // No Leaks
207     }
```

6.1.3.5 *Calc::CalcSubTotal()*

The Calc::CalcSubTotal() function computes a new total based on:

- The existing (current) total (stored in the data member total)

- The value of the new operand (stored as a resource in the display string)

- The indicated operation (as determined by the actual button pressed by the user)

After performing the indicated operation, the function invokes SetCalcDisplay() to display the new value. The variable clear_flag is used to indicate that a computation has completed and that, when the user presses the next digit button, the calculator can clear the display.

```
209     //
210     //          Calculate Subtotal
211     //
212     void Calc::CalcSubTotal()
```

```
213     {
214             long    tmp;
215             char    *old_str;
216             char    buf[ 256 ];
217
218             //
219             //      Get Current Display
220             //
221             old_str = XmTextGetString( display );
222             tmp = atol( old_str );
223
224             switch( operation )
225             {
226                     case '+':
227                             total += tmp;
228                             break;
229
230                     case '-':
231                             total -= tmp;
232                             break;
233
234                     case '*':
235                             total *= tmp;
236                             break;
237
238                     case '/':
239                             if( tmp != 0L )
240                                     total /= tmp;
241                             break;
242
243                     case '=':
244                             total = tmp;
245                             break;
246
247                     default:
248                             total = tmp;
249                             break;
250             }
```

```
251
252                //
253                //          Reset Display
254                //
255                sprintf( buf, "%ld", total );
256                SetCalcDisplay( buf );
257                operation = (char)NULL;
258                clear_flag++;
259
260                //
261                //          Cleanup
262                //
263                XtFree( old_str );                    // No Memory Leaks
264     }
```

6.1.3.6 Calc::Reset()

The Calc::Reset() function simply resets the calculator to an initial state. It is used in the constructor and whenever the user presses the 'clear' button.

```
266     //
267     //          Reset Calculator
268     //
269     void Calc::Reset()
270     {
271                total = 0L;
272                operation = (char)NULL;
273                SetCalcDisplay( "0" );
274                clear_flag = 0;
275     }
```

6.1.3.7 Calc::Static_Pushed()

The function Calc::Static_Pushed() serves a the bridge function between the toolkit and the object. It performs the following processing:

- It declares a button* and initializes it to point at client_data. Please keep in mind that when we registered the callbacks in the constructor, we passed a pointer to a button structure as client data.

- In a similar manner, it declares a pointer to a `Calc` object and sets it to point at the `object` member of the `button` structure. Recall that `static` member functions are not associated with any particular instance of an object. They are a class construct. Thus, a `static` member function does not 'know' for which object it was invoked. As a result, we passed the value of the `this` pointer as a member of the `button` structure. As an aside, note that this design provides for multiple, concurrent instances of `Calc` objects.

- After the two variable declarations, it becomes a simple matter to invoke the `Calc::Pushed()` member with appropriate arguments.

```
277    //
278    //          Bridge Function
279    //
280    void Calc::Static_Pushed( Widget widget, XtPointer client_data,
281                   XtPointer call_data )
282    {
283            button_struct *b = (button_struct *)client_data;
284
285            Calc *obj = (Calc *)b->object;
286
287            //
288            //          Pass on Callback
289            //
290            obj->Pushed( b->widget, (XtPointer)b->label,
                                  (XtPointer)call_data);
291    }
```

6.1.3.8 Calc::Pushed()

As we have just described, `Calc::Static_Pushed()` invokes `Calc::Pushed`. It is the work-horse routine for button callbacks. The basic operation of the function is quite simple. It begins by casting its `client_data` argument to a char. It then uses this value to determine the appropriate mathematical operation.

```
293    //
294    //          Pushbutton Callback Routine
```

```
295     //
296     void Calc::Pushed( Widget widget, XtPointer client_data,
                        XtPointer call_data )
297     {
298             char which_button = (char)client_data;
299
300             switch( which_button )
301             {
302                     case '0':
303                     case '1':
304                     case '2':
305                     case '3':
306                     case '4':
307                     case '5':
308                     case '6':
309                     case '7':
310                     case '8':
311                     case '9':
312                             if( clear_flag )
313                             {
314                                     SetCalcDisplay( "" );
315                                     clear_flag = 0;
316                             }
317                             AddToDisplay( which_button );
318                             break;
319
320                     case 'C':
321                             Reset();
322                             break;
323
324                     case '+':
325                     case '-':
326                     case '*':
327                     case '/':
328                             CalcSubTotal();
329                             operation = which_button;
330                             break;
```

```
331
332                    case '=':
333                            CalcSubTotal();
334                            operation = (char)NULL;
335                            break;
336            }
337    }
```

6.2 SUMMARY

This simple example has demonstrated some of the advantages of encapsulating widgets within a C++ class. They include:

PROGRAM INTERFACE Classes simplify the interface and operation of program components.

ENCAPSULATION Classes hide implementation details.

ABSTRACTION Classes create abstractions, which simplifies interaction with GUI components. Moreover, if we have done our job correctly, the client programmer can think in terms of the abstraction, rather than its implementation.

PORTABILITY An advantage of encapsulation is that we can maintain and enhance the private implementation of an object without the nasty ripple effects we've become accustomed to using traditional methodologies.

As it stands, this example also highlights some shortcomings of this, our initial approach:

NAMES We have not provided a way for users to access embedded component widgets by name.

CLEANUP The destructor function for our Calc class does not destroy its associated widgets. More importantly, objects might erroneously access widgets that have been destroyed by other means.

RESOURCES We have not, as yet, provided a systematic way to manage widget resources. How could a user set the background color of the `clear` button to red?

CODE REUSE One of the most important objectives of object-oriented programming is code reuse. As it stands, it is difficult for class designers to reuse the code contained in the `Calc` class.

We can address all these concerns through a core set of classes that can serve as a framework for GUI development. This is exactly the approach we will take in Section III. We will show you how to construct a C++ application framework for the Motif environment. However, before we can proceed, we must describe the basics of object-oriented analysis and design. The will be the central focus of Section II.

6.3 COMPLETE CALCULATOR PROGRAM LISTING

The following section contain the complete source code listing for our example calculator program.

6.3.1 main.cxx

```
 1   //
 2   //          TITLE:          MAIN.CXX
 3   //
 4   //        FUNCTION:         Driving Module for Calculator
 5   //
 6   #include          <iostream.h>
 7
 8   #include          "calc.h"
 9
10   int main( int ac, char *av[] )
11   {
12            register           i;
13            Arg                args[ 50 ];
14            XtAppContext       app;
```

```
15              Widget   top;                        // Toplevel Widget
16
17              //
18              //         Initialize Toolkit
19              //
20              top = XtAppInitialize( &app, "Calc", NULL, 0, &ac, av,
21                      NULL, NULL, 0 );
22
23              //
24              //         Create Calculator
25              //
26              Calc calc( top );
27
28              //
29              //         Realize Widgets
30              //
31              XtRealizeWidget( top );
32
33              //
34              //         Enter Main Loop
35              //
36              XtAppMainLoop( app );
37      }
```

6.3.2 calc.cxx

```
 1      //
 2      //          TITLE:          CALC.CXX
 3      //
 4      //          FUNCTION:       C++ Class to Create & Display a
                                    Simple Calculator
 5      //
 6      #include        <iostream.h>
 7
 8      #include        "calc.h"
 9      #include        "utility.h"
10
11      static char *cb[] =                 // Button Labels
```

```
12      {
13                      "1",  "2",  "3",  "/",
14                      "4",  "5",  "6",  "*",
15                      "7",  "8",  "9",  "-",
16                      "C",  "0",  "=",  "+"
17      };
18
19      //
20      //          Member Functions
21      //
22      Calc::~Calc()                         // Destructor
23      {
24                      delete buttons;       // Free Dynamic Memory
25      }
26
27      Calc::Calc( Widget top )              // Constructor
28      {
29
30                      Arg             args[ 50 ];
31                      int             i, index, row, col;
32                      XmString        labl;
33
34                      //
35                      //          Create Parent Form Widget
36                      //
37                      i = 0;
38                      mainform = XmCreateForm( top, "mainform", args, i );
39                      XtManageChild( mainform );
40
41                      //
42                      //   Create TextField Widget for Calculator Display
43                      //
44                      display = XtVaCreateManagedWidget( "display",
45
46                              xmTextFieldWidgetClass,            mainform,
47
48                              XmNeditable,                      False,
```

```
49                         XmNcursorPositionVisible,        False,
50                         XmNtraversalOn,                  False,
51
52          NULL );
53
54
55          //
56          //        Create Form to Hold Calculator Buttons
57          //
58          button_form = XtVaCreateManagedWidget( "buttonform",
59                    xmFormWidgetClass, mainform,
60
61                    XmNfractionBase,     4,
62
63                    XmNtopAttachment,    XmATTACH_WIDGET,
64                    XmNtopWidget,        display,
65
66                    XmNleftAttachment,   XmATTACH_FORM,
67                    XmNleftOffset,       0,
68
69                    XmNrightAttachment,  XmATTACH_FORM,
70                    XmNrightOffset,      0,
71
72                    XmNbottomAttachment, XmATTACH_FORM,
73                    XmNbottomOffset,     0,
74
75                    XmNlength,           200,
76                    XmNwidth,            200,
77
78                    NULL );
79
80
81          //
82          //        Allocate storage for callback
83          //
84          buttons = new button_struct[ max_rows * max_cols ];
85
```

```
86              //
87              //          Create Calculator Buttons
88              //
89              for( row = 0;  row < max_rows;  row++ )
90              {
91                      for( col = 0;  col < max_cols;  col++ )
92                      {
93                              index = (row * max_cols) + col;
94
95                              //
96                              //          Save state info
97                              //
98                              buttons[index].object = this;
99                              buttons[index].label =
                                      cb[index][0];
100
101                             //
102                             //          Create Label for Button
103                             //
104                             labl = XmStringCreateSimple
                                      ( cb[index] );
105
106                             //
107                             //          Create Button
108                             //
109                     buttons[index].widget =
                        XtVaCreateManagedWidget( "",
110
111                             xmPushButtonWidgetClass,
                                button_form,
112
113                             XmNlabelString,          labl,
114
115                             XmNtopAttachment,
                                XmATTACH_POSITION,
116                             XmNtopPosition,          row,
117
```

```
118                              XmNbottomAttachment,
                                 XmATTACH_POSITION,
119                              XmNbottomPosition,        row+1,
120

121                              XmNleftAttachment,
                                 XmATTACH_POSITION,
122                              XmNleftPosition,            col,
123

124                              XmNrightAttachment,
                                 XmATTACH_POSITION,
125                              XmNrightPosition,        col+1,
126

127                        NULL );
128

129                        //
130                        //        Register Callback
131                        //
132                        XtAddCallback(
                           buttons[index].widget,
133                              XmNactivateCallback,
134                              (XtCallbackProc)
                                 &Calc::Static_Pushed,
135                              (XtPointer)
                                 &buttons[index] );
136

137                        //
138                        //        Free String
139                        //
140                        XmStringFree( labl );
141                   }
142             }
143          Reset();
144    }
145

146    //
147    //      This Function Displays its String Argument
148    //
```

```
149     void Calc::SetCalcDisplay( char *str )
150     {
151             register        i;
152             short           cols;
153             Arg             args[ 50 ];
154             char            buf[ 256 ];
155
156             //
157             //          Determine Number of Columns
158             //
159             i = 0;
160             XtSetArg( args[i], XmNcolumns, &cols ); i++;
161             XtGetValues( display, args, i );
162
163             //
164             //          Format Buffer
165             //
166             sprintf( buf, "%*.*s", cols, cols, str );
167
168             //
169             //          Update Display
170             //
171             XmTextSetString( display, buf );
172     }
173
174     //
175     //          Function to Add a Character to the Display
176     //
177     void Calc::AddToDisplay( char c )
178     {
179             register        i;
180             short           cols;
181             Arg             args[ 50 ];
182             char            *old_str;
183             char            new_str[ 256 ];
184
185             //
```

```
186                 //              Determine Number of Columns
187                 //
188                 i = 0;
189                 XtSetArg( args[i], XmNcolumns, &cols ); i++;
190                 XtGetValues( display, args, i );
191
192                 //
193                 //          Get Current Display
194                 //
195                 old_str = XmTextGetString( display );
196                 rlb( old_str );                     // Remove blanks
197                 if( strcmp(old_str, "0") == 0 )
198                         *old_str = (char)NULL;
199
200                 if( strlen(old_str) < cols ) // Don't Overrun
201                 {
202                         sprintf( new_str, "%s%c", old_str, c );
203                         SetCalcDisplay( new_str );
204                 }
205
206                 XtFree( old_str );                  // No Leaks
207     }
208
209     //
210     //          Calculate Subtotal
211     //
212     void Calc::CalcSubTotal()
213     {
214             long    tmp;
215             char    *old_str;
216             char    buf[ 256 ];
217
218             //
219             //          Get Current Display
220             //
221             old_str = XmTextGetString( display );
222             tmp = atol( old_str );
```

```
223
224            switch( operation )
225            {
226                    case '+':
227                            total += tmp;
228                            break;
229
230                    case '-':
231                            total -= tmp;
232                            break;
233
234                    case '*':
235                            total *= tmp;
236                            break;
237
238                    case '/':
239                            if( tmp != 0L )
240                                    total /= tmp;
241                            break;
242
243                    case '=':
244                            total = tmp;
245                            break;
246
247                    default:
248                            total = tmp;
249                            break;
250            }
251
252        //
253        //        Reset Display
254        //
255        sprintf( buf, "%ld", total );
256        SetCalcDisplay( buf );
257        operation = (char)NULL;
258        clear_flag++;
259
```

```
260              //
261              //         Cleanup
262              //
263              XtFree( old_str );                    // No Memory Leaks
264      }
265
266      //
267      //         Reset Calculator
268      //
269      void Calc::Reset()
270      {
271              total = 0L;
272              operation = (char)NULL;
273              SetCalcDisplay( "0" );
274              clear_flag = 0;
275      }
276
277      //
278      //         Bridge Function
279      //
280      void Calc::Static_Pushed( Widget widget, XtPointer
                                     client_data,
281              XtPointer call_data )
282      {
283          button_struct *b = (button_struct *)client_data;
284
285          Calc *obj = (Calc *)b->object;
286
287          //
288          //         Pass on Callback
289          //
290          obj->Pushed(b->widget,(XtPointer)b->label,
                                 (XtPointer)call_data);
291      }
292
293      //
294      //         Pushbutton Callback Routine
```

```
295     //
296     void Calc::Pushed( Widget widget, XtPointer client_data,
                          XtPointer call_data )
297     {
298             char which_button = (char)client_data;
299
300             switch( which_button )
301             {
302                 case '0':
303                 case '1':
304                 case '2':
305                 case '3':
306                 case '4':
307                 case '5':
308                 case '6':
309                 case '7':
310                 case '8':
311                 case '9':
312                     if( clear_flag )
313                     {
314                         SetCalcDisplay( "" );
315                         clear_flag = 0;
316                     }
317                     AddToDisplay( which_button );
318                     break;
319
320                 case 'C':
321                     Reset();
322                     break;
323
324                 case '+':
325                 case '-':
326                 case '*':
327                 case '/':
328                     CalcSubTotal();
329                     operation = which_button;
330                     break;
```

```
331
332                         case '=':
333                                 CalcSubTotal();
334                                 operation = (char)NULL;
335                                 break;
336                 }
337     }
```

6.3.3 calc.h

```
1     //
2     //              TITLE:      CALC.H
3     //
4     //              FUNCTION:   Calc Class Definition
5     //
6     #ifndef _CALC_H
7     #define _CALC_H
8
9     #include <stdlib.h>
10    #include <string.h>
11
12    #include <Xm/Form.h>
13    #include <Xm/Text.h>
14    #include <Xm/TextF.h>
15    #include <Xm/PushB.h>
16    #include <Xm/RowColumn.h>
17
18    //
19    //        Declarations
20    //
21    class Calc;        // Class Declaration for Forward Reference
22
23    //
24    //        Constants
25    //
26    const int max_rows = 4;
27    const int max_cols = 4;
```

```
28
29    //
30    //          Button Structure - Serves as Client Data
31    //
32    struct button_struct {
33              char      label;
34              Calc      *object;
35              Widget    widget;
36    };
37
38    //
39    //          Class Definition
40    //
41    class Calc {
42    private:
43              Widget mainform;      // Main form widget
44              Widget display;       // Calculator Display
45              Widget button_form;   // Form for Buttons
46
47              long      total;      // Calculator Total
48              char      operation;  // Store Operation on Key Press
49              int       clear_flag; // Clear Display
50
51              button_struct *buttons; // Storage for Callbacks
52
53              //
54              //          Private Member Functions
55              //
56              void Calc::CalcSubTotal();
57              void Calc::AddToDisplay( char c );
58              void Calc::SetCalcDisplay( char *str );
59
60    public:
61              ~Calc();
62              Calc( Widget );
63
64              void Calc::Reset();
```

```
65                    void Calc::Pushed( Widget, XtPointer, XtPointer );
66                    static void Static_Pushed( Widget, XtPointer,
                                                 XtPointer );
67      };
68
69      #endif
```

6.3.4 utility.cxx

```
1       //
2       //              TITLE:          UTILITY.CXX
3       //
4       //              FUNCTION:           Utility functions
5       //
6
7       //
8       //              RTB():   Remove trailing Blanks from a String
9       //
10      void rlb( char *buf )
11      {
12              char *cp = buf;
13
14              while( *cp == ' ' )
15                      cp++;
16
17              if( cp != buf )
18                      while( *buf++ = *cp++ )
19                              ;
20      }
21
```

PART 2

INTRODUCTION TO OBJECT-ORIENTED ANALYSIS AND DESIGN

I N THE PREVIOUS SECTION, we began to combine C++ classes and Motif widgets. Specifically, we designed a calculator class that, when instantiated, created a complete GUI interface. Although it was an improvement over the basic widget API, this implementation had some shortcomings:

- The basic object (the calculator) was not developed using object-oriented analysis techniques.
- The individual components of the calculator (e.g., the display) are not, themselves, objects.
- Developers can not easily reuse the code contained in the program.

In essence, all we did was place a C++ wrapper around a C API. If we want to realize the full potential of the object-oriented environment, we must design applications with objects in mind. To accomplish this, we need to understand how to design and develop true object-oriented applications.

In Part 2, we begin to explore the power of the object-oriented paradigm. First, in Chapter 7 we describe a simple technique for performing object-oriented analysis and design. In Chapter 8, based on our newly acquired knowledge, we take another look at the design of our calculator program. Finally, in Chapter 9, we reimplement the calculator as a true object-oriented program.

CHAPTER 7

AN INTRODUCTION TO OO ANALYSIS AND DESIGN

As mentioned in Chapter 3, a programming paradigm requires analysis and design methodologies as well as an implementation language. To work well, the analysis and design techniques should support the underlying model. In addition, the development language should contain programming constructs that support the implementation of the model. As we will see, this holds true for C++ and the OO paradigm.

In traditional paradigms—most notably procedural—we have been trained to focus on *verbs*. This leads to programs whose major abstraction is the *procedure*. In the object-oriented paradigm, we reorient our approach and focus on data, or *nouns*. Specifically, we try to identify the important *objects* (i.e., classes) that our application will need. It is these classes and their relationships to each other that ultimately define the architecture of an OO application.

7.1. INTRODUCTION TO OBJECT-ORIENTED A&D

7.1.1 Overview

There are many well-known approaches to OO analysis and design (see the bibliography for a comprehensive list). However, none of the existing methodologies are complete; that is, from a practical perspective, no existing methodology is effective throughout the entire development process. For example, some methodologies work well during analysis, but fall short during design. For others, the opposite holds true. Thus, we will borrow ideas from several methodologies to create a synthesized approach that performs well throughout the entire development cycle.

The above notwithstanding, all of the prominent methodologies share one common feature, their almost zealot-like focus on classes. This is where we will begin our approach. Unfortunately, due to the nature and focus of this text, we cannot provide a complete treatise on object-oriented analysis and design. However, we will provide a solid foundation that will serve our needs throughout the remainder of this text.

7.1.2 *Object-Oriented System Development*

We can partition OO development into three phases, each with major components:

- Analysis
  - ◆ Understand the problem domain
  - ◆ Understand user requirements
  - ◆ Understand system behavior
- Design
  - ◆ Architectonic the software system
  - ◆ Designing classes
  - ◆ Designing interfaces
- Implementation
  - ◆ Implement classes
  - ◆ Implement relationships
  - ◆ Allocate objects to processors/processes

With the exception of implementation, the remainder of this chapter will discuss each of the above topics in detail. We will postpone discussion of implementation until Chapter 9.

7.2 OBJECT-ORIENTED ANALYSIS

7.2.1 *Understand the Problem Domain*

The main purpose of the analysis phase is to understand the problem we are trying to solve. We usually begin by defining the problem *domain*. A domain is a world unto itself. In programming terms, it is the world, or the piece of it, that we are going to automate. To a large degree, domains are independent of one another. Examples include:

- An industry
- An organization
- A business unit
- A product line
- A department
- Your little brother's bedroom (well beyond the scope of this book!)

The goals of domain analysis include:

- Obtain a thorough understanding of the problem we are trying to solve
- To identify a "vocabulary" to use when working within the environment
- To identify a set of interacting classes that represent the portion of the domain we are modeling

7.2.2 The Process

7.2.2.1 Objects and Classes
We begin by looking for objects. As noted previously, objects most often correspond to *nouns*. We proceed initially by "brainstorming"—that is, we enumerate a set of "candidate" classes. We then successively refine our list, pruning out unnecessary classes and adding new ones as needed.

7.2.2.2 Relationships
Next, we try to identify the relationships between classes. Relationships occur when classes depend on other classes or make references to other classes. We can group relationships into two[*] major categories:

---

*For purposes of this discussion, we will ignore other types of relationships.

SEMANTIC Semantic relationships are the important relationships that objects share in the real-world. For example:

- Person *works for* company

- Customer *purchases* products

These types of relationships depict object interaction in our problem domain.

OBJECT ORIENTED Object-oriented relationships include inheritance and containment (aggregation).

Relationships are most often associated with verbs or verb phrases. Some ideas of where to look include:

- Object actions: *moves, writes, drives*

- Object interaction: *talks to, sends*

- Object associations: *works for, manages, uses*

Once identified, we try to specify relationships with short phrases, such as:

- Person *drives* car

- Professor *teaches* student

- Employee *works for* company

2.2.3 Attributes

The next step is to identify the important *attributes* of each class. An attribute is a property of a class; it is a pure data value that maintains the state of the object. (As a result, we often refer to attributes as *state variables* or *state data.*) Every instantiated object of a given class receives and maintains its own copy of the state variables. Thus, if we tell one "car" object to "paint itself blue," the message will not affect the color of any other "car" object.

During the analysis phase, we focus our attention on attributes that are important to the application as a whole. We do not concern ourselves with minor attributes. We will leave them to the discretion of the class designers and implementors. For example, if we are designing a "car" class, we might identify "engine" as an important attribute, but ignore "color."

7.2.2.4 Operations

An operation is a function that is applied to objects. Operations report on, or change the value of, the state of an object. As an example, consider a graphical object that draws itself on a GUI terminal. Some useful operations might include:

- Move()
- Erase()
- Rotate()
- Invert()

As with attributes, we tend to direct our attention toward operations that are significant to the application as a whole. We will enumerate a complete set of operations for each class later in the development cycle.

7.2.2.5 The Deliverables

There are two major deliverables for this engineering activity: a *class diagram* and a *glossary*. Each is intended to convey the information we have gleaned during this phase.

7.2.2.5.1 Class Diagram

Class diagrams depict the types of objects and their relationships. A simple example appears in Figure 7.1.

We depict each class with a rectangle using its name listed inside. Important attributes are also included within each box. You may optionally list an attribute's type and initial value. Operations are listed below attributes. We usually draw a line to separate them visually. You may find it useful to specify the return type and arguments for important operations. We represent relationships by drawing lines connecting the interacting classes. As depicted in our example, we should provide a name for each relationship.

7.2.2.5.2 Glossary

The glossary lists and describes all of the classes and relationships in our model. It provides details about the behavior of classes (as they become known) and all assumptions that one might find difficult to infer from the class diagram.

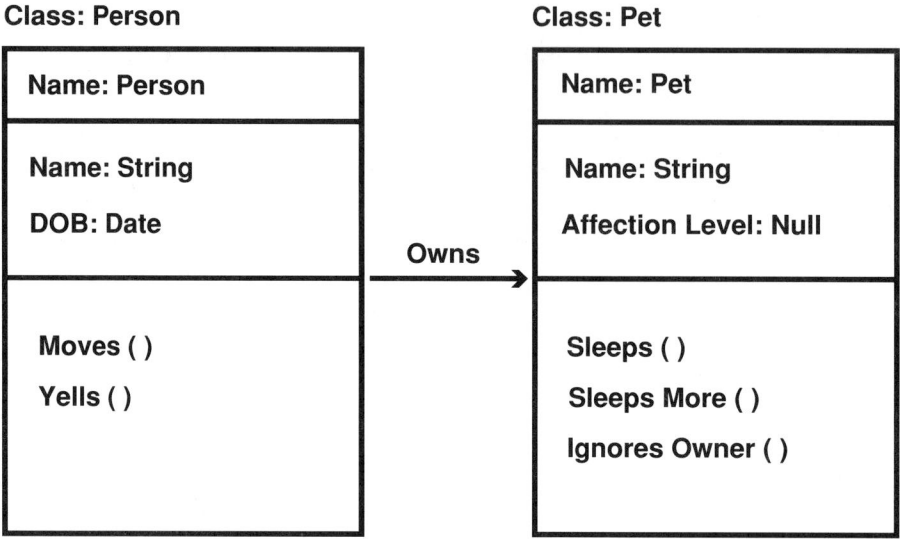

Class: Person

Name: Person
Name: String DOB: Date
Moves ( ) Yells ( )

Owns →

Class: Pet

Name: Pet
Name: String Affection Level: Null
Sleeps ( ) Sleeps More ( ) Ignores Owner ( )

FIGURE 7.1. Sample class diagram.

7.2.2.6 *Summary*

Note that the steps discussed in this section are not necessarily discrete. That is, as we identify classes, we might also discover relationships between classes; uncovering a new relationship might point out a missing class. As a rule, you should record all ideas as they occur.

7.2.3 *Understand User Requirements*

The third phase of analysis is understanding user requirements. The goal of this phase of analysis is to understand the operation of the system from the perspective of the user. To accomplish this, we must identify the potential users, the roles they play in the system, and the events that are generated as a result of their interaction.

7.2.3.1 *The Process*

7.2.3.1.1 *Actors & Their Roles for $100, Alex!* The fist step is to determine the *actors* and the *roles* they play within the system. An actor is anyone or anything external to the system that initiates processing within the application. The purpose of this activity is to identify the types of requests that the system must support.

7.2.3.1.2 Use Cases Once we determine the actors, the next step is to identify *use cases*. A use case is a complete course of events initiated by an actor. In effect, it specifies a set of interactions between a user and the application. For examples of some use cases, consider a typical banking application.

- Customer deposits money in a savings account
- Customer requests cash from an ATM terminal
- Customer transfers money from a savings account to a checking account (in the author's household, this is an all-too-common scenario)

7.2.3.1.3 Event Traces Although helpful in their own right, use cases do not provide developers with enough detail. As a result, we need to flesh them out. We accomplish this through the use of *scenarios* or *event traces*. A scenario is a sequences of events that portrays a single execution trace within the application.

For example, consider a vending machine that is composed of three objects: a *customer,* a *dispenser,* and a *coin collector.* An event trace might look something like the following:

- A. Customer deposits a quarter
- B. Customer deposits a dime
- C. Customer push selection button
- D. Dispenser queries coin collector
- E. Dispenser releases product
- F. Dispenser

Event traces such as the above help us several ways:

- They identify and define system behavior
- They identify required operations/services that individual classes must provide
- They identify omitted classes
- They serve as a check against our model to ensure its integrity

Event traces are not only easy to generate, they can actually exercise one's ingenuity. They are an indispensable part of a complete object-oriented analysis.

7.2.3.1.4 Adding Interface and Control Classes The classes we have identified to this point are called *entity* classes. They represent objects that exist in our problem domain. We now need to define two other types of classes: *interface* and *control.*

An interface class does just what its name implies: it encapsulates an interface. Interfaces can range from dumb ASCII terminals to X stations to sophisticated hardware device controllers. Taking this to its logical extreme, we could create a set of classes that would serve as foundation for a Motif-based application framework. (Excellent topic for a book!)

We use control classes to encapsulate behavior that is not otherwise associated with any of our other (entity or interface) classes. This is easier to understand with an example. Consider a simple banking transaction. A customer wants to transfer $100 from a savings account to a checking account. To simplify the lives of application programmers, you decide to provide this processing as a *transfer operation.* This begs the question: In which class should you place the transfer() method? We could try to force into one of the account objects. However, a better solution is to provide a control class called Transfer that performs the indicated operation. This type of solution encapsulates the relationship in another class. Figure 7.2 graphically illustrates this process.

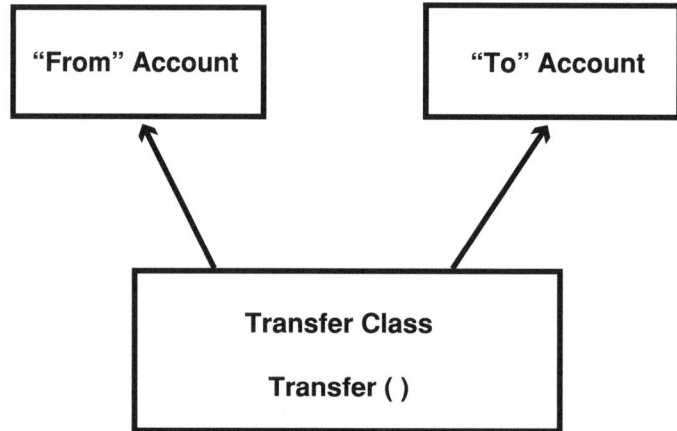

FIGURE 7.2. An example of a Control Class.

7.2.3.2 Deliverables
There are several deliverables required for this phase of analysis:

- Scenario listings
- Event trace listings
- Event trace diagrams

We also need to add the interface and control classes to our class diagram.

7.2.4 Understanding System Behavior

7.2.4.1 Overview
Classes, as depicted in our model, are static. Another way to view objects is to understand their behavior as they evolve over time. This gives us a more dynamic view of objects.

Moreover, an object's behavior (i.e., its responses to messages) may vary over time. That is, given a certain set of values for its attributes, an object may invoke behavior B_1 in response to message M_1; later, assuming its state has changed, the object may invoke behavior B_2 in response to the same message. We can envision an object's collective set of attribute values as a *state*. If any of the object's attribute values change, we can say that the object has changed state. We refer to such a change in state as a *transition*. We can represent states graphically in Harel diagrams as depicted in Figure 7.3.

We represent states as ovals. Solid dots represent the initial states; a dot within an enclosing circle represents a terminating, or result, state. The arrows represent transitions. We tag each transition with an *event/action* label. Event denotes the event that prompted the transition; action represents

FIGURE 7.3. State diagram notation.

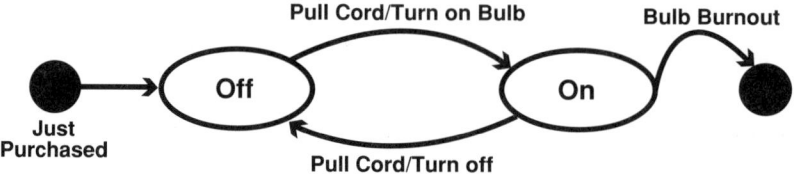

FIGURE 7.4. State diagram for a table lamp.

any processing the object must perform before effecting the transition. Figure 7.4 depicts the transition diagram for a simple table lamp with a pull cord.

7.2.4.2 Creating State Diagrams

We create state diagrams for objects as follows:

1. Begin by envisioning an initial state.
2. List all events (messages) that are possible in that state.
3. Select one of these events and name the state the object will transition to after it completes any processing.
4. If it is a new state, add it to the diagram.
5. Draw an arrow between the two states and label the transition.
6. Identify and name any action the object must perform (if other than just changing state).
7. Repeat steps 1–6 for all event or state combinations.

7.2.4.3 Deliverables

The deliverable at this phase is obviously a state transition diagram for all objects with life-cycles. However, although simple for humans, the state transition diagram is difficult to implement (as we will learn shortly.) Another way to represent a state diagram is with a state *transition matrix*. Figure 7.5 contains a state transition matrix for the table lamp example.

We list states vertically, with events across the top. Each cell in the matrix contains two parts. The top section denotes the action the machine should complete when it receives a given event; the bottom section indicates which state the machine should transition to after completing the action.

State \ Event	Buy	Pull Cord	Burn Out	
Initial	Plug In ——— Off State	Turn On Bulb ——— On State	Ignore	
On	Can't Happen	Turn Off Bulb ——— Off State	——— Halt	
Off	Ignore	Turn On Bulb ——— On State	Ignore	

FIGURE 7.5. Sample state diagram.

In addition to simplifying implementation, generating a state transition matrix affords us the following benefits:

- It verifies the integrity of the state transition diagram.
- It completely characterizes the life cycle of an object. (It even depicts events that cannot occur.) As a result, we can more accurately describe the actions and processing the object must undertake during transitions.

7.3 OBJECT-ORIENTED DESIGN

In the design phase, we begin to map our problem domain into the solution domain. That is, as a result of the analysis phase, we understand *what* the system must do. The design phases helps us formalize *how* the system will do it.

There is a raging debate among methodologists as to when we should transition to design. One extreme holds that we want to perform as much work as possible in the analysis phase so that we may focus on functionality. The other extreme contends that we do not want to remain too pure for too long for fear of having to radically alter our model when we are confronted with real-world limitations. The practical answer is somewhere in the middle: to remain pure in analysis, with an eye toward implementation.

We will partition design into two distinct phases:

- Designing the system architecture

- Designing individual objects

7.3.1 *Designing the System Architecture*

7.3.1.1 *The Process*

The purpose of this phase is to begin to allocate objects to processors (in multi- or distributed-processing environment) and to processes (in multitasking environments). To do this, we need to determine which objects use (i.e., call upon the services of) other objects. With respect to a client, there are two distinct ways in which one object may use another:

- An object may use another object as part of its public interface. For example, an object might have a member function `funct1()` that takes an object *B* as a parameter. In this case, the client might need to how to use objects of type *B*.

- An object may use another object as part of its implementation. For example, object *A* might contain an object *B* as a data member. In this case, the relationship between objects *A* and *B* would be transparent to the client. Indeed, the client may remain blissfully unaware of the arrangement.

We also must determine other attributes for our objects, such as *persistence, concurrency,* and *visibility.*

> **PERSISTENCE** Persistence is an important attribute of an object. How long will the object live? For all or part of the lifetime of a program or function? Or must the object transcend the execution of any particular program?

> **CONCURRENCY** Concurrency embodies two distinct facets:

> - Can the object coexist with other objects of the same class? For example, consider an object that is an interface to the single tape unit on some machine. Tape drives are usually 'opened' exclusively by a process.

> - Is the object, itself, concurrent? As an example, consider a "climate" object that can concurrently test and adjust the temperatures in several rooms.

> **VISIBILITY** An object's visibility is important to any other client or object that might want to use it. Is the object in my program? Is it in a different process but on the same machine? It the object on a different machine? Based on the above, how do we send it messages?

7.3.1.1 Deliverables

The deliverable at this phase is an updated list of classes with each of the above attributes described.

7.3.2 Designing Individual Objects

In this phase, we will design the individual classes whose objects will populate our application. In addition, we will need to design the implementation of relationships.

7.3.2.1 The Process

For each object that we cannot implement as a state machine (see below), we will need to develop algorithms and data structures. This is classic software development and is beyond the scope of this text.

For objects with lifecycles, we can construct their state machines in one of two ways. In the first method, we implement the state machine implicitly, as part of the normal flow-of-control logic. For example, refer back to the transition diagram depicted in Figure 7.4. We can implement the state machine implicitly using conventional coding constructs as illustrated by the pseudocode appearing in Listing 7.1.

```
1       if( cord pulled )
2               if( light is off )
3                       turn light on
4               else
5                       turn light on
```

LISTING 7.1. Implicit State Machine.

We can also code the state machine explicitly. The code fragment in Listing 7.2 provides an example.

```
1 class MyClass {

2 private:
3       enum State { State1, State2, ... };

4       State state;
5       //
6       //      Details Omitted
7       //

8 public:

9       void Event1()
10      {
11              switch( state )
12              {

13              case State1:
14                      //
15                      // Do Action
16                      //
```

```
17                    //
18                    // State Transition
19                    //
20                    state = NewState;
21                    break;

22            case State2:
23                    //
24                    // Details Omitted
25                    //
26            }
27      }

28      void Event2()
29      {
30              //
31              // Details Omitted
32              //
33      }

34      //
35      // Details Omitted
36      //
37 };
```

LISTING 7.2. Explicit state machine

We represent each event as a class method. The object maintains state in a `private` variable. In response to an event (i.e., the invocation of a member function), the object:

- Determines its current state
- Performs the appropriate action
- Transitions to a new state

Note that developing a state transition matrix makes the task of coding the class much simpler.

7.3.2.2 Deliverables
The deliverables at stage of the development cycle include:

- Additional class attributes
- Coding conventions
- State-machine design

7.3.3 Establishing Conventions

Unfortunately we will likely not have the luxury of working solely in the object-oriented paradigm. Reality dictates that any new object-based applications we are developing will more than likely interface with one or more legacy systems. Indeed, this book is about learning how to combine two distinct paradigms.

As a result, we may have to establish conventions that will support our foray into these dangerous waters. We may have to combine our C++ program with a procedural-based program, or we might need to support a relational database product. To minimize the difficulties of multiparadigm environments, we should establish and adopt strict conventions that define and control our interaction with non–object-oriented system components. One nice approach is to develop a set of C++ "class wrappers" that encapsulate the interface and insulate client programmers from the hardships of reality.

7.4 SUMMARY

This completes our overview of object-oriented analysis and design. In the next chapter, we will put this knowledge to work as we redesign our calculator program.

8

REDESIGNING THE CALCULATOR

In this chapter, we revisit the design of our calculator program. We will base our new design upon the synthesized methodology presented in the previous chapter. Our purpose is twofold. First, we want to show you how to design and implement the calculator program in a more object-oriented manner. Second, this material will serve as the foundation for the application framework that we will design in Section III.

8.1 ANALYSIS

8.1.1 Problem Specification

We need not dwell on the problem specification for this simple example. Our task is to re-implement the calculator program of Chapter 6. It will contain the identical components and function in the identical manner. As a convenience, Figure 8.1 depicts a copy of the interface.

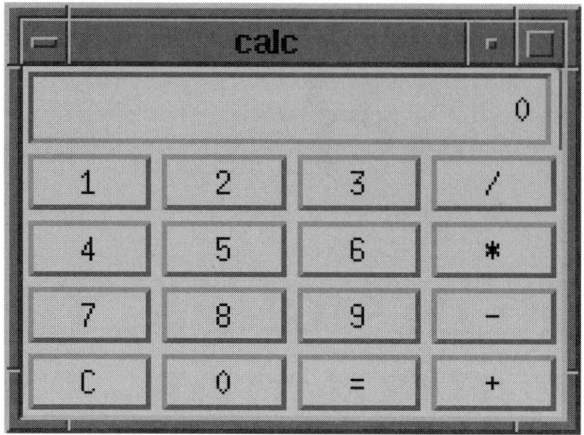

FIGURE 8.1. Calculator interface.

8.1.2 *Finding the Classes*

Based on the implementation discussed in Chapter 6, there appears to be only one class: `calc`. However, let's take a closer look. A calculator has a *keypad* and a *display*. Certainly, we can think of each of these items as individual objects:

- A keypad can function as an autonomous unit, sending key-press events to interested parties.
- A display object can function as a general-purpose display device.

In addition, we will need an object that will drive the operation of the calculator and respond to user commands. Let's call that object `calc_engine`. In effect, the engine will serve as the "brains" of the calculator.

Thus far we have identified three types of objects. Left as is, client programmers would have to understand and work with all three classes to create a working calculator. On the contrary, we would like the new programming interface to be as easy to use as the version in Chapter 6. As a result, we will create a fourth class, a control class, called *calc*. It will serve a wrapper for the other classes.

8.1.3 *Relationships*

Obviously, due to the minimal number of objects in this example, we need to address only a few relationships. Let's begin with the most obvious:

- To display the results of computations, the `calc_engine` class will need to send messages to a `display` object.

- Equally as obvious, the `calc_engine` object will also interact with a `keypad`.

   The final relationship we need to address is the one shared by `keypad` and `display`. At first, it might seem that the two objects should share a direct relationship. Consider that when a user presses a numeric button, the digit should appear on the display. With this in mind, we could argue that `keypad` should send messages directly to `display`. However, such a relationship would prompt the following concerns:

- With each key-press, a `keypad` object would need to send two messages: one to `display` and one to the `calc_engine`. This in and of itself is not a major concern. However, consider that as a result of a particular key-press, the engine and keypad each might want conflicting values displayed. For example, the engine might not want trailing zeros to display after a decimal point. This type of architecture would force classes to compete for resources.

- Not all keys presses will prompt a change in the display. For example, there are cases when the user presses an operator key, and the display remains unchanged. We would have a poor design if our `keypad` object had to "know" to which of several objects it should send each key press message. This would mean the `display` object would have to become application aware. On the contrary, to encourage code reuse, we want classes to be generic in nature. For example, a `display` object might be useful in other solutions such as a stopwatch or a data-entry application.

As a result, we will not implement this last relationship. Figure 8.2 depicts the set of relationships we will use.

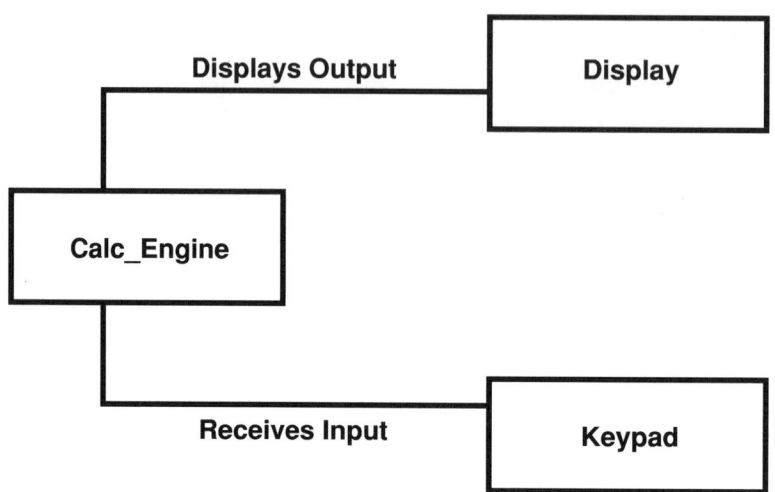

FIGURE 8.2. Calculator relationships.

8.1.4 Attributes

At this point, the important attributes of each class are as follows:

> calc_engine The calc_engine class will need attributes to maintain the following state data:
>
> - Current total
> - Current operand
> - Current operation
>
> display The display class will need an attribute to maintain the current contents of the display. As we will see, we will use widget resources to handle this requirement.
>
> keypad The keypad class will need an attribute to maintain its relationship with an calc_engine object.

8.1.5 Operations

The class calc_engine provides operations for all of the logical keys on a calculator (e.g., '+', '-', CLEAR, etc.). The display class must provide an opera-

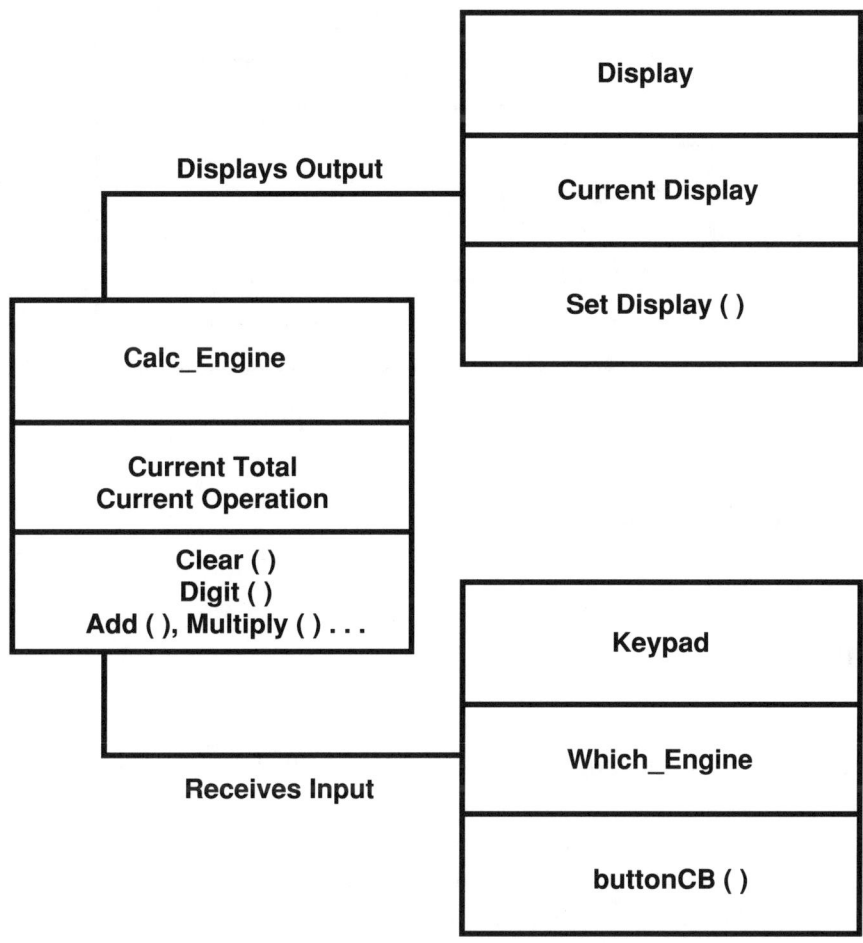

FIGURE 8.3. Calculator class diagram.

tion that will allow other objects to update its display. The keypad class does not provide any services to the other objects. It does, however, interface with Motif—via callbacks—to build and maintain the GUI frontend.

8.1.6 Deliverables

Figure 8.3 depicts the final version or our class diagram, Note that we have included attributes and operations in this version of the model.

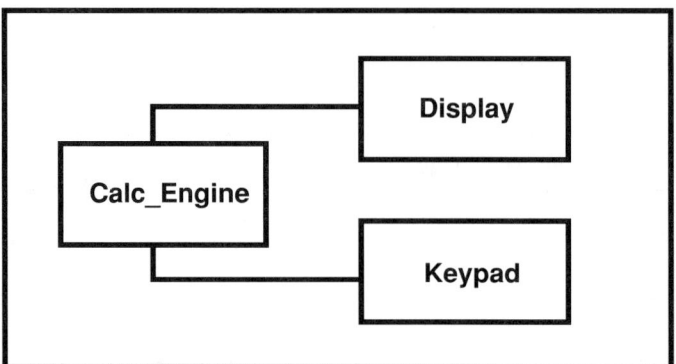

FIGURE 8.4. Updated Calc Class diagram.

8.1.7 *User Requirements*

8.1.7.1 *Actors/Roles*
Defining actors and roles for this application is trivial. We have one central actor: the user.

8.1.7.2 *Use Cases*
There are several important use cases for this application. We can describe them as follows:

A + B = This is a basic calculation. The user has entered the operator and its operand, and expects a direct result. Note that after pressing an operator key (in this case '+'), the user expects the display to clear with the press of the next digit key.

A + B -... This is a somewhat more complex operation. As above, the user expects the display to clear automatically. However, in this case, the user also expects an intermediate result to display with the press of the second operator key ('-').

A + B * / ... In this case, the user has changed the operation. That is, after pressing the ('*') key, the user decided that the correct operation was division. The display should remain the same and the engine should record the new operation.

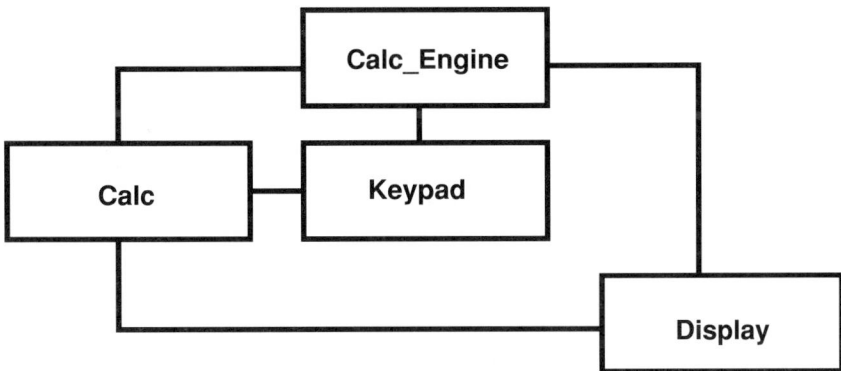

FIGURE 8.5. Calc class diagram: alternative view.

8.1.7.3 Interface Classes

Due to the nature of this application, we have already identified the interface classes, namely, keypad and display.

8.1.7.4 Control Classes

At first glance, it appears as if we have no need for control classes in this solution. However, note that as things stand, a client would have to instantiate three classes and implement two relationships just to create a single instance of a calculator.

As mentioned previously, we can simplify the lives of client programmers by creating a control class. This class, called calc, will address the more mundane matters associated with calculator initialization. Thus, clients would need to instantiate only one object. Figure 8.4 depicts our class diagram with the calc class included.

As an aside, many people like to view an enclosing control class (like calc), as a peer of the other classes. That is, instead of depicting a containment relationship, they prefer to represent control classes as having relationships with its contained classes. Figure 8.5 provides an example.

8.1.8 Understanding System Behavior

8.1.8.1 State Machines

There are several classes in our calculator program. Only calc_engine, however, is suitable for implementing as a state machine. That is, it gets instantiated,

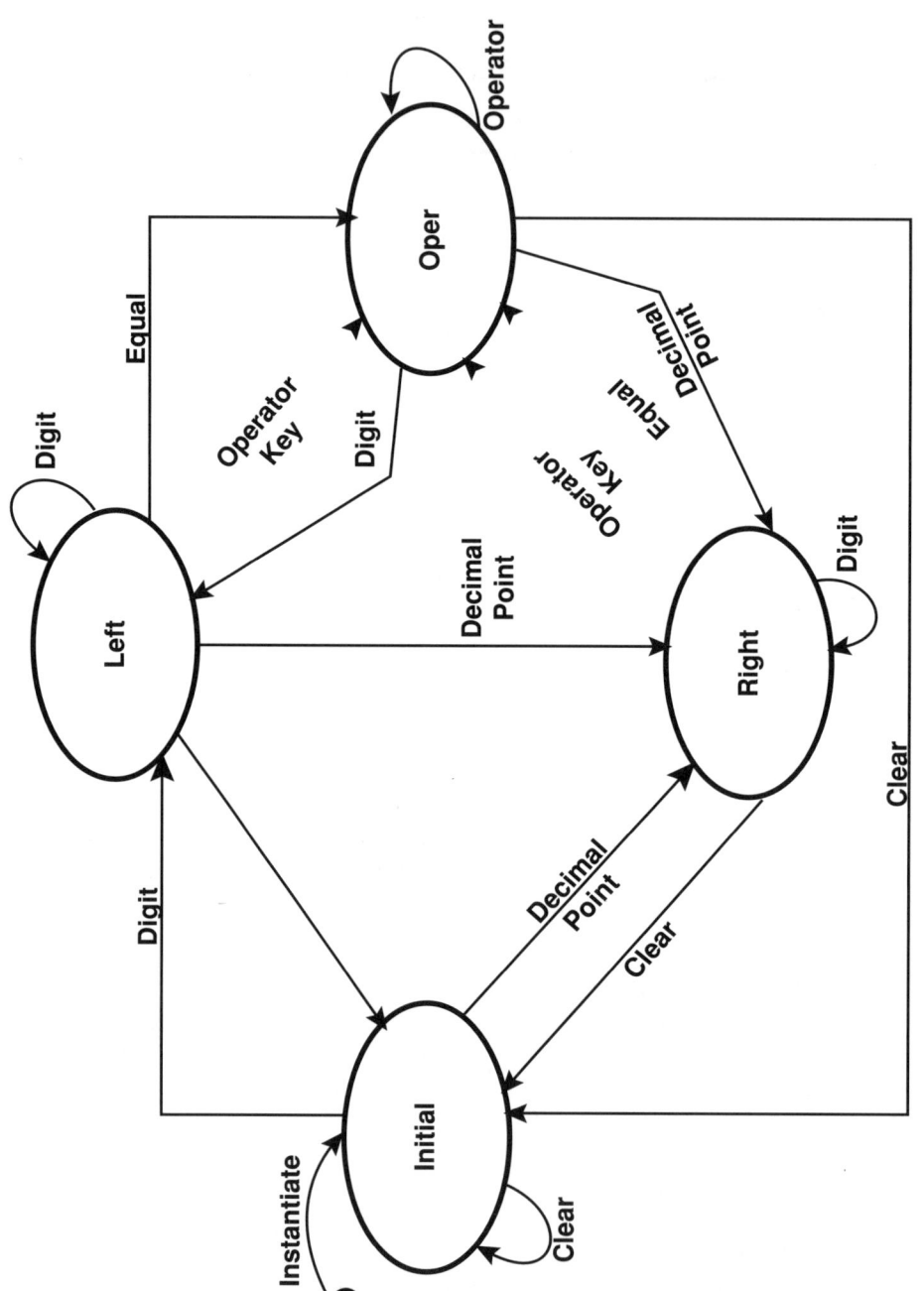

FIGURE 8.6. Calc_Engine state diagram.

responds to events (key presses), and then terminates.

As described in the Chapter 7, we begin our analysis by imagining the object in an initial state, say, just after instantiation. We then enumerate all possible events for that state and create transitions and states as required. Figure 8.6 contains the state diagram for our calculator program.

To ensure proper use of the decimal point, we use two states (left and right) to track the accumulation of digits. The machine remains in the left state until the user presses a decimal point; it then transitions to the right state. While in the right state, the machine ignores all subsequent presses of the decimal point key. Note also, the transition from oper back to oper on receipt of an operator event. This represents the case where the user changes operation (e.g., from '+' to '-').

8.2 DESIGN

8.2.1 System Architecture

For this tiny application, we need not be overly concerned with system architecture. In fact, this class structure is not intended to operate independently, but as part of a larger system.

8.2.2 Designing Individual Objects

For all objects with lifecycles, our next step is to convert the state diagram into a state transition matrix. We undertake this step to facilitate implementation. Figure 8.7 contains an example state transition matrix for the calc_engine class.

Each of the cells in the matrix is divided into two sections. The top section denotes the action required in each state as a result of a particular event. The bottom half specifies the new state to which the machine will transition after completing the action. Note that the actions are specified using a kind of pseudocode. We are thus not mired in detail at stage. Also, note that some of the cells specify an action of "ignore."

8.2.3 Other Classes

We will implement the other three classes in a more traditional manner, using algorithms and data structures, and postpone this discussion until Chapter 9.

Event (Key) \ State	Digit	Clear	Operator Key	Equal	Decimal Point
Init	Add Digit to Disp ---- Left	Reset ( ) Oper=Clear Disp (0.0) ---- Init	Ignore ---- Init	Ignore ---- Init	Add (.) to Disp ---- Right
Left	Add Digit to Disp ---- Left	Reset ( ) ---- Init	Push Operand Calc ( ) Oper=key Display Results ---- Oper	Push Operand Calc ( ) Display Oper= '=' ---- Oper	Add (.) to Disp ---- Right
Right	Add Digit to Disp ---- Right	Reset ( ) ---- Init	Push Operand Calc ( ) Disp Results Set Oper ---- Oper	Push Operand Calc ( ) Display Oper= '=' ---- Oper	Ignore ---- Right
Oper	Reset Disp Add Digit to Disp ---- Left	Reset ( ) ---- Init	Oper=New Oper ---- Oper	Ignore ---- Oper	Add (.) to Disp ---- Right

FIGURE 8.7. State transition matrix for Calc_Engine.

8.2.3.1 *Relationships*

Our last design task will be to determine the implementation of relationships. Again, owing to the lack of complexity, we will implement all relationships using simple pointer variables.

8.2.3.1 *Establish Conventions*

We need to establish a couple conventions for this exercise. To wit:

- All constructors will require a `widget` argument to serve as the parent for all `widgets` created within the classes.

- Each class will maintain an attribute of type `widget` to store the parent `widgets` ID.

8.3 SUMMARY

In this chapter, we have put to use many of the ideas discussed in Chapter 7. We have used object-oriented development techniques to revamp the design of our calculator program. The next step is the actual implementation, which we will discuss in Chapter 9. Based on our new design, the code should not look anything like our original version.

9

CALCULATOR
REVISITED: THE
IMPLEMENTATION

In this chapter, we turn our attention to the implementation of the new version of the calculator. Before we begin, we need to address several implementation considerations.

First, we need to decide how we should implement relationships. Specifically, we want to implement classes with code reuse in mind. We can describe the problem by discussing the relationship between Keypad and CalcEngine. The question is: How does a Keypad object inform a CalcEngine object that the user has pressed a particular key? If Keypad "knows" about CalcEngine, the classes are too tightly coupled. That is, we could never use a Keypad object without carrying a CalcEngine object around as baggage. Alternatively, we do not want the relationship to become so uncoupled as to become inefficient or difficult to use. We will address two solutions to this problem in this chapter; subsequent chapters will discuss others.

The second concern is from the client's perspective. Simply stated, we would like our Calc class to be as easy to use as possible. In particular, we do not want our clients to concern themselves with any details (e.g., implementing relationships). To that end, we will encapsulate all of the nasties in a control class.

9.1 IMPLEMENTATION

9.1.1 *Overview*

We will begin our discussions with the `Calc` class. This will provide us an overview of the implementation. Following that, we will discuss `CalcDisplay`, `Keypad`, and `CalcEngine` classes (in that order). We will then provide an example that demonstrates the way the classes are used.

9.1.2 *Caveats*

Please keep the following points in mind as you review the code.

- The `CalcEngine` class draws upon the service of a stack class. A professional implementation would typically draw upon a class library to provide such a service. However, for the purposes of this book, we did not want to tie the implementation to any compilation environment.* As a result, we developed a *simple* stack class to serve the needs of this exercise. We will not include its implementation as part of our discussions, but we do include its code as part of the complete listing that appears at the end of this chapter.

- We were not concerned with optimizing all of the FSA code. In particular, many of the FSA `case` blocks could have been combined. For pedagogical reasons, we kept some cases separate.

- We were also not overly concerned with programming attributes such as arithmetic precision or computational performance. For example, we could have employed a technique called *arbitrary precision arithmetic* to increase the accuracy of calculations. However, topics such as these are well beyond the scope of this book. Please refer to the bibliography for appropriate references.

9.1.3 *calc.h*

As stated previously, we will begin our discussions with the `Calc` class contained in the file `calc.h`. The module begins in typical fashion (i.e., include files and macro definitions), then defines the `Calc` class.

---

*In fact, the author used several compilation environments to test all of the code contained in this book.

```
1   //
2   //              TITLE:          CALC.H
3   //
4   //              FUNCTION:       Class definition for Calc
5   //
6   //
7
8   #ifndef _CALC_H_
9   #define _CALC_H_
10
11  #include <stdlib.h>
12  #include <string.h>
13
14  #include <Xm/Form.h>
15  #include <Xm/Text.h>
16  #include <Xm/TextF.h>
17  #include <Xm/PushB.h>
18  #include <Xm/RowColumn.h>
19
20  #include "keypad.h"
21  #include "display.h"
22  #include "calc_eng.h"
23
24  class Calc {
25
26  private:
27
28          Widget main_form;           // Parent Widget
29
30          Keypad          *keypad;    // Keypad Object
31          CalcEngine      *engine;    // Engine Object
32          CalcDisplay     *display;   // Display Object
```

As you may recall, Calc is a control class. As a result, it contains pointers to the other objects it will manage on the client's behalf. The first routine we encounter is disp(). This function serves as an interface between a Calc-Engine object and a CalcDisplay object. That is, it serves as a callback mechanism in that when the engine needs to modify the display, it calls disp() to pass the call on to the appropriate CalcDisplay object. This routine works by casting its obj argument to the appropriate type and then invoking SetDisplay() with str as a parameter. This design decouples CalcEngine from Display, fostering reuse of both classes individually rather than as a pair. The use of a control class (such as Calc) allows us to achieve this decoupling with minimal impact on client programmers:

```
34              //
35              // DISP():
36              //      "Callback" Routine used as an
37              //      interface to the Engine class.
38              //
39              //      disp() is called from a CalcEngine
40              //      and the call us passed on to a
41              //      display object. The "callback" is
42              //      "registered" in the constructor (Calc()).
43              //
44              static void disp( char *str, void *obj )
45              {
46                      ((Calc *)obj)->display->SetDisplay( str );
47              }
```

The Calc class definition closes with constructor and destructor declarations. We will discuss their definitions in the next section.

```
49      public:
50
51              Calc( Widget );
52              ~Calc();
53      };
```

9.1.4 calc.cxx

The module calc.cxx contains the definitions of the constructor and destructor for the Calc class. Let's begin with the constructor. Lines 15 and 16 create and manage a form widget to serve as the parent component for the rest of the calculator.

```
 8   #include "calc.h"
 9
10   Calc::Calc( Widget parent )
11   {
12           //
13           //        Create Form Widget
14           //
15           main_form = XmCreateForm( parent, "mainform", NULL, 0 );
16           XtManageChild( main_form );
```

Following that, on lines 21, 26, and 31, the function instantiates the other objects required by the calculator. Note that when we instantiate a Calc-Engine object (line 26) we pass the constructor pointers to implement the callback. Thus, the CalcEngine object now knows to whom it should send its display requests. Also, note that the constructors for both CalcDisplay and Keypad require a parent widget (main_form) as an argument. CalcEngine does not because it is not an interface class. This design simplifies the programming interface, but it also introduces some concerns that we will explore at the end of this chapter.

```
18           //
19           //        Create CalcDisplay Object
20           //
21           display = new CalcDisplay( main_form );
22
23           //
24           //        Create Engine Object
25           //
26           engine = new CalcEngine( disp, (void *)this );
27
28           //
29           //        Create Keypad
30           //
31           keypad = new Keypad( main_form, engine );
32   }
```

The only other function defined in this file is the destructor; it only needs to delete created objects.

```
34    Calc::~Calc( Widget p )
35    {
36            //
37            //          Clean-up
38            //
39            delete display;
40            delete engine;
41            delete keypad;
42    }
```

9.1.5 display.h

The next module we will discuss is display.h, which contains the definition of the class CalcDisplay. This class creates and manages the display component of the calculator. It begins with a declaration of a private Widget variable.

```
 1    //
 2    //          TITLE:          DISPLAY.H
 3    //
 4    //          FUNCTION:       Complete implementation of the
                                  CalcDisplay Class.
 5    //
 6
 7    #ifndef _CALC_DISPLAY_
 8    #define _CALC_DISPLAY_
 9
10    #include <Xm/Text.h>
11    #include <Xm/TextF.h>
12
13    class CalcDisplay
14    {
15
16    private:
17
18            Widget display;
```

Next, we define two public functions. The constructor creates a TextField widget to serve as the display. To insure that is operates as a write-only screen component, we set three resources—XmNeditable, XmNcursorPosition-Visible, and XmNtraversalOn—to False.

```
20      public:
21
22              //
23              //        Constructor:
24              //
25              CalcDisplay( Widget parent )
26              {
27                      //
28                      //        Create TextField Widget for Display
29                      //
30                      display = XtVaCreateManagedWidget( "display",
31
32                      xmTextFieldWidgetClass,              parent,
33
34                      XmNeditable,                    False,
35                      XmNcursorPositionVisible,       False,
36                      XmNtraversalOn,                 False,
37
38                      NULL );
39              }
```

The other public function is called SetDisplay(). Its job is to take a string argument and display it in the TextField widget. To ensure nicely formatted output, SetDisplay() queries the TextField widget to determine the number of columns currently visible.

```
41              //
42              //        This Function Displays its String Arg
43              //
44              void SetDisplay( char *str )
45              {
46                      register            i;
47                      short               cols;
```

```
48                      Arg                    args[ 50 ];
49                      char                   buf[ 256 ];
50
51                      //
52                      //          Determine Number of Columns
53                      //
54                      i = 0;
55                      XtSetArg( args[i], XmNcolumns, &cols ); i++;
56                      XtGetValues( display, args, i );
57
58                      //
59                      //          Format Buffer
60                      //
61                      sprintf( buf, "%*.*s", cols, cols, str );
62
63                      //
64                      //          Update Display
65                      //
66                      XmTextSetString( display, buf );
67              }
68      };
69
70      #endif
```

9.1.6 *keypad.h*

The file keypad. h contains the definition of the class Keypad. This class contains two private data members, button_form and engine. The former is type Widget and serves as the parent of this screen component; the latter is of type CalcEngine* and points to the object to which Keypad will send its screen event messages.

```
1      //
2      //          TITLE:          KEYPAD.H
3      //
4      //          FUNCTION:       Definition of the class Keypad.
5      //
6
```

```
 7   #ifndef _Keypad_H_
 8   #define _Keypad_H_
 9
10   #include <stdlib.h>
11   #include <string.h>
12
13   #include <Xm/Form.h>
14   #include <Xm/PushB.h>
15   #include <Xm/RowColumn.h>
16
17   class CalcEngine;                         // Declare Engine Class
18
19   //
20   //       Constants (for button alignment)
21   //
22   const int max_rows = 4;
23   const int max_cols = 4;
24
25   //
26   //       Class Definition
27   //
28   class Keypad {
29
30   private:
31
32            Widget button_form;        // Form to hold buttons
33
34            CalcEngine *engine;        // Pointer to Engine Object
```

The class also contains three public functions: a constructor and two routines to implement a pushbutton callback. We will discuss their implementation in the next section.

```
38            Keypad( Widget, CalcEngine* );
39
40            //
41            //       Callback Functions
42            //
```

```
43      static void ButtonPressedCB( Widget, XtPointer, XtPointer );
44      virtual void ButtonCB( Widget, XtPointer, XtPointer );
45      };
```

9.1.7 keypad.cxx

This module contains the definition of the three member functions of the Keypad class. After some normal housekeeping code, the module contains a structure definition, called button_struct, that will serve as client data for the callback mechanism.

```
10      //
11      //      Button Structure - Serves as "client data"
12      //      in callbacks.
13      //
14      struct button_struct {
15              char    label;
16              Keypad  *object;
17              Widget  widget;
18      };
```

Next, we declare an array of character pointers to serve as convenient storage for button labels.

```
20      //
21      //      Button Labels
22      //
23      static char *cb[] =
24      {
25              "1",  "2",  "3",  "/",
26              "4",  "5",  "6",  "*",
27              "7",  "8",  "9",  "-",
28              "C",  "0",  "=",  "+"
29      };
```

The first function defined in the file is the constructor. It requires two arguments. The first, as usual, it the parent widget ID; the second is a pointer to the CalcEngine object that will be the recipient of its keypress events.

```
31      //
32      //        Constructor
33      //
34      Keypad::Keypad( Widget parent, CalcEngine *e )
35      {
36
37              Arg              args[ 50 ];
38              int              i, index, row, col;
39              XmString         lab;
40              button_struct    *buttons;
```

The constructor begins by saving the CalcEngine pointer in a private state variable.

```
42              //
43              //        Save pointer to CalcEngine object
44              //
45              engine = e;
```

Next, the function begins constructing the user interface for the keypad. It begins with a form widget. Note that we set the XmNfractionBase equal to 4 to simplify button alignment.

```
47              //
48              //        Create Form to Hold Calculator Buttons
49              //
50              button_form = XtVaCreateManagedWidget( "keypad",
51
52                      xmFormWidgetClass,      parent,
53
54                      XmNfractionBase,        4,
55
56                      XmNlength,              200,
57                      XmNwidth,               200,
58
59              NULL );
```

Following the creation of the parent form, the constructor creates an array
of `button_struct` structures. Each array element will serve as client data in
a pushbutton callback.

```
61              //
62              //          Allocate storage for button callback structs
63              //
64              buttons = new button_struct[ max_rows * max_cols ];
```

The function closes with a set of nested `for` loops that construct the rows
and columns of buttons. Note that for each button, we store in its associated
`button_struct` the value of the `this` pointer (line 78), the button's label
(line 79), and, on line 89, the pushbutton's widget ID.

```
66              //
67              //          Create Calculator Buttons
68              //
69              for( row = 0; row < max_rows; row++ )
70              {
71                      for( col = 0; col < max_cols; col++ )
72                      {
73                              index = (row * max_cols) + col;
74
75                              //
76                              //          Save state info
77                              //
78                              buttons[index].object = this;
79                              buttons[index].label =
                                        cb[index][0];
80
81                              //
82                              //          Create Label
83                              //
84                              lab = XmStringCreateSimple(
                                        cb[index] );
85
```

In the above text, we noted that we set XmNfractionBase equal to 4. As a result, we can align our buttons in the form by using an attachment type of XmATTACH_POSITION (lines 97 and 98). In effect, we have divided the form into quarters (both vertically and horizontally), and we can position buttons using what amounts to row/column coordinates.

```
86                      //
87                      //          Create Button
88                      //
89                      buttons[index].widget = XtVaCreateManagedWidget(
89
91                      cb[index],
92
93                      xmPushButtonWidgetClass,  button_form,
94
95                      XmNlabelString,           lab,
96
97                      XmNtopAttachment,         XmATTACH_POSITION,
98                      XmNtopPosition,           row,
99
100                     XmNbottomAttachment,      XmATTACH_POSITION,
101                     XmNbottomPosition,        row+1,
102
103                     XmNleftAttachment,        XmATTACH_POSITION,
104                     XmNleftPosition,          col,
105
106                     XmNrightAttachment,       XmATTACH_POSITION,
107                     XmNrightPosition,         col+1,
108
109                     NULL );
```

Lines 110 through 118 register a XmNactivateCallback callback for the newly created pushbutton. Note that for each callback, we register the same static function (ButtonPressedCB) and set the client data to pointer to the appropriate element in the button[] array.

```
111                     //
112                     //          Register Callback
```

```
113                          //
114                          XtAddCallback( buttons[index].widget,
115                              XmNactivateCallback,
116                              (XtCallbackProc)ButtonPressedCB,
117                              (XtPointer)&buttons[index]
118                          );
119
120                          //
121                          //          Free String
122                          //
123                          XmStringFree( lab );
124                  }
125          }
126  }
```

The next function defined in the file is ButtonPressedCB(). Its job is to pass on the callback to the appropriate Keypad instance. As you may recall, we stored the pertinent data in the button[] array. Thus, ButtonPressedCB () can pass on the callback by simply creating a pointer to a Keypad object and assigning to it the value contained in the object member of the button structure passed as client data in the callback. The function also extracts the value of the label member and passes it on as client data to the nonstatic member function.

```
128  //
129  //          Static Callback Function
130  //
131  void Keypad::ButtonPressedCB( Widget widget,
132          XtPointer client_data, XtPointer call_data )
133  {
134          button_struct *b = (button_struct *)client_data;
135
136          Keypad *obj = (Keypad *)b->object;
137
138          //
139          //          Pass on callback to actual object
140          //
```

```
141                    obj->ButtonCB( b->widget, (XtPointer)b->label,
142                           (XtPointer)call_data );
143      }
```

The final function defined in keypad.cxx is ButtonCB(). This function actually carries out all of the work involved in processing a key-press event. In this example, the work is not too extensive. The function merely determines which button the user pressed and sends the appropriate message to the engine.

```
145      //
146      //        Pushbutton Callback Routine
147      //
148      void Keypad::ButtonCB( Widget widget,
149             XtPointer client_data, XtPointer call_data )
150      {
151             char which_button = (char)client_data;
152
153
154             switch( which_button )
155             {
156                    case '0':
157                    case '1':
158                    case '2':
159                    case '3':
160                    case '4':
161                    case '5':
162                    case '6':
163                    case '7':
164                    case '8':
165                    case '9':
166                            //
167                            // Pass on digit to engine
168                            //
169                            engine->digit( which_button-'0' );
170                            break;
171
```

```
172                    case 'C':
173                            //
174                            // Clear button pressed
175                            //
176                            engine->clear();
177                            break;
178
179                    case '+':
180                            //
181                            // Add operation
182                            //
183                            engine->add();
184                            break;
185
186                    case '-':
187                            //
188                            // Subtraction operation
189                            //
190                            engine->sub();
191                            break;
192
193                    case '*':
194                            //
195                            // Multiply operation
196                            //
197                            engine->mul();
198                            break;
199
200                    case '/':
201                            //
202                            // Division operation
203                            //
204                            engine->div();
205                            break;
206
207                    case '=':
208                            //
209                            // Compute & display result
```

```
210                                    //
211                                    engine->equal();
212                                    break;
213                    }
214        }
```

9.1.8 calc_eng.h

The file calc_eng.h contains the definition of the CalcEngine class. Calc-
Engine uses a stack class to perform its arithmetic operations (see the end of
this chapter for a complete listing). The use of a stack might seem like overkill
for the simple arithmetic computations performed in this version of the calculator, but we decided to implement the class in this manner to allow for future
extension.

```
1     //
2     //            TITLE:        CALC_ENG.H
3     //
4     //            FUNCTION:     Class definition for the "engine"
5     //                          portion of the calculator program.
6     //
7     //                          This class is implemented as
8     //                          a "State Machine".
9     //
10
11    #ifndef _CalcEngine_
12    #define _CalcEngine_
13
14    #include <string.h>
15    #include <stdlib.h>
16
17    #include <iostream.h>              // For 'CERR'
18
19    #include "stack.h"
```

As you may recall, this class is implemented as a state machine. To simplify
coding, the class definition begins with two enum declarations: one for State
and one for Operation.

```
21      class CalcEngine {
22
23      private:
24
25              //
26              //          Internal State
27              //
28              enum State { INIT, LEFT, RIGHT, OPERATOR };
29
30              //
31              //          Operations
32              //
33              enum Operation { ADD, SUB, MUL, DIV, EQUAL, CLEAR };
```

Next, the class defines several internal variables to track state, operation, operand, and an instance of a Stack class.

```
35              Stack s;                // The calculator stack
36              State state;            // Master "state" variable
37              Operation oper;         // Operation flag
38              char str[ 100 ];        // Operand (display) value
```

The next section of code implements the callback mechanism for displaying results via the CalcDisplay class. The two variables, display_function and cd, are set in the class constructor and point to the display function and client data, respectively. The function display() uses these values to invoke display functionality without being tightly coupled to another class.

```
40              //
41              //          These next two variables implement a kind
42              //          of "callback" mechanism for displaying
43              //          values computed by an engine.
44              //
45              void *cd;                       // Pointer to "client_data"
46              void (*display_function)( char *, void * );
47
48              //
49              // DISPLAY():
```

```
50              // Display a new value. Implemented as a "callback"
51              // so that Engine class is not tightly coupled to
52              //          some other class (e.g., CalcDisplay).
53              //
54              void display()
55              {
56                      //
57                      // If "callback" is registered, call routine
58                      // with display string and client data
59                      //
60                      if( display_function ) // (In)Sanity Check
61                              display_function( str, cd );
62              }
```

Lines 64 through 92 contain one declaration and two definitions of private 'worker' functions.

calc() The calc() function performs all computations for the calculator. We will discuss its implementation in the next section.

reset() This function resets the calculator to an initial state: it empties the stack, sets state to INIT, sets the operation to CLEAR, and sets the display string to 0.00.

error() The function error() generates errors messages for the class. In this version, it simply emits a diagnostic on the error channel and exits. In a more robust implementation, it should throw an exception.

```
65              //
66              // CALC():
67              // Calculation Routine: this performs all the basic
68              // operations of the calculator (add, sub, ...)
69              //
70              void calc();
71
72              //
73              // RESET():
```

```
74              //          Reset the engine to the INIT state.
75              //
76              void reset()
77              {
78                      s.reset();
79                      oper = CLEAR;
80                      state = INIT;
81                      strcpy( str, "0.00" );
82              }
83
84              //
85              // ERROR():
86              //          Error handler. Should use Exceptions.
87              //
88              void error( char *arg )
89              {
90                cerr << "CalcEngine: **ERROR: " << arg << "\\n";
91                exit( -1 );
92              }
```

The public section of the class contains one constructor (note the arguments), the definition of the clear() function, and declarations for all the member functions that manage key-press events.

```
95    public:
96        //
97        // Constructor:
98        //          Objects require 2 args: a display function
99        //          to invoke and optional client data.
100       //
101       CalcEngine( void (*f)(char*, void*), void *client_data )
102           {
103                   //
104                   // Save callback info
105                   //
106                   cd = client_data;
```

```
107                         display_function = f;
108
109                 //
110                 // Reset  engine.
111                 //
112                 reset();
113                 display();
114             }
115
116             //
117             // CLEAR():
118             //      Clear engine.  Invoked when user press
119             //      the "C" key on the keypad.
120             //
121             void clear()
122             {
123                     reset();
124                     display();
125             }
126
127             //
128             // Declarations for "event" functions.
129             //
130             void add();
131             void sub();
132             void mul();
133             void div();
134             void equal();
135             void digit( int );
136             void decimal_point();
137      };
138
139     #endif
```

9.1.9 calc_eng.cxx

This file contains the remaining implementation of the CalcEngine class. As noted, we implemented this class as a state machine. This is best demonstrated beginning on line 10 with the definition of the `digit()` method. The invocation of this function is equivalent to an event being received by the object. The function begins its processing by determining its current state (the `switch` statement beginning on line 20). It then performs the appropriate actions and transitions to the next state. All the key-press functions operate in basically the same manner.

```
10    //
11    // DIGIT():
12    //        Received a new digit from the keypad
13    //
14    void CalcEngine::digit( int d )
15    {
16            char buf[ 256 ];
17
18            sprintf( buf, "%1d", d );
19
20            switch( state )
21            {
22
23            case INIT:
24                    strcpy( str, buf );
25                    display();
26                    state = LEFT;
27                    break;
28
29            case LEFT:
30                    strcat( str, buf );
31                    display();
32                    state = LEFT;
33                    break;
34
35            case OPERATOR:
36                    strcpy( str, buf );
37                    display();
38                    state = LEFT;
39                    break;
40
```

```
41                    case RIGHT:
42                            strcat( str, buf );
43                            display();
44                            state = RIGHT;
45                            break;
46                    }
47      }
48
49      //
50      // DECIMAL_POINT():
51      //      User entered a decimal point - only
52      //      allow 1 as part of a number.
53      //
54      void CalcEngine::decimal_point()
55      {
56              switch( state )
57              {
58
59              case OPERATOR:
60                      strcpy( str, "." );
61                      display();
62                      state = RIGHT;
63                      break;
64
65              case INIT:
66                      strcat( str, "." );
67                      display();
68                      state = RIGHT;
69                      break;
70
71              case LEFT:
72                      strcat( str, "." );
73                      display();
74                      state = RIGHT;
75                      break;
76              }
77      }
```

The `calc()` method performs the indicated arithmetic operation. Note that, as it pops operands off the stack, it is careful to maintain proper evaluation order (refer to the DIV case).

```
79    //
80    // CALC():
81    //       Perform indicated operation.
82    //
83    void CalcEngine::calc()
84    {
85            double ans, operand1, operand2;
86
87            switch( oper )
88            {
89
90            case ADD:
91                    if( s.pop(&operand2) != Stack::OK )
92                            error( "ADD: Missing Operand2" );
93                    if( s.pop(&operand1) != Stack::OK )
94                            error( "ADD: Missing Operand1" );
95                    ans = operand1 + operand2;
96                    s.push( ans );
97                    sprintf( str, "%f", ans );
98                    break;
99
100           case SUB:
101                   if( s.pop(&operand2) != Stack::OK )
102                           error( "SUB: Missing Operand2" );
103                   if( s.pop(&operand1) != Stack::OK )
104                           error( "SUB: Missing Operand1" );
105                   ans = operand1 - operand2;
106                   s.push( ans );
107                   sprintf( str, "%f", ans );
108                   break;
109
110           case MUL:
111                   if( s.pop(&operand2) != Stack::OK )
112                           error( "MUL: Missing Operand2" );
```

```
113                          if( s.pop(&operand1) != Stack::OK )
114                                  error( "MUL: Missing Operand1" );
115                          ans = operand1 * operand2;
116                          s.push( ans );
117                          sprintf( str, "%f", ans );
118                          break;
119
120                  case DIV:
121                          if( s.pop(&operand2) != Stack::OK )
122                                  error( "DIV: Missing Operand2" );
123                          if( s.pop(&operand1) != Stack::OK )
124                                  error( "DIV: Missing Operand1" );
125                          if( operand2 == 0.0 )
126                                  error( "DIV: Division by Zero" );
127                          ans = operand1 / operand2;
128                          s.push( ans );
129                          sprintf( str, "%f", ans );
130                          break;
131                  }
132
133                  display();
134          }
135
136  //
137  // ADD():
138  //       Add top two numbers on the stack - push answer
139  //
140  void CalcEngine::add()
141  {
142
143          switch( state )
144          {
145
146          case LEFT:
147          case RIGHT:
148                  s.push( atof(str) );
149                  calc();
150                  oper = ADD;
```

```
151                     state = OPERATOR;
152                     break;
153
154             case OPERATOR:
155                     oper = ADD;
156                     break;
157             }
158     }
159
160     //
161     // SUB():
162     //      Subtract top 2 numbers on stack - push ans
163     //
164     void CalcEngine::sub()
165     {
166
167             switch( state )
168             {
169
170             case LEFT:
171             case RIGHT:
172                     s.push( atof(str) );
173                     calc();
174                     oper = SUB;
175                     state = OPERATOR;
176                     break;
177
178             case OPERATOR:
179                     oper = SUB;
180                     break;
181             }
182     }
183
184     //
185     // MUL():
186     //      Mult top 2 numbers on stack - push ans
187     //
188     void CalcEngine::mul()
```

```
189     {
190
191             switch( state )
192             {
193
194             case LEFT:
195             case RIGHT:
196                     s.push( atof(str) );
197                     calc();
198                     oper = MUL;
199                     state = OPERATOR;
200                     break;
201
202             case OPERATOR:
203                     oper = MUL;
204                     break;
205             }
206     }
207
208     //
209     // DIV():
210     //      Divide top two numbers on the stack - push answer
211     //      Ensure proper order of operands and check of
212     //      division by zero.
213     //
214     void CalcEngine::div()
215     {
216
217             switch( state )
218             {
219
220             case LEFT:
221             case RIGHT:
222                     s.push( atof(str) );
223                     calc();
224                     oper = DIV;
225                     state = OPERATOR;
226                     break;
```

```
227
228              case OPERATOR:
229                      oper = DIV;
230                      break;
231              }
232      }
233
234      //
235      // EQUAL():
236      //        Perform indicated operation and display result
237      //
238      void CalcEngine::equal()
239      {
240              switch( state )
241              {
242
243              case LEFT:
244              case RIGHT:
245                      s.push( atof(str) );
246                      calc();
247                      oper = EQUAL;
248                      state = OPERATOR;
249                      break;
250              }
251      }
```

9.1.10 *main.cxx*

This file contains a small test module for our new version of the calculator. It performs toolkit initialization, instantiates a Calc, and enters the main event loop.

On lines 42–61, the program registers a callback on the WM_DELETE_WINDOW property of the window manager. The toolkit will invoke the function win_closeCB() (line 85) whenever the user selects the window manager's close option.

```
1    //
2    //           TITLE:        MAIN.CXX
3    //
```

```
 4    //          FUNCTION:           Tear module for calculator
 5    //
 6
 7    #include <iostream.h>
 8
 9    #include <Xm/AtomMgr.h>
10    #include <Xm/Protocols.h>
11
12    #include "calc.h"
13
14    //
15    // Window Manger Callback Routine
16    //
17    void win_closeCB( Widget widget, XtPointer client_data,
18            XtPointer call_data );
19
20    int main( int ac, char *av[] )
21    {
22            register        i;
23            Arg             args[ 50 ];
24            XtAppContext    app;
25            Widget          top;
26            Atom            Delete_Window;   // WinMgr Protocol
27
28            //
29            //      Initialize Toolkit
30            //
31            top = XtAppInitialize( &app, "Calc2", NULL, 0,
32                    &ac, av, NULL, NULL, 0 );
33
34
35            //
36            //      Handle "Close" Message from Window Manager
37            //      Two steps:
38            //              - Retrieve Atom
39            //              - Register Callback
40            //
```

```
41
42          //
43          //          Get WM Protocol Atom
44          //
45          Delete_Window = XmInternAtom
46          (
47                  XtDisplay(top),         /* X Display        */
48                  "WM_DELETE_WINDOW",     /* Name             */
49                  False                   /* Ignore?          */
50          );
51
52          //
53          //          Register WM Callback Routine
54          //
55          XmAddWMProtocolCallback
56          (
57                  top,                    /* Widget           */
58                  Delete_Window,          /* Atom Type        */
59                  win_closeCB,            /* Callback Routine */
60                  NULL                    /* Client Data      */
61          );
62
63
64          //
65          //          Create a Calculator
66          //
67          Calc c( top );
68
69          //
70          //          Realize Widgets
71          //
72          XtRealizeWidget( top );
73
74          //
75          //          Enter Main Loop
76          //
77          XtAppMainLoop( app );
78  }
```

```
79
80    //
81    //  WIN_CLOSECB():
82    //          This  routine  is  called  when  the  user  selects
83    //          the  "close"  option  from  the  window  manager.
84    //
85    void  win_closeCB( Widget  widget,  XtPointer  client_data,
86              XtPointer  call_data )
87    {
88              exit( 0 );          // Just Exit
89    }
```

9.1.11 *Calc2*

The file `Calc2` contains resource definitions for the `calc2` program. Its contents should be self-explanatory.

```
1    !
2    !         Resource  File  for  New  Version  of  Calculator  Program
3    !
4    *background:          lightblue
5    *display.columns:     30
6    *keypad.y:            35
```

9.2 SUMMARY

In this chapter, we presented the implementation of our new, object-oriented version of the calculator. This material completes our discussion of object-oriented analysis, design, and implementation. There are, however, a number of issues that arise from the above implementation. They include:

- How do we get control back from calculator? That is, what if rather than a program unto itself, the calculator was just one feature of an application?

- What if we wanted `Calc` to function as a stand-alone screen component? It would need a shell widget to serve as its parent.

- In line with the previous comment, we would have a difficult time attaching a `Calc` to another form.

- We have no way to manage and unmanage a `Calc` object as a whole, or any of its component widgets.

- As a rule, our destructors are relinquishing all resources that their classes have claimed. However, they are *not* destroying widgets when C++ class objects go out of scope. Moreover, as implemented, our objects will never know if and when one of their associated widgets has been destroyed. As a result, they might erroneously reference a widget that has been destroyed by other means.

- Note that there really is no need for a class to store its parent's widget ID. Member functions can always invoke `XtGetParent()`.

- In general, we need a way to handle active objects like Keypad. That is, we need a way to define new callbacks and override behavior (e.g., `Keypad::buttonCB()`) in derived classes.

The answers to these questions will serve as the foundation for the next section, wherein we discuss the need for, and the implementation of, an application framework.

9.3 COMPLETE CODE LISTING

The following is the complete listing for the new version of the calculator program.

9.3.1 *calc.h*

```
1    //
2    //          TITLE:    CALC.H
3    //
4    //          FUNCTION:    Class definition for Calc -
                              the controlling class
5    //                       for the calculator program.
6    //
7
```

```
 8     #ifndef _CALC_H_
 9     #define _CALC_H_
10
11     #include <stdlib.h>
12     #include <string.h>
13
14     #include <Xm/Form.h>
15     #include <Xm/Text.h>
16     #include <Xm/TextF.h>
17     #include <Xm/PushB.h>
18     #include <Xm/RowColumn.h>
19
20     #include "keypad.h"
21     #include "display.h"
22     #include "calc_eng.h"
23
24     class Calc {
25
26     private:
27
28             Widget main_form;       // Parent Widget
29
30             Keypad      *keypad;    // Pointer to Keypad Object
31             CalcEngine  *engine;    // Pointer to Engine Object
32             CalcDisplay *display;   // Pointer to Display Object
33
34             //
35             // DISP():
36             //        "Callback" Routine used as an
37             //        interface to the Engine class.
38             //
39             //        disp() is called from a CalcEngine
40             //        and the call is passed on to a
41             //        display object. The "callback" is
42             //        "registered" in the constructor (Calc()).
43             //
44             static void disp( char *str, void *obj )
45                     {
```

```
46                          ((Calc *)obj)->display->SetDisplay( str );
47                  }
48
49      public:
50
51                  Calc( Widget );
52                  ~Calc();
53      };
54
55      #endif
```

9.3.2 calc_eng.h

```
1       //
2       //          TITLE:      CALC_ENG.H
3       //
4       //          FUNCTION:   Class definition for the "engine"
5       //                      portion of the calculator program.
6       //
7       //                      This class is implemented as
8       //                      a "State Machine".
9       //
10
11      #ifndef _CalcEngine_
12      #define _CalcEngine_
13
14      #include <string.h>
15      #include <stdlib.h>
16
17      #include <iostream.h>               // For 'cerr'
18
19      #include "stack.h"
20
21      class CalcEngine {
22
23      private:
24
25                  //
```

```
26              //          Internal State
27              //
28              enum State { INIT, LEFT, RIGHT, OPERATOR };
29
30              //
31              //          Operations
32              //
33              enum Operation { ADD, SUB, MUL, DIV, EQUAL, CLEAR };
34
35              Stack s;             // The calculator stack
36              State state;         // Master "state" variable
37              Operation oper;      // Operation flag
38              char str[ 100 ]; // Operand (display) value
39
40              //
41              //          These next two variables implement a kind
42              //          of "callback" mechanism for displaying
43              //          values computed by an engine.
44              //
45              void *cd;             // Pointer to "client_data"
46              void (*display_function)( char *, void * );
47
48              //
49              // DISPLAY():
50              //   Display a new value.
51              //   so that Engine class is not tightly coupled to
52              //          some other class (e.g., CalcDisplay).
53              //
54              void display()
55              {
56                      //
57                      // If "callback" is registered, call routine
58                      // with display string and client data
59                      //
60                      if( display_function )    // (In)Sanity Check
61                      display_function( str, cd );
62              }
63
```

```
64
65              //
66              // CALC():
67              //      Calculation Routine: performs all basic
68              //      operations of the calculator (add, sub, ...)
69              //
70              void calc();
71
72              //
73              // RESET():
74              //      Reset the engine to the INIT state.
75              //
76              void reset()
77              {
78                      s.reset();
79                      oper = CLEAR;
80                      state = INIT;
81                      strcpy( str, "0.00" );
82              }
83
84              //
85              // ERROR():
86              //      Error handler. Should use Exceptions.
87              //
88              void error( char *arg )
89              {
90                cerr << "CalcEngine: **ERROR: " << arg << "\\n";
91                exit( -1 );
92              }
93
94
95  public:
96              //
97              // Constructor:
98              //      Requires two arguments: a display function
99              //      to invoke and optional client data.
```

```
100             //
101             CalcEngine( void (*f)(char*, void*),
                            void *client_data )
102             {
103                     //
104                     // Save callback info
105                     //
106                     cd = client_data;
107                     display_function = f;
108
109                     //
110                     // Reset engine.
111                     //
112                     reset();
113                     display();
114             }
115
116             //
117             // CLEAR():
118             //      Clear engine.  Invoked when user press
119             //      the "C" key on the keypad.
120             //
121             void clear()
122             {
123                     reset();
124                     display();
125             }
126
127             //
128             // Declarations for "event" functions.
129             //
130             void add();
131             void sub();
132             void mul();
133             void div();
134             void equal();
135             void digit( int );
136             void decimal_point();
```

```
137    };
138
139    #endif
```

9.3.3 keypad.h

```
 1    //
 2    //            TITLE:           KEYPAD.H
 3    //
 4    //            FUNCTION:        Definition of the class Keypad.
 5    //
 6
 7    #ifndef _Keypad_H_
 8    #define _Keypad_H_
 9
10    #include <stdlib.h>
11    #include <string.h>
12
13    #include <Xm/Form.h>
14    #include <Xm/PushB.h>
15    #include <Xm/RowColumn.h>
16
17    class CalcEngine;                    // Declare Engine Class
18
19    //
20    //        Constants (for button alignment)
21    //
22    const int max_rows = 4;
23    const int max_cols = 4;
24
25    //
26    //        Class Definition
27    //
28    class Keypad {
29
30    private:
31
```

```
32                Widget button_form;      // Form to hold buttons
33
34                CalcEngine *engine;      // Pointer to Engine Object
35
36     public:
37
38                Keypad( Widget, CalcEngine* );
39
40                //
41                //        Callback Functions
42                //
43                static void ButtonPressedCB( Widget, XtPointer,
                   XtPointer );
44                virtual void ButtonCB( Widget, XtPointer, XtPointer
                   );
45     };
46
47     #endif
```

9.3.4 *display.h*

```
 1     //
 2     //        TITLE:   DISPLAY.H
 3     //
 4     //    FUNCTION:   Complete implementation of the CalcDisplay.
 5     //
 6
 7     #ifndef _CALC_DSIPLAY_
 8     #define _CALC_DSIPLAY_
 9
10     #include <Xm/Text.h>
11     #include <Xm/TextF.h>
12
13     class CalcDisplay
14     {
15
16     private:
17
```

```
18              Widget display;
19
20      public:
21
22              //
23              //    Constructor: Requires Parent Widget as Argument
24              //
25              CalcDisplay( Widget parent )
26              {
27                  //
28                  //   Create TextField Widget for Calculator Display
29                  //
30                  display = XtVaCreateManagedWidget( "display",
31
32                          xmTextFieldWidgetClass,        parent,
33
34                          XmNeditable,                   False,
35                          XmNcursorPositionVisible,      False,
36                          XmNtraversalOn,                False,
37
38                      NULL );
39              }
40
41              //
42              //       Display a String
43              //
44              void SetDisplay( char *str )
45              {
46                      register        i;
47                      short           cols;
48                      Arg             args[ 50 ];
49                      char            buf[ 256 ];
50
51                      //
52                      //       Determine Number of Columns
53                      //
54                      i = 0;
```

```
55                         XtSetArg( args[i], XmNcolumns, &cols ); i++;
56                         XtGetValues( display, args, i );
57
58                         //
59                         //          Format Buffer
60                         //
61                         sprintf( buf, "%*.*s", cols, cols, str );
62
63                         //
64                         //          Update Display
65                         //
66                         XmTextSetString( display, buf );
67              }
68      };
69
70      #endif
```

9.3.5 *main.cxx*

```
1       //
2       //        TITLE:    MAIN.CXX
3       //
4       //    FUNCTION:    Driving module for the calculator program
5       //
6
7       #include <iostream.h>
8
9       #include <Xm/AtomMgr.h>
10      #include <Xm/Protocols.h>
11
12      #include "calc.h"
13
14      //
15      // Window Manger Callback Routine
16      //
17      void win_closeCB( Widget widget, XtPointer client_data,
18              XtPointer call_data );
```

```
19
20     int main( int ac, char *av[] )
21     {
22              register          i;
23              Arg               args[ 50 ];
24              XtAppContext      app;
25              Widget            top;
26              Atom              Delete_Window;
27
28              //
29              //        Initialize Toolkit
30              //
31              top = XtAppInitialize( &app, "Calc2", NULL, 0,
32                      &ac, av, NULL, NULL, 0 );
33
34
35              //
36              //        Handle "Close" Message from WM
37              //        Two steps:
38              //                - Retrieve Atom
39              //                - Register Callback
40              //
41
42              //
43              //        Get WM Protocol Atom
44              //
45              Delete_Window = XmInternAtom
46              (
47                      XtDisplay(top),         /* X Display    */
48                      "WM_DELETE_WINDOW",     /* Name         */
49                      False                   /* Ignore?      */
50              );
51
52              //
53              //        Register WM Callback Routine
54              //
55              XmAddWMProtocolCallback
```

```
56                  (
57                              top,                     /* Widget           */
58                              Delete_Window,           /* Atom Type         */
59                              win_closeCB,             /* Callback Routine  */
60                              NULL                     /* Client Data       */
61                  );
62
63
64                  //
65                  //        Create a Calculator
66                  //
67                  Calc c( top );
68
69                  //
70                  //        Realize Widgets
71                  //
72                  XtRealizeWidget( top );
73
74                  //
75                  //        Enter Main Loop
76                  //
77                  XtAppMainLoop( app );
78      }
79
80      //
81      // WIN_CLOSECB():
82      //        This routine is called when the user selects
83      //        the "close" option from the window manager.
84      //
85      void win_closeCB( Widget widget, XtPointer client_data,
86              XtPointer call_data )
87      {
88              exit( 0 );           // Just Exit
89      }
```

9.3.6 calc.cxx

```
1     //
2     //          TITLE:          CALC.CXX
3     //
4     //          FUNCTION:       Member function definitions for
5     //                          the Calc class.
6     //
7
8     #include "calc.h"
9
10    Calc::Calc( Widget parent )
11    {
12            //
13            //          Create Form Widget
14            //
15            main_form = XmCreateForm( parent, "mainform",
                            NULL, 0 );
16            XtManageChild( main_form );
17
18            //
19            //          Create CalcDisplay Object
20            //
21            display = new CalcDisplay( main_form );
22
23            //
24            //          Create Engine Object
25            //
26            engine = new CalcEngine( disp, (void *)this );
27
28            //
29            //          Create Keypad
30            //
31            keypad = new Keypad( main_form, engine );
32    }
33
```

```
34    Calc::~Calc( Widget p )
35    {
36            //
37            //          Clean-up
38            //
39            delete display;
40            delete engine;
41            delete keypad;
42    }
```

9.3.7 *calc_eng.cxx*

```
1     //
2     //        TITLE:              CALC_ENG.CXX
3     //
4     //    FUNCTION:               Implements the CalcEngine
5     //                            class as a state machine.
6     //
7
8     #include "calc_eng.h"
9
10    //
11    // DIGIT():
12    //      Received a new digit from the keypad
13    //
14    void CalcEngine::digit( int d )
15    {
16            char buf[ 256 ];
17
18            sprintf( buf, "%1d", d );
19
20            switch( state )
21            {
22
23            case INIT:
24                    strcpy( str, buf );
25                    display();
26                    state = LEFT;
```

```
27                      break;
28
29              case LEFT:
30                      strcat( str, buf );
31                      display();
32                      state = LEFT;
33                      break;
34
35              case OPERATOR:
36                      strcpy( str, buf );
37                      display();
38                      state = LEFT;
39                      break;
40
41              case RIGHT:
42                      strcat( str, buf );
43                      display();
44                      state = RIGHT;
45                      break;
46              }
47      }
48
49      //
50      // DECIMAL_POINT():
51      //      User entered a decimal point - only
52      //      allow 1 as part of a number.
53      //
54      void CalcEngine::decimal_point()
55      {
56              switch( state )
57              {
58
59              case OPERATOR:
60                      strcpy( str, "." );
61                      display();
62                      state = RIGHT;
63                      break;
64
```

```
65                case INIT:
66                        strcat( str, "." );
67                        display();
68                        state = RIGHT;
69                        break;
70
71              case LEFT:
72                        strcat( str, "." );
73                        display();
74                        state = RIGHT;
75                        break;
76              }
77      }
78
79      //
80      // CALC():
81      //       Perform indicated operation.
82      //
83      void CalcEngine::calc()
84      {
85              double ans, operand1, operand2;
86
87              switch( oper )
88              {
89
90              case ADD:
91                      if( s.pop(&operand2) != Stack::OK )
92                              error( "ADD: Missing Operand2" );
93                      if( s.pop(&operand1) != Stack::OK )
94                              error( "ADD: Missing Operand1" );
95                      ans = operand1 + operand2;
96                      s.push( ans );
97                      sprintf( str, "%f", ans );
98                      break;
99
100             case SUB:
101                     if( s.pop(&operand2) != Stack::OK )
102                             error( "SUB: Missing Operand2" );
```

```
103                         if( s.pop(&operand1) != Stack::OK )
104                                 error( "SUB: Missing Operand1" );
105                         ans = operand1 - operand2;
106                         s.push( ans );
107                         sprintf( str, "%f", ans );
108                         break;
109
110              case MUL:
111                         if( s.pop(&operand2) != Stack::OK )
112                                 error( "MUL: Missing Operand2" );
113                         if( s.pop(&operand1) != Stack::OK )
114                                 error( "MUL: Missing Operand1" );
115                         ans = operand1 * operand2;
116                         s.push( ans );
117                         sprintf( str, "%f", ans );
118                         break;
119
120              case DIV:
121                         if( s.pop(&operand2) != Stack::OK )
122                                 error( "DIV: Missing Operand2" );
123                         if( s.pop(&operand1) != Stack::OK )
124                                 error( "DIV: Missing Operand1" );
125                         if( operand2 == 0.0 )
126                                 error( "DIV: Division by Zero" );
127                         ans = operand1 / operand2;
128                         s.push( ans );
129                         sprintf( str, "%f", ans );
130                         break;
131              }
132
133         display();
134    }
135
136    //
137    // ADD():
138    //       Add top two numbers on the stack - push answer
139    //
140    void CalcEngine::add()
```

```
141    {
142
143            switch( state )
144            {
145
146            case LEFT:
147            case RIGHT:
148                    s.push( atof(str) );
149                    calc();
150                    oper = ADD;
151                    state = OPERATOR;
152                    break;
153
154            case OPERATOR:
155                    oper = ADD;
156                    break;
157            }
158    }
159
160    //
161    // SUB():
162    //      Subt top 2 numbers on stack - push answer
163    //
164    void CalcEngine::sub()
165    {
166
167            switch( state )
168            {
169
170            case LEFT:
171            case RIGHT:
172                    s.push( atof(str) );
173                    calc();
174                    oper = SUB;
175                    state = OPERATOR;
176                    break;
177
178            case OPERATOR:
```

```
179                      oper = SUB;
180                      break;
181               }
182   }
183
184   //
185   // MUL():
186   //      Multiply top 2 numbers on stack - push ans
187   //
188   void CalcEngine::mul()
189   {
190
191            switch( state )
192            {
193
194            case LEFT:
195            case RIGHT:
196                      s.push( atof(str) );
197                      calc();
198                      oper = MUL;
199                      state = OPERATOR;
200                      break;
201
202            case OPERATOR:
203                      oper = MUL;
204                      break;
205            }
206   }
207
208   //
209   // DIV():
210   //      Divide top 2 numbers on stack - push ans
211   //      Ensure proper order of operands and check for
212   //      division by zero.
213   //
214   void CalcEngine::div()
```

```
215     {
216
217             switch( state )
218             {
219
220             case LEFT:
221             case RIGHT:
222                     s.push( atof(str) );
223                     calc();
224                     oper = DIV;
225                     state = OPERATOR;
226                     break;
227
228             case OPERATOR:
229                     oper = DIV;
230                     break;
231             }
232     }
233
234     //
235     // EQUAL():
236     //      Perform indicated operation and display result
237     //
238     void CalcEngine::equal()
239     {
240             switch( state )
241             {
242
243             case LEFT:
244             case RIGHT:
245                     s.push( atof(str) );
246                     calc();
247                     oper = EQUAL;
248                     state = OPERATOR;
249                     break;
250             }
251     }
```

9.3.8 keypad.cxx

```
1    //
2    //      TITLE:       KEYPAD.CXX
3    //
4    //    FUNCTION:      Functions to process keystrokes
5    //
6
7    #include "keypad.h"
8    #include "calc_eng.h"
9
10   //
11   //      Button Structure - Serves as "client data"
12   //      in callbacks.
13   //
14   struct button_struct {
15           char    label;
16           Keypad  *object;
17           Widget  widget;
18   };
19
20   //
21   //      Button Labels
22   //
23   static char *cb[] =
24   {
25           "1",  "2",  "3",  "/",
26           "4",  "5",  "6",  "*",
27           "7",  "8",  "9",  "-",
28           "C",  "0",  "=",  "+"
29   };
30
31   //
32   //      Constructor
33   //
34   Keypad::Keypad( Widget parent, CalcEngine *e )
35   {
36
```

```
37              Arg                args[ 50 ];
38              int                i, index, row, col;
39              XmString           labl;
40              button_struct*     buttons;
41
42              //
43              //        Save pointer to CalcEngine object
44              //
45              engine = e;
46
47              //
48              //        Create Form to Hold Calculator Buttons
49              //
50              button_form = XtVaCreateManagedWidget( "keypad",
51
52                      xmFormWidgetClass,     parent,
53
54                      XmNfractionBase,       4,
55
56                      XmNlength,             200,
57                      XmNwidth,              200,
58
59              NULL );
60
61              //
62              //        Allocate storage for button callbacks
63              //
64              buttons = new button_struct[ max_rows * max_cols ];
65
66              //
67              //        Create Calculator Buttons
68              //
69              for( row = 0; row < max_rows; row++ )
70              {
71                      for( col = 0; col < max_cols; col++ )
72                      {
73                          index = (row * max_cols) + col;
74
```

```
75                          //
76                          //   Save state info in callback struct
77                          //
78                          buttons[index].object = this;
79                          buttons[index].label = cb[index][0];
80
81                          //
82                          //   Create Label String for Button
83                          //
84                          labl = XmStringCreateSimple( cb[index] );
85
86                          //
87                          //       Create Button
88                          //
89                          buttons[index].widget =
                            XtVaCreateManagedWidget(
90
91                             cb[index],
92
93                             xmPushButtonWidgetClass, button_form,
94
95                             XmNlabelString,   labl,
96
97                             XmNtopAttachment, XmATTACH_POSITION,
98                             XmNtopPosition,   row,
99
100                            XmNbottomAttachment,
                               XmATTACH_POSITION,
101                            XmNbottomPosition, row+1,
102
103                            XmNleftAttachment, XmATTACH_POSITION,
104                            XmNleftPosition,   col,
105
106                            XmNrightAttachment, |
                               XmATTACH_POSITION,
107                            XmNrightPosition, col+1,
108
109                         NULL );
```

```
110
111                         //
112                         //          Register Callback
113                         //
114                         XtAddCallback( buttons[index].widget,
115                             XmNactivateCallback,
116                             (XtCallbackProc)ButtonPressedCB,
117                             (XtPointer)&buttons[index]
118                         );
119
120                         //
121                         //          Free String
122                         //
123                         XmStringFree( labl );
124                     }
125             }
126     }
127
128     //
129     //          Static Callback Function
130     //
131     void Keypad::ButtonPressedCB( Widget widget,
132             XtPointer client_data, XtPointer call_data )
133     {
134             button_struct *b = (button_struct *)client_data;
135
136             Keypad *obj = (Keypad *)b->object;
137
138             //
139             //          Pass on callback to actual object
140             //
141             obj->ButtonCB( b->widget, (XtPointer)b->label,
142                     (XtPointer)call_data );
143     }
144
145     //
146     //          Pushbutton Callback Routine
147     //
```

```
148     void Keypad::ButtonCB( Widget widget,
149             XtPointer client_data, XtPointer call_data )
150     {
151             char which_button = (char)client_data;
152
153
154             switch( which_button )
155             {
156                     case '0':
157                     case '1':
158                     case '2':
159                     case '3':
160                     case '4':
161                     case '5':
162                     case '6':
163                     case '7':
164                     case '8':
165                     case '9':
166                             //
167                             // Pass on digit to engine
168                             //
169                             engine->digit( which_button-'0' );
170                             break;
171
172                     case 'C':
173                             //
174                             // Clear button pressed
175                             //
176                             engine->clear();
177                             break;
178
179                     case '+':
180                             //
181                             // Add operation
182                             //
183                             engine->add();
184                             break;
```

```
185
186                     case '-':
187                         //
188                         // Subtraction operation
189                         //
190                         engine->sub();
191                         break;
192
193                     case '*':
194                         //
195                         // Multiply operation
196                         //
197                         engine->mul();
198                         break;
199
200                     case '/':
201                         //
202                         // Division operation
203                         //
204                         engine->div();
205                         break;
206
207                     case '=':
208                         //
209                         // Compute & display result
210                         //
211                         engine->equal();
212                         break;
213                 }
214     }
```

9.3.9 *Calc2*

```
1       !
2       !        Resource File for New Version of Calculator Program
3       !
```

```
4     *background:          lightblue
5     *display.columns:     30
6     *keypad.y:            35
```

9.3.10 stack.h

```
1     //
2     //         TITLE:        STACK.H
3     //
4     //         FUNCTION:     Quick and dirty implementation of
5     //                       a Stack - for used as a part of
6     //                       the Engine class.
7     //
8
9     #ifndef _Stack_H_
10    #define _Stack_H_
11
12    #include <stdio.h>
13    #include <string.h>
14    #include <stdlib.h>
15
16    class Stack {
17
18    private:
19
20            const int max_stack;     // Stack Size
21            double *stack;           // The Stack
22            int top;                 // Top of Stack
23
24    public:
25
26        //
27        //        Return Codes
28        //
29        enum StackVal { EMPTY, OVERFLOW, UNDERFLOW, OK, FAIL };
30
31        //
32        // Constructor:
```

```
33         //          Initialize Stack
34         //
35         Stack( int stk_size = 200 )
36         :            max_stack(stk_size)
37             {
38                         stack = new double[ max_stack ];
39                         top = -1;
40             }
41
42         //
43         // PUSH():
44         //          Push a new value on the stack.
45         //
46         StackVal push( double v )
47             {
48                         if( max_stack - top > 1 )
49                         {
50                                     stack[ ++top ] = v;
51                                     return( OK );
52                         } else {
53                                     return( OVERFLOW );
54                         }
55             }
56
57         //
58         // POP():
59         //          remove the top value from the stack.
60         //
61         StackVal pop( double *v )
62             {
63                         if( top == -1 )
64                                 return( EMPTY );
65                         *v = stack[ top- ];
66                         return( OK );
67             }
68
69         //
70         // PEEK():
```

```
71                  //          Return (w/o removing) top value.
72                  //
73                  StackVal peek( double *v )
74                  {
75                          if( top == -1 )
76                                  return( EMPTY );
77                          *v = stack[ top ];
78                          return( OK );
79                  }
80
81                  //
82                  // RESET():
83                  //          Reset stack to initial state.
84                  //
85                  StackVal reset()
86                  {
87                          top = -1;
88                          return( OK );
89                  }
90          };
91
92      #endif
```

P A R T 3

THE MWL
LIBRARY

THUS FAR, WE HAVE EXAMINED SEVERAL WAYS to combine the GUI and object-oriented paradigms. However, we have only demonstrated how to make the paradigms work together. This begs the question: Is that enough? That is, have we achieved the greatest degree of integration between the models?

Well, obviously based on the number of pages remaining in this book the answer to that question is a resounding "no." What we need is a structure or *framework* that will serve as a cohesive development model. The goal is to create a solution that is greater than the sum of its parts. This is not a new idea. Indeed, Motif itself creates a new model that simplifies the development of X clients. We will extend this basic idea to incorporate the advantages of the object-oriented paradigm.

The application framework we will develop is based on the Model-View-Controller architecture—more on this later. We will call the resulting class library MWL (for Motif Windows Library). We will begin by building a base class that addresses many of the concerns we identified in Section II. We will then design a complete library that can serve as an object-oriented framework for GUI-based application development.

APPLICATION FRAMEWORKS

There are several important reasons for developing an application framework. They include:

- Most GUI applications share many common features (e.g., menus and dialogs). We can encapsulate common features and behavior into classes. This reduces development costs by allowing client programmers to draw upon common classes when developing applications.

- We can use an application framework to create and enforce a consistent look-and-feel across programs and applications.

- Although an unpopular notion, developers are people, too. We can minimize some of their programming drudgery by encapsulating mundane tasks into classes.

- We can create classes that act as one screen element, but comprise multiple widgets (and windows). Also, we can incorporate low-level (X and Xt) functionality into our library without violating the abstractions we create. We can thus extend and modify the basic behavior of otherwise "canned" widgets.

- We can take full advantage of all the benefits of the object-oriented paradigm. For example, we can employ inheritance to extend and customize the MWL classes.

Chapter 10 introduces the Motif Windows Library. We begin our discussion by describing its foundation class: `ScreenComponent`.

CHAPTER 10

THE ScreenComponent CLASS

10.1 THE ScreenComponent CLASS

10.1.1 *The* ScreenComponent *Class: Version 1*

The best way to begin our discussions is by diving right in. Listings 10.1 and 10.2 comprise version 1 of the ScreenComponent class. As the previous sentence implies, this first attempt is not complete. After introducing this version, we will discuss some of its weaknesses and correct them. We have taken this approach in the hope that readers will gain some insight into the design process.

10.1.2 *The* ScreenComponent *Header File*

```
1    //
2    //          TITLE:  scrn_cmp.h
3    //
4    //          FUNCTION:  Version 1 of the ScreenComponent class.
5    //
6
7    #ifndef _SCREEN_COMPONENT_H_
```

```
8      #define _SCREEN_COMPONENT_H_
9
10     #include <string.h>                        // For strcpy()
11
12     #include <Xm/Xm.h>                          // Motif header
13
14     class ScreenComponent {
15     protected:
16             //
17             // Protected data to allow derived classes
18             // direct access
19             //
20             char*   _widget_name;       // Name for resource DB
21             Widget  _main_widget;       // Main "parent" widget
22
23             //
24             // Protected constructor: we do not want
25             // this class to be instantiated - only
26             // derived from.
27             //
28             ScreenComponent( char* name );
29
30     public:
31             //
32             //       Basic Features
33             //
34             virtual ~ScreenComponent();    // Destructor
35
36             Widget main_widget()           // Return widget
37             {
38                     return( _main_widget );
39             }
40
41             char* widget_name()            // widget's name
42             {
43                     char *t = new char[ strlen(_widget_name)+1 ];
44                     strcpy( t, _widget_name );
```

```
45
46                        //
47                        // N.B.: Client must "free" storage
48                        //
49                        return( t );
50           }
51
52           //
53           //        Virtual Functions
54           //
55           virtual void manage();          // Manage   widget
56           virtual void unmanage();        // Unmanage widget
57    };
58
59    #endif
```

LISTING 10.1. Version 1: scrn_cmp.h.

Throughout these discussions (and the remainder of the text) keep in mind that we are designing for reuse. We want to make our classes easy to use for both clients and designers. To that end, the ScreenComponent class defines several protected data members:

_widget_name This member records the widget's name as set by a client. This name is used to uniquely identify each screen component in the same way we name widgets in Motif programs.

_main_widget We will make a basic assumption that each screen component will define a main widget to serve the parent for all other widgets contained in the class. That is, many classes will create screen interfaces composed of multiple widgets. Such classes will usually have a main manager widget serve as the parent for the overall instance tree.

Following the data members, line 28 declares a protected constructor. We do this to ensure that clients cannot instantiate this class. Its only intended use is as a base class for derivation.

Line 30 begins the public section of the class. In particular, line 34 declares the destructor virtual. A virtual destructor helps to ensure that derived class can clean up after themselves (by ensuring that their destructors execute).

The functions `main_widget()` (lines 36–39) and `widget_name()` (lines 41–50) are convenience routines that return the ID of the parent widget and the component name, respectively. Note that the latter function creates dynamic storage that the caller must delete. This is a reasonable approach considering the infrequent use of this type of function. (Clients usually set—and therefore should remember—the names of their widgets.)

Lines 55 and 56 declare two additional functions: `manage()` and `unmanage()`. As their names imply, these functions manage and unmanage the component. Note that they, too, are declared `virtual`. Thus, if need be, derived classes can modify their behavior.

10.1.3 *The* ScreenComponent *Class Implementation File*

```
1    //
2    //            TITLE: scrn_cmp.cxx
3    //
4    //       FUNCTION: Version 1 of ScreenComponent
5    //
6    #include "scrn_cmp.h"
7
8    ScreenComponent::ScreenComponent( char* name )
9    {
10          _main_widget = (Widget)NULL;
11
12          _widget_name = new char[ strlen(name)+1 ];
13          strcpy( _widget_name, name );
14   }
15
16   virtual ScreenComponent::~ScreenComponent()
17   {
18          //
19          // Destroy main widget if it has not
20          // been done already
21          //
22          if( _main_widget != (Widget)NULL )
23                  XtDestroyWidget( _main_widget );
```

```
24
25              //
26              // Relinquish dynamic memory
27              //
28              delete [] _widget_name;
29      }
30
31      virtual void ScreenComponent::manage()
32      {
33              //
34              // Only manage if we have a widget
35              //
36              if( _main_widget != (Widget)NULL )
37                      XtManageChild( _main_widget );
38      }
39
40      virtual void ScreenComponent::unmanage()
41      {
42              //
43              // Only unmanage if we have a widget
44              //
45              if( _main_widget != (Widget)NULL )
46                      XtUnmanageChild( _main_widget );
47      }
```

LISTING 10.2. Version 1: scrn_cmp.cxx.

Listing 10.2 contains the definitions for the remaining undefined member functions. The constructor (lines 8–14) performs two simple tasks. First, it sets _main_widget to NULL. We can perform this initialization precisely because this is a base class: constructors for derived classes—where widgets are actually created—execute only after this constructor terminates.

The constructor's second task is to allocate storage for the widget's name. Note that we do not use a routine based on malloc() (such as strdup()). It is potentially dangerous to mix calls to new and malloc() in C++ programs.

The destructor (lines 16–29) calls XtDestroyWidget() if the base widget has not yet been destroyed by other means. (Note that XtDestroyWidget()

is a recursive procedure. We will return to this point later in the chapter.) It
then relinquishes the dynamic memory it allocated for the widget's name.

The routines manage() (lines 31–38) and unmanage() (lines 40–47) call
their respective toolkit counterparts XtManageChild() and XtUnman-
ageChild(). Notice that, as a sanity check, both functions verify that
_main_widget is not NULL.

10.1.4 A Simple Example

Before we go any further, let's take a look a simple example of how we can put
the ScreenCompnent class to use. Listing 10.3 contains a complete program
that creates a new class called Label, derived from ScreenComponent. The
new class will not win any prizes for complexity: it simply creates and displays
a label. However, it does clearly demonstrate how clients can use the Screen-
Component class.

```
1    //
2    //              TITLE:  ScrnTest.cxx
3    //
4    //        FUNCTION:  Simple test of the first version of the
5    //                   ScreenComponent class.
6    //
7    #include <iostream.h>
8
9    #include "scrn_cmp.h"
10
11   #include <Xm/Label.h>
12
13   //
14   // Derive a simple label class
15   //
16   class Label : public ScreenComponent {
17
18   public:
19            Label( Widget, char* );
20   };
21
```

```
22    Label::Label( Widget parent, char *name )
23              : ScreenComponent(name)
24    {
25            _main_widget = XtVaCreateWidget( name,
26                    xmLabelWidgetClass,    parent,
27                    XmNwidth,              200,
28                    XmNheight,             100,
29            NULL );
30    }
31
32    int main( int ac, char *av[] )
33    {
34            Widget          top;   // Top level shell
35            XtAppContext    app;   // Application Context
36
37            //
38            // Initialize toolkit
39            //
40            top = XtAppInitialize( &app, "T1",
41                    NULL, 0, &ac, av, NULL, NULL, 0
42            );
43
44            //
45            // Create a new label
46            //
47            Label *pb = new Label( top, "label1" );
48
49            //
50            // Manage widget
51            //
52            pb->manage();
53
54            //
55            // Realize widgets
56            //
57            XtRealizeWidget( top );
58
```

```
59              //
60              // Enter main event loop
61              //
62              XtAppMainLoop( app );
63        }
```

LISTING 10.3. ScreenCompnent test program.

On line 9, we include the header file for the ScreenComponent class. Lines 16–20 contain the definition of Label. It is derived (publicly) from Screen-Component and contains only one new function, a constructor (lines 22–30) that requires two arguments. The first is the ID of the widget that will serve as the parent for the interface. It passes the second, name, as an argument to its base class constructor. In the body of the constructor, we create our new interface, in this case, a simple label widget. Note that we create the widget by invoking XtCreateWidget(), that is, the widget is not managed.

The definition of main() is much like any other Xt/Xm program. The difference is in the way we create the interface. On line 47 we instantiate a Label. This creates the widget, which ultimately creates a window on the server. On line 52, we manage the underlying widget, which *maps* the associated window.

10.1.5 Implementation Summary

The ScreenComponent class provides basic functionality for all screen component classes. It supplies hooks to create and manage the display and to ensure resources are relinquished upon object destruction. There are several points to keep in mind regarding the its use:

- The class declares a variable _main_widget to serve as the main parent widget.

- Derived classes should expect a parent widget passed as a constructor argument.

- Derived classes need not store the widget ID of their parent. They can always retrieve it via a call to XtParent().

- ScreenComponent's constructor sets _main_widget to NULL. The actual interface is built in the constructor of the derived class.

- Screen component classes require a name supplied by clients. Just like widgets, these names should be unique within the program.

- As implemented, the <$iScreenComponent> class provides several convenience routines:

  main_widget() Returns widget ID of the parent widget.

  widget_name() Returns the name of the screen component. Note that clients are responsible for deleting the storage created by this function.

  manage() Manages the main widget.

  unmanage() Unmanages main widget.

- The class was designed with code reuse in mind:

  - We have declared as virtual the manage(), unmanage(), and destructor functions. Thus, subclasses can override their behavior.

  - The two data members are declared as protected.

The important question is whether we are done. Obviously not (hence, the question.) Two important issues have not yet been discussed: widget destruction and resource management. We will address these concerns in the next section.

10.2 THE ScreenComponent CLASS REVISITED

10.2.1 *Widget Destruction*

As stated several times, one of the goals of the MWL library is code reuse. To be considered reusable, classes must manage resources (e.g., memory, files, etc.) efficiently. This can be problematic when C++ classes serve as wrappers for non–object-oriented APIs (e.g., Motif). Consider widget destruction. At first glance, it appears that the initial version of the ScreenComponent class handles the problem adequately: The destructor calls XtDestroyWidget() whenever a ScreenComponent object goes out of scope. However, we know that XtDestroyWidget() is recursive. When we destroy a widget, we also destroy all of its children. This may seem helpful since a screen component object can have all of its widgets destroyed with one simple call.

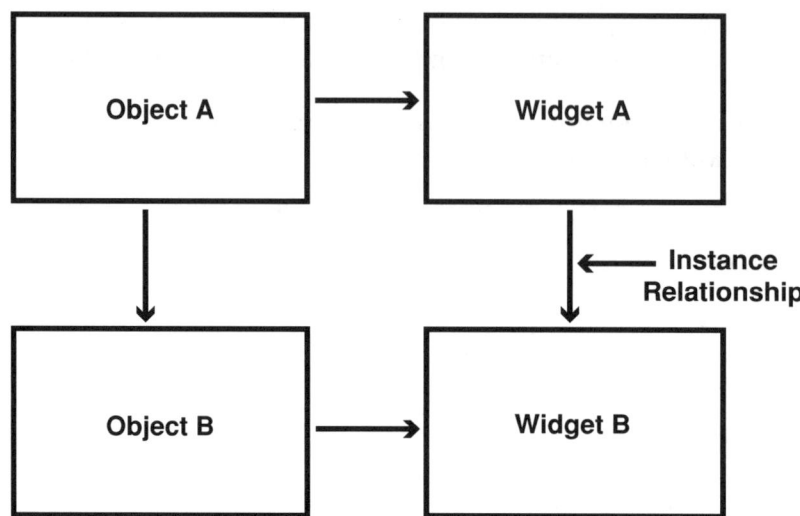

FIGURE 10.1. Class/Widget Instance Hierarchy.

However, some of these child widgets may reside within other objects. That means we have, in effect, breached one of the most fundamental laws of object-oriented development: encapsulation. Through some seemingly benign action, one object can now modify the internal state of another.

For example, consider the instance hierarchy depicted in Figure 10.1. There is an Instance relationship between objects *A* and *B*. Note that each of those objects have instantiated widgets that also share a parent/child instance relationship. If we were to invoke `XtDestroyWidget()` on widget *A* (let's say in its destructor), we would also destroy widget *B* (it is a descendent of *A*). This might surprise the member functions of object *B*.

To address this problem, we will add three member functions to the `ScreenComponent` class:

- `void registerDestroyCB()`
- `static void destroyCB( Widget, XtPointer, XtPointer )`
- `virtual void destroyWidget()`

The first function, `void registerDestroyCB()`, registers an XmNde-stroyCallback for the widget. The routine, `static void destroyCB()`, is a bridge function that passes on the destroy callback to the appropriate object. The `virtual` member function `void destroyWidget()` sets the data member _main_widget equal to NULL. Thus, the object now knows that the widget has been destroyed. We need only test the value of _main_widget in each member function before we undertake any widget processing. Listing 10.4 contains the code for the new functions.

```
73    void ScreenComponent::registerDestroyCB()
74    {
75            //
76            // Register an XmNdestroyCallback
77            // for class
78            //
79            if( _main_widget != (Widget)NULL )
80                    XtAddCallback(
81                            _main_widget,
82                            XmNdestroyCallback,
83                            &ScreenComponent::destroyCB,
84                            (XtPointer)this
85                    );
86    }
87
88    virtual void ScreenComponent::destroyWidget()
89    {
90            //
91            // Record that the widget has been destroyed
92            //
93            _main_widget = (Widget)NULL;
94    }
95
96    void ScreenComponent::destroyCB( Widget w,
97            XtPointer client, XtPointer call )
98    {
99        //
100       // Static CB function - pass on callback
101       //
102       ScreenComponent* the object = (ScreenComponent*)client;
```

```
103
104          the object->destroyWidget();
105      }
```

LISTING 10.4. Destroy Callback Processing.

To complete this new processing, we must also remove the destroy call-back whenever a C++ object goes out of scope. If we omit this step, the tool-kit can invoke a `static` callback function, which, in turn, would try to pass on the callback to an object that no longer exists. The `ScreenComponent` destructor is the natural location for this processing. Listing 10.5 contains the revised definition.

```
16      virtual ScreenComponent::~ScreenComponent()
17      {
18              if( _main_widget != (Widget)NULL )
19              {
20                      //
21                      // Remove Destroy Callback
22                      //
23                      XtRemoveCallback(
24                              _main_widget,
25                              XmNdestroyCallback,
26                              &ScreenComponent::destroyCB,
27                              (XtPointer)this
28                      );
29              }
```

LISTING 10.5. Updated Destructor Function.

There is one minor drawback to this scheme. The `ScreenComponent` con-structor cannot register the destroy callback: no widgets are created during this function's lifetime. Thus, we must rely on clients to call `registerDe-stroyCB()`.

10.2.2 *Resources*

When we create a GUI component based on the `ScreenComponent` class, we are creating a self-contained object, much like a widget. Users can customize widgets and screen elements using the Xt Toolkit resource mechanism. It would be nice if our clients and users could customize our GUI components in the same manner. For example, we could let the user, through a resource setting, determine the number of decimal places in the calculator's display.

Most Xt programmers are familiar with the toolkit function XtGetApplicationResources(). The routine allows developers to modify the behavior of their Xt/Motif–based programs using user-customizable resources. However, we should view objects as components or building blocks, not as entire programs. As a result, application-wide resources are too general to be useful.

Fortunately, the Xt toolkit provides another capability, XtGetSubresources(), which we can adapt to our needs. That is, it will allow us to retrieve and set resources by individual GUI component (i.e., object). The idea is that we can view each object derived from ScreenComponent as subtree in the widget hierarchy. Thus, each component can retrieve resources based on its name and class (more on this shortly).

The function XtGetSubresources() takes a number of arguments:

```
void XtGetSubresources(
        Widget          w,        // The Widget
        XtPointer       data,     // Pointer to Application Data
        String          name,     // Subpart Name
        String          class,    // Subpart Class
        XtResourceList  res,      // Resource Array
        Cardinal        numb,     // Number of Resources
        ArgList         args,     // Override Resources
        Cardinal        numb      // Number of Args
    );
```

The routine is similar to its cousin XtGetApplicationResources(): programmers develop a list of resources, along with default values, and the resource manager updates application data fields with appropriate values. We specify resources using an array of type XtResource:

```
typedef struct {
    String          resource_name;        // Resource Name
    String          resource_class;       // Resource Class
```

```
    String        resource_type;      // Resource Type
    Cardinal      resource_size;      // Resource Size
    Cardinal      resource_offset;    // Offset of Member
    String        default_type;       // Default Type
    XtPointer     default_addr;       // Default Address
} XtResource;
```

We will not need to use the last two items.

The easiest way to understand how all this processing works is through an example. Let's say we created a struct that contained some application-specific data.

```
typedef struct _AppData {
    .
    .

    .
    int no_dec_places;
    .

    .

    .
} AppData;
```

To enable the user to set the value of no_dec_places via <$iresources>, the program must perform the following processing:

- Define an instance of our application data structure:
        AppData MyData;

- Define an <$iXtResource [ ]> array, one element for each resource:
XtResource MyResources[] = {
{
        "decimal places",   // Resource Name
        "Decimal places",   // Class
        XmRInt,   // Resource Type
        sizeof(int),   // Resource Size
        XtOffset(AppData*,no_dec_places), // Offset
```
```

```
        XmRString,                          // Default Type
        (XtPointer)"4"                      // Default Addr
    },
    {
        // Another Resource ...
    },
    .
    .
    .
};
```

- Create screen interface using the normal Xt/Motif conventions.
  ```
  Widget label;
  label = XmCreateLabel( parent_widget, "name", ... );
  ```

- Load resources:
  ```
  void XtGetSubresources(
      label,                              // The Widget
      (XtPointer)&MyData,                 // Ptr to Application Data
      "decimal places",                   // Subpart Name
      "Decimal places",                   // Subpart Class
      MyResources,                        // Resource Array
      XtNumber(MyResources),              // Num of Resources
      NULL,                               // Override Resources

      0                                   // Number of Args

  );
  ```

- The final step is to use the values set in MyData to customize program behavior.

Using the above processing, users can set resources in the normal manner:

```
    *decimal places:         10
    program*decimal places:  10
    program*Decimal places:  10
```

We can easily adapt this feature to support MWL classes. First, every object will need both an instance name and a class name. We have already provided for the instance name as part of the constructor. We need only add a member function that returns a class name. We will declare this function `virtual` to allow subclasses to define unique class names. The following code is from the revised version of ScreenComponent:

```
79              virtual const char* class_name() const
80              {
81                      return("ScreenComponent");
82              }
```

Next, we can take advantage of our knowledge of class implementation. As we have stated, under the object-oriented paradigm, objects contain both data and behavior (procedures). However, it would be too costly to implement objects that way. Consider that the code contained in member functions does not change from object to object. Thus, we really only need to store one copy of each member function and allow all objects to share it. As a result, when we instantiate an object, we really only create storage for the data portion of the object. (Hence the need for a `this` pointer: member functions need to know which object to process.) Thus, `this` pointers really point to the equivalent of a C `struct`. As a result, we can use `this` pointers as the data structure in calls to XtGetSubresources(). To simplify use, we will supply a convenience routine. The following code is also from the revised version of the ScreenComponent class:

```
107    //
108    // Routine to Get Component Resources
109    // Called from Derived Classes
110    //
111    void ScreenComponent::getComponentResources(
112            const XtResourceList res, const int cnt )
113    {
114            XtGetSubresources(
115                    parent_widget(),    // Parent Widget
116                    (XtPointer)this,    // Data Structure
117                    _widget_name,       // Instance Name
```

```
118                               class_name(),        // Class Name
119                               res,                 // Resource Array
120                               cnt,                 // Num of Resources
121                               NULL,                // Arg Array
122                               0                    // Number of Args
123                 );
124    }
```

The function getComponentResources() takes two arguments: a resource list and a count. It can then set class data members by using the this pointer. The function parent_widget() is a convenience routine that simply makes a call to XtParent().

To use this facility, derived classes need only:

- Provided their own version of the class_name() member

- Define a custom resource array

- Call the convenience routine getComponentResources()

MWL objects now function as self-contained GUI components.

10.3 ScreenComponent CLASS: FINAL VERSION

10.3.1 The ScreenComponent *Header File*

```
1    //
2    //           TITLE: scrn_cmp.h
3    //
4    //           FUNCTION: Version 2 of the ScreenComponent class.
5    //
6
7    #ifndef _SCREEN_COMPONENT_H_
8    #define _SCREEN_COMPONENT_H_
9
10   #include <string.h>                       // For strcpy() ...
11
```

```
12   #include <Xm/Xm.h>                          // Motif header file
13
14   class ScreenComponent {
15
16   protected:
17
18           //
19           // Protected data to allow derived classes
20           // direct access
21           //
22           char*   _widget_name;   // Widget Name
23           Widget  _main_widget;   // Main widget
24
25           //
26           // Protected constructor: we do not want
27           // this class to be instantiated - only
28           // derived from.
29           //
30           ScreenComponent( char* name );
31
32   public:
33           //
34           //       Basic Features
35           //
36           virtual ~ScreenComponent();   // Destructor
37
38           Widget main_widget()          // Return widget
39           {
40                   return( _main_widget );
41           }
42
43           char* widget_name()                // Widget's name
44           {
45                   char *t = new char[ strlen(_widget_name)+1 ];
46                   strcpy( t, _widget_name );
47
48                           //
```

```
49                        // N.B.: Client must "free" storage
50                        //
51                        return( t );
52              }
53
54              //
55              //        Virtual Functions
56              //
57              virtual void manage();          // Manage widget
58              virtual void unmanage();        // Unmanage widget
59
60              //
61              //                    Additional Features
62              //
63
64              //
65              //        Widget Destruction
66              //
67              void registerDestroyCB();
68              virtual void destroyWidget();
69              static void destroyCB( Widget, XtPointer, XtPointer );
70
71              //
72              // Resource Management Functions
73              //
74              Widget parent_widget()
75              {
76                      return( XtParent(_main_widget) );
77              }
78
79              virtual const char* class_name() const
80              {
81                      return("ScreenComponent");
82              }
83
84              void getComponentResources( const XtResourceList,
                                            const int );
85      };
```

```
86
87    #endif
```

LISTING 10.6. Version 2: scrn_cmp.h

10.3.2 *The* ScreenComponent *Class Implementation File*

```
1    //
2    //            TITLE: scrn_cmp.cxx
3    //
4    //            FUNCTION: Version 2 of the ScreenComponent class.
5    //
6    #include "scrn_cmp.h"
7
8    ScreenComponent::ScreenComponent( char* name )
9    {
10           _main_widget = (Widget)NULL;
11
12           _widget_name = new char[ strlen(name)+1 ];
13           strcpy( _widget_name, name );
14    }
15
16    virtual ScreenComponent::~ScreenComponent()
17    {
18           if( _main_widget != (Widget)NULL )
19           {
20                   //
21                   // Remove Destroy Callback
22                   //
23                   XtRemoveCallback(
24                           _main_widget,
25                           XmNdestroyCallback,
26                           &ScreenComponent::destroyCB,
27                           (XtPointer)this
28                   );
29           }
30
31                   //
```

```
32                  // Relinquish dynamic memory
33                  //
34                  delete [] _widget_name;
35      }
36
37      virtual void ScreenComponent::manage()
38      {
39                  //
40                  // Only manage if we have a widget
41                  //
42                  if( _main_widget != (Widget)NULL )
43                  {
44                    XtManageChild( _main_widget );
45
46                    //
47                    // Verify destroy handler has been registered by
48                    // if not - register it now
49                    //
50                    // This is not foolproof - this routine is virtual
51                    // and can be redefined in a derived class
52                    //
53                    if( XtHasCallbacks(_main_widget, XmNdestroyCallback)
54                            != XtCallbackHasSome )
55                        {
56                            registerDestroyCB();
57                        }
58                  }
59      }
60
61      virtual void ScreenComponent::unmanage()
62      {
63                  //
64                  // Only unmanage if we have a widget
65                  //
66                  if( _main_widget != (Widget)NULL )
67                        XtUnmanageChild( _main_widget );
68      }
```

```
69
70    //
71    // Routines to manage widget destruction
72    //
73    void ScreenComponent::registerDestroyCB()
74    {
75        //
76        // Convenience routine to register an XmNdestroyCallback
77        // for class
78        //
79        if( _main_widget != (Widget)NULL )
80                XtAddCallback(
81                    _main_widget,
82                    XmNdestroyCallback,
83                    &ScreenComponent::destroyCB,
84                    (XtPointer)this
85                  );
86    }
87
88    virtual void ScreenComponent::destroyWidget()
89    {
90            //
91            // Record that the widget has been destroyed
92            //
93            _main_widget = (Widget)NULL;
94    }
95
96    void ScreenComponent::destroyCB( Widget w,
97            XtPointer client, XtPointer call )
98    {
99            //
100           // Static CB function - pass on to object
101           //
102           ScreenComponent* the_object =
                  (ScreenComponent*)client;
103
104           the_object->destroyWidget();
105    }
```

```
106
107     //
108     // Routine to Get Component Resources
109     // Called from Derived Classes
110     //
111     void ScreenComponent::getComponentResources(
112            const XtResourceList res, const int cnt )
113     {
114            XtGetSubresources(
115               parent_widget(),           // Parent Widget
116               (XtPointer)this,           // Data Structure
117               _widget_name,              // Instance Name
118               class_name(),              // Class Name
119               res,                       // Resource Array
120               cnt,                       // # of Resources
121               NULL,                      // Arg Array
122               0                          // Number of Args
123                   );
124     }
```

LISTING 10.7. Version 2: scrn_cmp.cxx

10.3.3 Another Simple Example

Before we continue our discussions, let's return to the example of Listing 10.3. As you may recall, the program ScrnTest.cxx, created a simple interface using the first version of the ScreenComponent class. Let's reimplement the program using the new version of the class. Listing 10.8 contains the code.

```
1     //
2     //             TITLE: ScrnTest2.cxx
3     //
4     //             FUNCTION: Simple test of the second version of the
5     //                       ScreenComponent class.
6     //
7     #include <iostream.h>
8
9     #include "scrn_cmp.h"
```

```
10
11      #include <Xm/PushB.h>
12
13      //
14      // Derive a simple pushbutton class
15      //
16      class PB : public ScreenComponent {
17
18      private:
19
20              //
21              // Some Private Data Members to Exercise
22              // Resource DB Processing
23              //
24              XmString my_label;
25              static XtResource PB_resources[];
26
27      public:
28              PB( Widget, char* );
29
30              static void pbCB( Widget, XtPointer, XtPointer );
31
32              //
33              // Redefine Classname
34              //
35              virtual const char* class_name() const
36              {
37                      return("PB");
38              }
39      };
40
41      //
42      // Class/Component Resources
43      //
44      XtResource PB::PB_resources[] = {
45              {
46                      "pblabel",                      // Resource Name
```

```
47                    "PBlabel",                 // Resource Class
48                    XmRXmString,               // Data Type
49                    sizeof(XmString),          // Size
50                    XtOffset(PB*, my_label),  // Offset
51                    XmRString,                 // Default Type
52                    (XtPointer)"T2 Pgm"        // Default Value
53             }
54    };
55
56    PB::PB( Widget parent, char *name )
57             : ScreenComponent(name)
58    {
59          int i;
60          Arg args[ 10 ];
61
62          _main_widget = XtVaCreateWidget( name,
63                  xmPushButtonWidgetClass,    parent,
64                  XmNwidth,                   200,
65                  XmNheight,                  100,
66          NULL );
67
68          //
69          // Add Destroy CB
70          //
71          registerDestroyCB();
72
73          //
74          // Add an Activate Callback
75          //
76          XtAddCallback(
77                  _main_widget, XmNactivateCallback,
78                  &PB::pbCB, (XtPointer)NULL
79          );
80
81          //
82          // Query Resource DB
83          //
```

```
84                       getComponentResources( PB_resources,
85                               XtNumber(PB_resources) );
86
87               //
88               // Use a "Class" Resource to Change the Label
89               //
90               i = 0;
91               XtSetArg( args[i], XmNlabelString, my_label ); i++;
92               XtSetValues( _main_widget, args, i );
93       }
94
95     //
96     // Use a Button Press to Test destroyCB Code
97     //
98     void PB::pbCB( Widget w, XtPointer c, XtPointer x )
99     {
100              XtDestroyWidget( w );
101      }
102
103    int main( int ac, char *av[] )
104    {
105              Widget              top;  // Top Level Shell
106              XtAppContext        app;   // Application Context
107
108              //
109              // Initialize Xt Toolkit
110              //
111              top = XtAppInitialize( &app, "T2",
112                      NULL, 0, &ac, av, NULL, NULL, 0
113              );
114
115              //
116              // Create New Pushbutton
117              //
118              PB *pb = new PB( top, "pb1" );
119
120              //
```

```
121                // Manage Widget
122                //
123                pb->manage();
124
125                //
126                // Realize Widgets
127                //
128                XtRealizeWidget( top );
129
130                //
131                // Enter Main Event Loop
132                //
133                XtAppMainLoop( app );
134     }
```

LISTING 10.8. ScreenCompnent test program revisited.

In addition to the simple interface change, there are several other coding differences in this version. On line 25, we added a declaration for an XtResource array called PB_resources[]. We define the array on lines 44–54. For this simple example, we are using the class resource mechanism to determine the initial label displayed by the pushbutton.

The constructor's definition begins with line 56. After we create the interface (lines 62–66), we register the destroy handler on line 71. On lines 85 and 85, we invoke the inherited member getComponentResources() to access our class resources. We uses the values we obtained on lines 90–92 to set the button's label.

10.4 CALCULATOR REVISITED

10.4.1 The calc.cxx File

Once again, let's return to our calculator example and reimplement the program using the ScreenComponent class. Specifically, we will derive all user interface classes from ScreenComponent. Listing 10.9 presents the file calc.cxx.

```
 1     //
 2     //              TITLE:        CALC.CXX
 3     //
 4     //              FUNCTION:     Member function definitions for
 5     //                            the Calc class.
 6     //
 7
 8     #include "calc.h"
 9
10     #include "scrn_cmp.h"
11
12     //
13     // Calc Class Resources
14     //
15     XtResource Calc::Calc_resources[] = {
16             {
17                     "initDisplay",              // Resource Name
18                     "InitDisplay",              // Resource Class
19                     XmRString,                  // Data Type
20                     sizeof(String),             // Size
21                     XtOffset(Calc*, label),     // Offset
22                     XmRString,                  // Default Type
23                     (XtPointer)"WELCOME"        // Default Value
24             }
25     };
26
27     Calc::Calc( Widget parent, char* name )
28             : ScreenComponent(name)
29     {
30             //
31             //        Create Form Widget
32             //
33             _main_widget = XmCreateForm( parent, name, NULL, 0 );
34
35             //
36             // Add Destroy CB
37             //
```

```
38              registerDestroyCB();
39
40              //
41              // Query Resource DB
42              //
43              getComponentResources( Calc_resources,
44                      XtNumber(Calc_resources) );
45
46              //
47              //      Create CalcDisplay Object
48              //
49              display = new CalcDisplay( _main_widget, "display" );
50
51              //
52              //      Create Engine Object
53              //
54              engine  = new CalcEngine( disp, (void *)this );
55
56              //
57              //      Create Keypad
58              //
59              keypad = new Keypad( _main_widget, "keypad", engine );
60
61              //
62              //      Manage Sub-components
63              //
64              keypad->manage();
65              display->manage();
66
67              //
68              // Use a "Class" resource to initialize display
69              //
70              display->SetDisplay( label );
71      }
72
73      Calc::~Calc( Widget p )
```

```
74      {
75                  //
76                  //          Clean-up
77                  //
78                  delete display;
79                  delete engine;
80                  delete keypad;
81      }
```

LISTING 10.9. Revised Calc constructor

On lines 15–25 we define our resource array. For this example, we have defined a class resource to determine the initial display string. Line 30 contains the call to register the destroy handler, and lines 43 and 44 retrieve resources from the database.

We made similar changes to the CalcDisplay and Keypad classes as well. Note that we did not modify CalcEngine or Stack. ScreenComponent should serve as a base class for only GUI classes. The entire listing appears in the next section.

10.4.2 calc: *Complete Listing*

The following is the complete listing for the newest version of the calculator program.

10.4.2.1 calc.h

```
1    //
2    //          TITLE:          CALC.H
3    //
4    //          FUNCTION:       Class definition for cals
5    //
6    //
7
8    #ifndef _CALC_H_
9    #define _CALC_H_
10
11   #include <stdlib.h>
12   #include <string.h>
```

```
13
14      #include <Xm/Form.h>
15      #include <Xm/Text.h>
16      #include <Xm/TextF.h>
17      #include <Xm/PushB.h>
18      #include <Xm/RowColumn.h>
19
20      #include "keypad.h"
21      #include "display.h"
22      #include "calc_eng.h"
23
24      #include "scrn_cmp.h"
25
26      class Calc : public ScreenComponent {
27
28      private:
29
30              Keypad          *keypad;        // Ptr to Keypad
31              CalcEngine      *engine;        // Ptr to Engine
32              CalcDisplay     *display;       // Ptr to Display
33
34              //
35              //      Resource Array for Class Resources
36              //
37              char* label;
38              static XtResource Calc_resources[];
39
40              //
41              // DISP():
42              //      "Callback" Routine used as an
43              //      interface to the Engine class.
44              //
45              //      disp() is called form a calculator
46              //      and the call us passed on to a
47              //      display object. The "callback" is
48              //      "registered" in the constructor.
49              //
```

```
50          static void disp( char *str, void *obj )
51          {
52                  ((Calc *)obj)->display->SetDisplay( str );
53          }
54
55   public:
56
57          Calc( Widget, char* );
58          virtual ~Calc();
59
60          //
61          // Redefine Classname
62          //
63          virtual const char* class_name() const
64          {
65                  return( "Calc" );
66          }
67   };
68
69   #endif
```

10.4.2.2 calc_eng.h

```
 1   //
 2   //            TITLE:       CALC_ENG.H
 3   //
 4   //            FUNCTION:    Class definition for the "engine"
 5   //                         portion of the calculator program.
 6   //
 7   //                         This class is implemented as
 8   //                         a "State Machine".
 9   //
10
11   #ifndef _CalcEngine_
12   #define _CalcEngine_
13
14   #include <string.h>
15   #include <stdlib.h>
```

```
16
17      #include <iostream.h>              // For 'CERR'
18
19      #include "stack.h"
20
21      class CalcEngine {
22
23      private:
24
25              //
26              //          Internal State
27              //
28              enum State { INIT, LEFT, RIGHT, OPERATOR };
29
30              //
31              //          Operations
32              //
33              enum Operation { ADD, SUB, MUL, DIV, EQUAL, CLEAR };
34
35              Stack s;               // The calculator stack
36              State state;           // Master "state" variable
37              Operation oper;        // Operation flag
38              char str[ 100 ];       // Operand (display) value
39
40              //
41              //          These next two variables implement a kind
42              //          of "callback" mechanism for displaying
43              //          values computed by an engine.
44              //
45              void *cd;              // Ptr to "client_data"
46              void (*display_function)( char *, void * );
47
48              //
49              // DISPLAY():
50              // Display a new value. Implemented as a "callback"
51              // so that Engine class is not tightly coupled to
52              // some other class (e.g., CalcDisplay).
```

```
53                  //
54                  void display()
55                  {
56                          //
57                          // If registered, call routine
58                          // with display string and client data
59                          //
60                          if( display_function )
61                                  display_function( str, cd );
62                  }
63
64
65                  //
66                  // CALC():
67                  //      Calculation Routine: performs the basic
68                  //      operations of the calculator
69                  //
70                  void calc();
71
72                  //
73                  // RESET():
74                  //      Reset the engine to the INIT state.
75                  //
76                  void reset()
77                  {
78                          s.reset();
79                          oper = CLEAR;
80                          state = INIT;
81                          strcpy( str, "0.00" );
82                  }
83
84                  //
85                  // ERROR():
86                  //      Error handler. Should use Exceptions.
87                  //
88                  void _error( char *arg )
89                  {
```

```
90                              cerr << "CalcEngine:  **ERROR:  "  <<  arg
                                    <<  "\\n";
91                              exit( -1 );
92                  }
93
94
95      public:
96              //
97              // Constructor:
98              //      Reqs 2 args: a display function
99              //      to invoke and optional client data.
100             //
101             CalcEngine( void (*f)(char*, void*),
                        void *client_data )
102               {
103                     //
104                     // Save callback info
105                     //
106                     cd = client_data;
107                     display_function = f;
108
109                     //
110                     // Reset engine.
111                     //
112                     reset();
113                     display();
114               }
115
116             //
117             // CLEAR():
118             //      Clear engine.  Invoked when user press
119             //      the "C" key on the keypad.
120             //
121              void clear()
122             {
123                     reset();
124                     display();
125             }
```

```
126
127                 //
128                 // Declarations for "event" functions.
129                 //
130                 void add();
131                 void sub();
132                 void mul();
133                 void div();
134                 void equal();
135                 void digit( int );
136                 void decimal_point();
137      };
138
139      #endif
```

10.4.2.3 keypad.h

```
1    //
2    //              TITLE:          KEYPAD.H
3    //
4    //              FUNCTION:       Definition for the class Keypad.
5    //                              This version derived from the
6    //                              ScreenComponent class.
7    //
8
9    #ifndef _Keypad_H_
10   #define _Keypad_H_
11
12   #include <stdlib.h>
13   #include <string.h>
14
15   #include <Xm/Form.h>
16   #include <Xm/PushB.h>
17   #include <Xm/RowColumn.h>
18
19   #include "scrn_cmp.h"
20
21   class CalcEngine;                        // Declare Engine Class
```

```
22
23   //
24   //          Constants (for button alignment)
25   //
26   const int max_rows = 4;
27   const int max_cols = 4;
28
29   //
30   //          Class Definition
31   //
32   class Keypad : public ScreenComponent {
33
34   private:
35
36          CalcEngine *engine;                      // Ptr to Engine
37
38   public:
39
40          Keypad( Widget, char*, CalcEngine* );
41
42          //
43          //          Callback Functions
44          //
45          static void ButtonPressedCB( Widget, XtPointer,
                                         XtPointer );
46          virtual void ButtonCB( Widget, XtPointer, XtPointer );
47
48          //
49          // Redefine Classname
50          //
51          virtual const char* class_name() const
52          {
53                  return( "Keypad" );
54          }
55   };
56
57   #endif
```

10.4.2.4 display.h

```
1    //
2    //              TITLE:       DISPLAY.H
3    //
4    //              FUNCTION:    Definition of the CalcDisplay Class.
5    //                           Derived from ScreenComponent.
6    //
7
8    #ifndef _CALC_DSIPLAY_
9    #define _CALC_DSIPLAY_
10
11   #include <Xm/Text.h>
12   #include <Xm/TextF.h>
13
14   #include "scrn_cmp.h"
15
16   class CalcDisplay : public ScreenComponent
17   {
18
19   public:
20
21            //
22            //       Constructor: Requires A Parent Widget
23            //
24            CalcDisplay( Widget parent, char* name )
25                    : ScreenComponent(name)
26            {
27                    //
28                    //       Create TextField Widget
29                    //
30                    _main_widget = XtVaCreateWidget( name,

32                            xmTextFieldWidgetClass,     parent,

34                            XmNeditable,                False,
35                            XmNcursorPositionVisible,   False,
36                            XmNtraversalOn,             False,
```

```
37
38                        NULL );
39
40                        //
41                        // Add Destroy CB
42                        //
43                        registerDestroyCB();
44              }
45
46              //
47              // Redefine Classname
48              //
49              virtual const char* class_name() const
50              {
51                        return( "CalcDisplay" );
52              }
53
54              //
55              //        Displays A String Argument
56              //
57              void SetDisplay( char *str )
58              {
59                        register          i;
60                        short             cols;
61                        Arg               args[ 50 ];
62                        char              buf[ 256 ];
63
64                        //
65                        //        Determine Number of Columns
66                        //
67                        i = 0;
68                 XtSetArg( args[i], XmNcolumns, &cols ); i++;
69                 XtGetValues( _main_widget, args, i );
70
71                        //
72                        //        Format Buffer
73                        //
```

```
74                     sprintf( buf, "%*.*s", cols, cols, str );
75
76              //
77              //        Update Display
78              //
79              XmTextSetString( _main_widget, buf );
80          }
81   };
82
83   #endif
```

10.4.2.5 main.cxx

```
 1   //
 2   //          TITLE:        MAIN.CXX
 3   //
 4   //          FUNCTION:        Driving module for calc
 5   //
 6
 7   #include <iostream.h>
 8
 9   #include <Xm/AtomMgr.h>
10   #include <Xm/Protocols.h>
11
12   #include "calc.h"
13
14   //
15   // Window Manger Callback Routine
16   //
17   void win_closeCB( Widget widget, XtPointer client_data,
18          XtPointer call_data );
19
20   int main( int ac, char *av[] )
21   {
22          register          i;
23          Arg               args[ 50 ];
24          XtAppContext      app;
25          Widget            top;
26          Atom              Delete_Window;
```

```
27
28          //
29          //          Initialize Toolkit
30          //
31          top = XtAppInitialize( &app, "Calc", NULL, 0,
32                      &ac, av, NULL, NULL, 0 );
33
34          //
35          //          Get WM Protocol Atom
36          //
37          Delete_Window = XmInternAtom
38          (
39                  XtDisplay(top),
40                  "WM_DELETE_WINDOW",
41                  False
42          );
43
44          //
45          //          Register  WM  Callback  Routine
46          //
47          XmAddWMProtocolCallback
48          (
49                  top,
50                  Delete_Window,
51                  win_closeCB,
52                  NULL
53          );
54
55
56          //
57          //          Create  a  Calculator
58          //
59          Calc c( top, "mycalc" );
60          c.manage();
61
62          //
63          //          Realize Widgets
```

```
64              //
65              XtRealizeWidget( top );
66
67              //
68              //          Enter Main Loop
69              //
70              XtAppMainLoop( app );
71      }
72
73      //
74      // WIN_CLOSECB():
75      //          This routine is called when the user selects
76      //          the "close" option from the window manager.
77      //
78      void win_closeCB( Widget widget, XtPointer client_data,
79              XtPointer call_data )
80      {
81              exit( 0 );          // Just Exit
82      }
```

10.4.2.6 calc.cxx

```
1       //
2       //              TITLE:       CALC.CXX
3       //
4       //          FUNCTION:        Member function definitions for
5       //                           the Calc class.
6       //
7
8       #include "calc.h"
9
10      #include "ScrnCmpnt.h"
11
12      //
13      // Calc Class Resources
14      //
15      XtResource Calc::Calc_resources[] = {
```

```
16                 {
17                         "initDisplay",              // Name
18                         "InitDisplay",              // Class
19                         XmRString,                  // Data Type
20                         sizeof(String),             // Size
21                         XtOffset(Calc*, label),     // Offset
22                         XmRString,                  // Default Type
23                         (XtPointer)"WELCOME"        // Default Val
24                 }
25      };
26
27      Calc::Calc( Widget parent, char* name )
28                 : ScreenComponent(name)
29      {
30              //
31              //      Create Form Widget
32              //
33              _main_widget = XmCreateForm( parent, name, NULL, 0 );
34
35              //
36              // Add Destroy CB
37              //
38              registerDestroyCB();
39
40              //
41              // Query Resource DB
42              //
43              getComponentResources( Calc_resources,
44                      XtNumber(Calc_resources) );
45
46              //
47              //      Create CalcDisplay Object
48              //
49              display = new CalcDisplay( _main_widget, "display" );
50
51              //
52              //      Create Engine Object
```

```
53              //
54              engine   = new CalcEngine( disp, (void *)this );
55
56              //
57              //        Create Keypad
58              //
59              keypad = new Keypad( _main_widget, "keypad", engine );
60
61              //
62              //        Manage Sub-components
63              //
64              keypad->manage();
65              display->manage();
66
67              //
68              // Use a "Class" resource to initialize display
69              //
70              display->SetDisplay( label );
71      }
72
73      Calc::~Calc( Widget p )
74      {
75              //
76              //        Clean-up
77              //
78              delete display;
79              delete engine;
80              delete keypad;
81      }
```

10.4.2.7 calc_eng.cxx

```
1       //
2       //        TITLE:    CALC_ENG.CXX
3       //
4       //        FUNCTION:    This file implements the CalcEngine
5       //                     class as a state machine.
6       //
```

```
7
8      #include "calc_eng.h"
9
10     //
11     // DIGIT():
12     //        Received a new digit from the keypad
13     //
14     void CalcEngine::digit( int d )
15     {
16             char buf[ 256 ];
17
18             sprintf( buf, "%1d", d );
19
20             switch( state )
21             {
22
23             case INIT:
24                     strcpy( str, buf );
25                     display();
26                     state = LEFT;
27                     break;
28
29             case LEFT:
30                     strcat( str, buf );
31                     display();
32                     state = LEFT;
33                     break;
34
35             case OPERATOR:
36                     strcpy( str, buf );
37                     display();
38                     state = LEFT;
39                     break;
40
41             case RIGHT:
42                     strcat( str, buf );
43                     display();
```

```
44                      state = RIGHT;
45                      break;
46              }
47      }
48
49      //
50      // DECIMAL_POINT():
51      //      User entered a decimal point - only
52      //      allow 1 as part of a number.
53      //
54      void CalcEngine::decimal_point()
55      {
56              switch( state )
57              {
58
59              case OPERATOR:
60                      strcpy( str, "." );
61                      display();
62                      state = RIGHT;
63                      break;
64
65              case INIT:
66                      strcat( str, "." );
67                      display();
68                      state = RIGHT;
69                      break;
70
71              case LEFT:
72                      strcat( str, "." );
73                      display();
74                      state = RIGHT;
75                      break;
76              }
77      }
78
79      //
80      // CALC():
```

```
81        //        Perform indicated operation.
82        //
83        void CalcEngine::calc()
84        {
85                double ans, operand1, operand2;
86
87                switch( oper )
88                {
89
90                case ADD:
91                        if( s.pop(&operand2) != Stack::OK )
92                                _error( "ADD: Missing Op2" );
93                        if( s.pop(&operand1) != Stack::OK )
94                                _error( "ADD: Missing Op1" );
95                        ans = operand1 + operand2;
96                        s.push( ans );
97                        sprintf( str, "%f", ans );
98                        break;
99
100                case SUB:
101                        if( s.pop(&operand2) != Stack::OK )
102                                _error( "SUB: Missing Op2" );
103                        if( s.pop(&operand1) != Stack::OK )
104                                _error( "SUB: Missing Op1" );
105                        ans = operand1 - operand2;
106                        s.push( ans );
107                        sprintf( str, "%f", ans );
108                        break;
109
110                case MUL:
111                        if( s.pop(&operand2) != Stack::OK )
112                                _error( "MUL: Missing Op2" );
113                        if( s.pop(&operand1) != Stack::OK )
114                                _error( "MUL: Missing Op1" );
115                        ans = operand1 * opd2;
116                        s.push( ans );
117                        sprintf( str, "%f", ans );
```

```
118                      break;
119
120            case DIV:
121                      if( s.pop(&operand2) != Stack::OK )
122                              _error( "DIV: Missing Op2" );
123                      if( s.pop(&operand1) != Stack::OK )
124                              _error( "DIV: Missing Op1" );
125                      if( operand2 == 0.0 )
126                              _error( Div by Zero" );
127                      ans = operand1 / operand2;
128                      s.push( ans );
129                      sprintf( str, "%f", ans );
130                      break;
131            }
132
133            display();
134    }
135
136    //
137    // ADD():
138    //      Add top two numbers on the stack - push answer
139    //
140    void CalcEngine::add()
141    {
142
143            switch( state )
144            {
145
146            case LEFT:
147            case RIGHT:
148                      s.push( atof(str) );
149                      calc();
150                      oper = ADD;
151                      state = OPERATOR;
152                      break;
153
```

```
154              case OPERATOR:
155                        oper = ADD;
156                        break;
157            }
158    }
159
160    //
161    // SUB():
162    //        Subtract top two numbers - push answer
163    //
164    void CalcEngine::sub()
165    {
166
167            switch( state )
168            {
169
170            case LEFT:
171            case RIGHT:
172                      s.push( atof(str) );
173                      calc();
174                      oper = SUB;
175                      state = OPERATOR;
176                      break;
177
178            case OPERATOR:
179                        oper = SUB;
180                        break;
181            }
182    }
183
184    //
185    // MUL():
186    //        Multiply top two numbers - push answer
187    //
188    void CalcEngine::mul()
189    {
190
```

```
191             switch( state )
192             {
193
194             case LEFT:
195             case RIGHT:
196                     s.push( atof(str) );
197                     calc();
198                     oper = MUL;
199                     state = OPERATOR;
200                     break;
201
202             case OPERATOR:
203                     oper = MUL;
204                     break;
205             }
206     }
207
208     //
209     // DIV():
210     //      Divide top two numbers - push answer
211     //      Ensure proper order of operands and check for
212     //      division by zero.
213     //
214     void CalcEngine::div()
215     {
216
217             switch( state )
218             {
219
220             case LEFT:
221             case RIGHT:
222                     s.push( atof(str) );
223                     calc();
224                     oper = DIV;
225                     state = OPERATOR;
226                     break;
227
```

```
228              case OPERATOR:
229                      oper = DIV;
230                      break;
231          }
232      }
233
234      //
235      // EQUAL():
236      //       Perform indicated operation and display result
237      //
238      void CalcEngine::equal()
239      {
240          switch( state )
241          {
242
243          case LEFT:
244          case RIGHT:
245                  s.push( atof(str) );
246                  calc();
247                  oper = EQUAL;
248                  state = OPERATOR;
249                  break;
250          }
251      }
```

10.4.2.8 keypad.cxx

```
1    //
2    //          TITLE:     KEYPAD.CXX
3    //
4    //          FUNCTION:  Functions to process keystrokes for the
5    //                     calc program.
6    //
7
8    #include "keypad.h"
9    #include "calc_eng.h"
10
```

```
11    //
12    //        Button Structure - Serves as "client data"
13    //        in callbacks.
14    //
15    struct button_struct {
16            char      label;
17            Keypad    *object;
18            Widget    widget;
19    };
20
21    //
22    //        Button Labels
23    //
24    static char *cb[] =
25    {
26            "1",  "2",  "3",  "/",
27            "4",  "5",  "6",  "*",
28            "7",  "8",  "9",  "-",
29            "C",  "0",  "=",  "+"
30    };
31
32    //
33    //        Constructor
34    //
35    Keypad::Keypad( Widget parent, char* name, CalcEngine* e )
36            : ScreenComponent(name)
37    {
38
39            Arg              args[ 50 ];
40            int              i, index, row, col;
41            XmString         labl;
42            button_struct*   buttons;
43
44            //
45            //        Save pointer to CalcEngine object
46            //
47            engine = e;
```

```
48
49            //
50            //          Create Form to Hold Calculator Buttons
51            //
52            _main_widget = XtVaCreateWidget( name,
53
54                    xmFormWidgetClass,      parent,
55
56                    XmNfractionBase,        4,
57
58                    XmNlength,              200,
59                    XmNwidth,               200,
60
61            NULL );
62
63            //
64            // Add Destroy CB
65            //
66            registerDestroyCB();
67
68            //
69            //          Allocate storage for button callbacks
70            //
71            buttons = new button_struct[ max_rows * max_cols ];
72
73            //
74            //          Create Calculator Buttons
75            //
76            for( row = 0;  row < max_rows;  row++ )
77            {
78                    for( col = 0;  col < max_cols;  col++ )
79                    {
80                            index = (row * max_cols) + col;
81
82                            //
83                            //          Save state info
84                            //
```

```
85              buttons[index].object = this;
86              buttons[index].label =
                cb[index][0];
87
88              //
89              //      Create Label String
90              //
91              labl = XmStringCreateSimple(
                cb[index] );
92
93              //
94              //      Create Button
95              //
96              buttons[index].widget =
                XtVaCreateManagedWidget(
97
98               cb[index],
99
100                 xmPushButtonWidgetClass,
                    _main_widget,
101
102                 XmNlabelString,         labl,
103
104                 XmNtopAttachment,
                    XmATTACH_POSITION,
105                 XmNtopPosition,         row,
106
107                 XmNbottomAttachment,
                    XmATTACH_POSITION,
108                 XmNbottomPosition,      row+1,
109
110                 XmNleftAttachment,
                    XmATTACH_POSITION,
111                 XmNleftPosition,        col,
112
113                 XmNrightAttachment,
                    XmATTACH_POSITION,
```

```
114                                    XmNrightPosition,       col+1,
115
116                         NULL );
117
118                         //
119                         //        Register Callback
120                         //
121                         XtAddCallback( buttons[index].widget,
122                         XmNactivateCallback,
123                      (XtCallbackProc)ButtonPressedCB,
124                            (XtPointer)&buttons[index]
125                         );
126
127                         //
128                         //        Free String
129                         //
130                         XmStringFree( labl );
131                    }
132                }
133      }
134
135      //
136      //        Static Callback Function
137      //
138      void Keypad::ButtonPressedCB( Widget widget,
139              XtPointer client_data, XtPointer call_data )
140      {
141              button_struct *b = (button_struct *)client_data;
142
143              Keypad *obj = (Keypad *)b->object;
144
145              //
146              //        Pass on callback to actual object
147              //
148              obj->ButtonCB( b->widget, (XtPointer)b->label,
149                      (XtPointer)call_data );
150      }
```

```
151
152     //
153     //          Pushbutton Callback Routine
154     //
155     void Keypad::ButtonCB( Widget widget,
156             XtPointer client_data, XtPointer call_data )
157     {
158             char which_button = (char)client_data;
159
160
161             switch( which_button )
162             {
163                     case '0':
164                     case '1':
165                     case '2':
166                     case '3':
167                     case '4':
168                     case '5':
169                     case '6':
170                     case '7':
171                     case '8':
172                     case '9':
173                             //
174                             // Pass on digit to engine
175                             //
176                             engine->digit( which_button-'0' );
177                             break;
178
179                     case 'C':
180                             //
181                             // Clear button pressed
182                             //
183                             engine->clear();
184                             break;
185
186                     case '+':
187                             //
```

```
188                         // Add operation
189                         //
190                         engine->add();
191                         break;
192
193             case '-':
194                         //
195                         // Subtraction operation
196                         //
197                         engine->sub();
198                         break;
199
200             case '*':
201                         //
202                         // Multiply operation
203                         //
204                         engine->mul();
205                         break;
206
207             case '/':
208                         //
209                         // Division operation
210                         //
211                         engine->div();
212                         break;
213
214             case '=':
215                         //
216                         // Compute & display result
217                         //
218                         engine->equal();
219                         break;
220         }
221     }
```

10.4.2.9 Calc

```
1     !
2     !              Resource File for Calculator Program
3     !
4     *background:                lightblue
5     *display.columns:          30
6     *keypad.y:                 35
7     calc.mycalc.initDisplay:   WELCOME
```

10.4.2.10 stack.h

```
1     //
2     //              TITLE:       STACK.H
3     //
4     //              FUNCTION:    Quick and dirty implementation of
5     //                           a Stack - for used as a part of
6     //                           the Engine class.
7     //
8
9     #ifndef _Stack_H_
10    #define _Stack_H_
11
12    #include <stdio.h>
13    #include <string.h>
14    #include <stdlib.h>
15
16    class Stack {
17
18    private:
19
20            const int max_stack;      // Stack Size
21            double *stack;            // The Stack
22            int top;                  // Top of Stack
23
24    public:
25
26            //
27            //        Return Codes
```

```
28                 //
29                 enum StackVal { EMPTY, OVERFLOW, UNDERFLOW, OK, FAIL };
30
31                 //
32                 // Constructor:
33                 //       Initialize Stack
34                 //
35                 Stack( int stk_size = 200 )
36                 :       max_stack(stk_size)
37                 {
38                         stack = new double[ max_stack ];
39                         top = -1;
40                 }
41
42                 //
43                 // PUSH():
44                 //       Push a new value on the stack.
45                 //
46                 StackVal push( double v )
47                 {
48                         if( max_stack - top > 1 )
49                         {
50                                 stack[ ++top ] = v;
51                                 return( OK );
52                         } else {
53                                 return( OVERFLOW );
54                         }
55                 }
56
57                 //
58                 // POP():
59                 //       remove the top value from the stack.
60                 //
61                 StackVal pop( double *v )
62                 {
63                         if( top == -1 )
64                                 return( EMPTY );
```

```
65                      *v = stack[ top⁻ ];
66                      return( OK );
67              }
68
69              //
70              // PEEK():
71              //      Return (w/o removing) top value.
72              //
73              StackVal peek( double *v )
74              {
75                      if( top == -1 )
76                              return( EMPTY );
77                      *v = stack[ top ];
78                      return( OK );
79              }
80
81              //
82              // RESET():
83              //      Reset stack to initial state.
84              //
85              StackVal reset()
86              {
87                      top = -1;
88                      return( OK );
89              }
90      };
91
92      #endif
```

10.5 SUMMARY

In this chapter, we constructed the foundation class for the MWL library, ScreenComponent. In subsequent chapters, we will build upon this class to create an entire application framework. Before we proceed, let's take a moment to review some of ScreenComponent's features:

- Classes derived from ScreenComponent can support interfaces that comprise multiple widgets. Each component roots its instance tree in a main widget variable (_main_widget).

- Derived classes will typically create screen interfaces in their constructor functions, but strictly speaking, this is not a requirement.

- Derived classes should register a destructor callback using register-DestroyCB().

- Derived class constructors should accept at least two arguments, an instance name and a parent widget.

- Derived classes can allow the user to use the toolkit's resource database to customize behavior. As a consequence of the processing, all derived classes should override the class_name() member function inherited from ScreenComponent.

CHAPTER *11*

MWL—THE BASIC COMPONENTS

In Chapter 10 we discussed the design and implementation of the `Screen-Component` class. This class will serve as the foundation for other MWL components. In this chapter, we will build on the knowledge gained thus far and develop several additional component classes. Our goals include:

- Demonstrate how to derive new components from existing classes
- Provide examples of how easy the resulting screen component objects are to use
- Supply some practical examples of MWL usage

In effect, this chapter begins to highlight the true power of "objectifying" *Motif.*

There is one caveat, however. For the sake of brevity and pedagogical discourse, we cannot discuss every detail of every class. However, we will present many examples of each technique. Thus, will you will understand how to add features to your classes.

11.1 THE Label CLASS

Label is one of the simplest and most commonly used widgets. Let's begin our discussion by creating a Label class derived from the ScreenComponent class. Listing 11.1 contains the definition.

11.1.1 The Header File

```
1      //
2      //            TITLE:        label.h
3      //
4      //            FUNCTION:       Label class definition
5      //
6
7      #ifndef _LABEL_H_
8      #define _LABEL_H_
9
10     #include "scrn_cmp.h"
11     #include "mwlr.h"
12     #include "cs.h"
13
14     #include <Xm/Label.h>
15
16     class Label : public ScreenComponent {
17
18     private:
19
20            static XtResource LabelResources[];
21
22     protected:
23
24            XmString my_label;
25
26     public:
27            //
28            //        Constructors
29            //
30            Label( Widget parent, char* name,
31                   WidgetClass wclass = xmLabelWidgetClass,
```

```
32                              MWLResourceList res = MWLNoResources );
33
34                  Label(Widget parent, char* name, MWLResourceList res )
35                         : ScreenComponent(name)
36                  {
37
38                          _main_widget = XmCreateLabel( parent,
                                                  name, res, res );
39
40                          //
41                          //        Register Destroy Handler
42                          //
43                          registerDestroyCB();
44                  }
45
46                  //
47                  //        Destructor
48                  //
49                  ~Label()
50                  {
51                          XmStringFree( my_label );
52                  }
53
54                  //
55                  //   Redefine Class name
56                  //
57                  virtual const char* class_name() const
58                  {
59                          return("Label");
60                  }
61
62                  //
63                  //        Set Label String (char*)
64                  //
65                  void setLabelString( char* str )
66                  {
67                          CompoundString cs = str;
```

```
68                         XtVaSetValues( _main_widget,
69                              XmNlabelString, (XmString)cs,
70                         NULL );
71             }
72
73             //
74             //      Set Label String (XmString)
75             //
76             void setLabelString( XmString xmstring )
77             {
78                         XtVaSetValues( _main_widget, XmNlabel-
                                   String, xmstring, NULL );
79             }
80
81             //
82             //      Set Label String (CompoundString)
83             //
84             void setLabelString( CompoundString cs )
85             {
86                         XtVaSetValues(_main_widget,XmNlabelString,
                                   XmString(cs),NULL);
87             }
88     };
89
90     #endif
```

LISTING 11.1. label.h

We begin the class definition on line 16 where we derive Label from ScreenComponent. Line 20 contains a declaration for a private resource array (as discussed in the previous chapter). Line 24 contains a declaration for an XmString attribute used by the resource mechanism.

Line 30 begins a declaration for a constructor. The first argument, parent, is the ID of the widget that will serve as the label's instance parent. The second argument, name, will perform double duty, serving as the name used in the XtCreateLabel() function call, and an argument passed to the base class. As an aside, we will use the same first two arguments in all of our component classes.

With line 34, we begin the definition of another constructor. The function passes its name argument on to its base class (line 35), creates the label widget (line 38), and registers the destroy handler (line 43). As you might recall, the constructor for ScreenComponent class cannot register a destroy handler because it creates no widgets.

Additional member functions follow the constructors. The destructor (line 49) is trivial; it simply frees the label. Line 57 contains the redefinition of the class_name() member. Following that, we provide three overloaded definitions for convenience functions that set the widget's label. The first two expect a C string and an XmString, respectively. Although simple, this example demonstrates how we can make life a little easier for client programmers. We will defer discussion of the third signature until Chapter 12.

11.1.2 *The Implementation File*

Listing 11.2 contains the code from the implementation file label.cxx. However, the code is straightforward and requires no additional comment. We would like to draw your attention to the references made to the MWLResourceList class. Part of the MWL library, this class manages Motif resources. We will discuss its implementation in Chapter 12.

```
1    //
2    //          TITLE:        label.cxx
3    //
4    //          FUNCTION:     Label class definitions
5    //
6
7    #include "label.h"
8
9    //
10   //      Label Class/Component Resources
11   //
12   XtResource Label::LabelResources[] = {
13           {
14                   "LabelString",              // Resource
15                   "labelString",              // Class
16                   XmRXmString,                // Data Type
17                   sizeof(XmString),           // Size
```

```
18                    XtOffset(Label*, my_label),  // Offset
19                    XmRString,                   // Type
20                    (XtPointer)""                // Value
21              }
22      };
23
24      //
25      //         Label Constructor
26      //
27      Label::Label( Widget parent, char* name, WidgetClass wclass,
28              MWLResourceList res )
29              : ScreenComponent(name)
30      {
31              MWLResourceList rl;
32
33              _main_widget = XtCreateWidget( name, wclass, parent,
                                            res, res );
34
35              //
36              //         Register Destroy Handler
37              //
38              registerDestroyCB();
39
40              //
41              //         Query Resource DB
42              //
43              LabelResources[0].default_addr = (XtPointer)
                                            _widget_name;
44              getComponentResources( LabelResources,
                                    XtNumber(LabelResources) );
45
46              //
47              //         Use Class Resources to Change/Set Label
48              //
49              rl.setArg( XmNlabelString, my_label );
50              setValues( rl );
51      }
```

LISTING 11.2. label.cxx.

11.1.3 Label *Class Usage*

Using the Label class, clients can create a label widget by simply instantiating a Label object. Thus, application programmers need not concerns themselves with programming details associated with X, Xt, and Motif. The following code fragment contains several examples.

```
Widget form;

        .
        .               // Normal Startup Code
        .

Label label1( form, "name" );
Label* lptr = new Label( form, "name" );

label1.setLabelString( "OBJECTIFYING MOTIF IS MY LIFE" );
lptr->setLabelString( "MINE TOO!" );

label1.manage();
lptr->manage();

        .
        .               // Rest of Program
        .
```

11.2 THE PushButton CLASS

11.2.1 *A Question of Inheritance*

Another very commonly used widget is the pushbutton. We could create a PushButton class in much the same way we created the Label class: derive from ScreenComponent and create the new interface. However, after a moment's pause, we might reconsider. One of the basic precepts of object-oriented programming is code reuse. Specifically, we should look for every opportunity to inherit rather than rewrite. Thus, a better approach is to *derive* PushButton from Label. Unfortunately, after some additional reflection, we realize that inheritance might not be as easy as it seems. The reason is that most GUI classes will create widgets in their constructors. As such, if we blindly derive `PushButton` from `Label`, we would create a label widget each time we instantiated a pushbutton.

This begs the obvious question: Is there a better way? The answer is yes. We could allow base class constructors to accept an argument that determines the type of widget they should create. Moreover, this argument could be *defaulted* to simplify instantiation of the base class itself. For example, if we instantiate a `Label`, the constructor creates a label widget by default. However, if we instantiate a `PushButton`, the `PushButton` constructor passes an argument to its base class constructor (i.e., `Label`) that causes it to create a pushbutton widget.

An example is in order. Please recall that in Listing 11.1 we provided the following constructor signature for `Label`:

```
30              Label( Widget parent, char* name,
31                        WidgetClass wclass = xmLabelWidgetClass,
32                        MWLResourceList res = MWLNoResources );
```

By default (literally) the argument `wclass` is set to `xmLabelWidgetClass`. The constructor (Listing 11.2) executes the following code to create the widget:

```
33              _main_widget = XtCreateWidget( name, wclass, parent,
                                                res, res );
```

Note that it uses the generic widget creation function `XtCreateWidget()` and passes `wclass` as the second argument. We can now derive the `PushButton` class without any nasty side effects. We need only pass the appropriate value to the `Label` constructor, as in:

```
27    PushButton::PushButton( Widget parent, char* name )
28              : Label( parent, name, xmPushButtonWidgetClass )
```

As you will see, we employ this technique quite often within the MWL classes. The next two sections continue the discussion of the `PushButton` class.

11.2.2 *The* PushButton *Class Definition*

Listing 11.3 contains the PushButton class definition.

```
 1    //
 2    //          TITLE:          pb.h
 3    //
 4    //          FUNCTION:          PushButton class definition
 5    //
 6
 7    #ifndef _PUSHBUTTON_H_
 8    #define _PUSHBUTTON_H_
 9
10    #include "label.h"
11    #include "mwlr.h"
12
13    #include <Xm/PushB.h>
14
15    //
16    //      PushButton class definition
17    //
18    class PushButton : public Label {
19
20    private:
21
22            static XtResource PushButtonResources[];
23
24    public:
25
26            //
27            //        Constructor
28            //
29            PushButton( Widget, char*, MWLResourceList =
                                        MWLNoResources );
30
31
32            //
```

```
33              //          Destructor
34              //
35              ~PushButton()
36              {
37                      // Empty
38              }
39
40              //
41              //          Redefine Class name
42              //
43              virtual const char* class_name() const
44              {
45                      return("PushButton");
46              }
47
48              //
49              //          Set Accelerator
50              //
51              void setAccelerator( char* acc_label, char* acc_key );
52
53              //
54              //          Add an Activate Callback
55              //
56              void addActivateCallback( XtCallbackProc proc,
                                    XtPointer data )
57              {
58                      XtAddCallback(_main_widget,XmNactivateCall-
                                back,proc,data);
59              }
60
61              //
62              //          Set Button Mnemonic
63              //
64              void setMnemonic( char mnem )
65              {
66                  XtVaSetValues( _main_widget, XmNmnemonic, mnem,
                            NULL );
```

```
67                    }
68      };
69
70      #endif
```

LISTING 11.3. pb.h.

We have included several convenience functions as members of the class. The function setAccelerator() sets the button's accelerator key and label; setMnemonic() sets the button's mnemonic when its used as part of a menu. In addition, we have included a function that registers an XmNactivate-Callback callback procedure. We can extend this feature in several ways. We could modify the function to take an additional argument that identifies which callback to use. Or, we could provide a convenience function for every callback supported by a widget. We will return to this topic when we discuss extensions to the ScreenComponent class later in Chapter 12.

11.2.3 PushButton *Class Implementation*

The file pb.cxx contains only one function worthy of note: setAccelerator(). Listing 11.4 contains its definition.

```
52 void PushButton::setAccelerator( char* acc_label, char* acc_key )
53 {
54             MWLResourceList res;
55             CompoundString acceleratorText = acc_label;
56
57             res.setArg( XmNaccelerator, acc_key );
58             res.setArg( XmNacceleratorText, acceleratorText );
59             XtSetValues( _main_widget, res, res );
60 }
```

LISTING 11.4. PushButton::setAccelerator().

11.2.4 *The* MainWindow *Class Definition*

Many Motif programs contain a similar structure: menu bar, work area, message area. Motif's Main Window widget encapsulates all of those components. MWL contains a convenience class that creates and manages a Main Window widget. Listing 11.5 presents the class definition.

```
 1      //
 2      //           TITLE:          mainwin.h
 3      //
 4      //           FUNCTION:        Definition of the MainWindow Class
 5      //
 6
 7      #ifndef _MW_H_
 8      #define _MW_H_
 9
10      #include "scrn_cmp.h"
11
12      #include "Xm/MainW.h"
13
14      class MainWindow : public ScreenComponent {
15
16      private:
17
18              //
19              //        Main Window Areas
20              //
21              Widget menuBar;
22              Widget workArea;
23              Widget messageArea;
24              Widget commandArea;
25
26
27      public:
28
29              MainWindow( Widget, char* );            // Constructor
30
31              ~MainWindow()                            // Destructor
32              {
33                      XtDestroyWidget( menuBar );
34                      XtDestroyWidget( workArea );
35                      XtDestroyWidget( messageArea );
36                      XtDestroyWidget( commandArea );
37              }
```

```
38
39              //
40              //          Redefine Class name
41              //
42              virtual const char* class_name() const
43              {
44                      return("MainWindow");
45              }
46

47              //
48              //          Convenience Routines
49              //
50              void setMenuBar( Widget w )
51              {
52                menuBar = w;
53                XtVaSetValues( _main_widget, XmNmenuBar, w, NULL );
54              }
55              Widget getMenuBar() { return( menuBar ); }
56

57              void setWorkArea( Widget w )
58              {
59                workArea = w;
60                XtVaSetValues( _main_widget, XmNworkWindow, w, NULL );
61              }
62              Widget getWorkArea() { return( workArea ); }
63

64              void setMessageArea( Widget w )
65              {
66                messageArea = w;
67                XtVaSetValues( _main_widget, XmNmessageWindow, w,
                               NULL );
68              }
69              Widget getMessageArea() { return( messageArea ); }
70

71              void setCommandArea( Widget w )
72              {
73                      commandArea = w;
```

```
74                  XtVaSetValues( _main_widget, XmNcommandWindow, w,
                            NULL );
75              }
76              Widget getCommandArea() { return( commandArea ); }
77
78              void setSeparators( Boolean v = False )
79              {
80               XtVaSetValues( _main_widget, XmNshowSeparator, v );
81              }
82      };
83
84      #endif
```

LISTING 11.5. mainwin.h.

Note that we have provided clients with several convenience functions to set and retrieve the widget IDs associated with the various areas managed by a Main Window. From a practical standpoint, we have found this minimal set sufficient for most of our needs. Obviously, you can extend the basic ideas presented in this section to add as many additional functions as you see fit.

11.2.5 MainWindow *Implementation*

The only function contained in the file mainwin.cxx is the constructor. Listing 11.6 contains its definition.

```
1     //
2     //          TITLE:        mainwin.cxx
3     //
4     //          FUNCTION:         Definition of the MainWindow Class
5     //
6
7     #include "mainwin.h"
8
9     //
10    //       Constructor
11    //
12    MainWindow::MainWindow( Widget parent, char* name )
13                : ScreenComponent( name )
```

```
14      {
15                  //
16                  //        Create a MainWindow
17                  //
18                  _main_widget = XtVaCreateWidget(
19                      name,                          // Name
20                      xmMainWindowWidgetClass,       // Widget Class
21                      parent,                        // Parent ID
22
23                      XmNscrollBarDisplayPolicy,  XmAS_NEEDED,
24                      XmNscrollingPolicy,         XmAUTOMATIC,
25
26                      NULL );
27
28                  //
29                  //        Register Destroy Handler
30                  //
31                  registerDestroyCB();
32      }
```

LISTING 11.6. `mainwin.cxx`.

Note that we have set several resources. As we will see in Chapter 12, we can allow clients to modify these values directly.

11.3 MENUS

Very few (if any) Motif programs do not use menus. A simple, intuitive menu structure greatly simplifies program interaction for the user. However, as convenient as menus are for users, they are equally as tedious to implement. Objectifying menu components can greatly simplify development effort.

11.3.1 The MenuBar Class

MWL contains two classes that simplify menu creation and usage: MenuBar and MenuPane. As its name implies, MenuBar creates a Motif menu bar. Its class definition appears in Listing 11.7.

```
 1    //
 2    //             TITLE:        menubar.h
 3    //
 4    //             FUNCTION:      MenuBar Class Definition
 5    //
 6
 7    #ifndef _MENUBAR_H_
 8    #define _MENUBAR_H_
 9
10    #include "scrn_cmp.h"
11
12    #include <Xm/RowColumn.h>
13    #include <Xm/CascadeB.h>
14    #include <Xm/Separator.h>
15
16    class MenuBar : public ScreenComponent {
17
18    private:
19
20    public:
21
22            //
23            // Constructor
24            //
25            MenuBar( Widget parent, char* name )
                    : ScreenComponent(name)
26            {
27                    _main_widget = XmCreateMenuBar( parent,
                                        name, NULL, 0 );
28
29                    //
30                    //        Register Destroy Handler
31                    //
32                    registerDestroyCB();
33            }
34
35            //
```

```
36              //         Redefine Class name
37              //
38              virtual const char* class_name() const
39              {
40                     return("MenuBar");
41              }
42
43              //
44              //         Identify the 'Help' Button
45              //
46              void setHelpButton( Widget w )
47              {
48               XtVaSetValues( _main_widget, XmNmenuHelpWidget, w,
                             NULL );
49              }
50
51              //
52              //         Add a CascadeButton to Menu Bar
53              //
54              Widget addBar( char* label, char mnem, Widget pane );
55      };
56
57      #endif
```

LISTING 11.7. menubar.h.

The class creates a Motif menu bar in the constructor. It also provides a convenience function to identify the Help button. As an extension to this class, you might consider encapsulating a set of buttons (e.g., File, Help, etc.) in the constructor. In this manner, you can enforce organizational standards.

The real work of the class is performed in the function addBar(). Listing 11.8 presents the file menubar.cxx, which contains the function's definition.

```
1 //
2 //            TITLE:       menubar.h
3 //
4 //            FUNCTION:    MenuBar Member Function Definitions
5 //
```

```
 6
 7 #include "cs.h"
 8 #include "mwlr.h"
 9 #include "menubar.h"
10
11 //
12 //         Add option to MenuBar
13 //
14 Widget MenuBar::addBar( char* label, char mnemonic, Widget pane )
15 {
16             Widget cascade;
17             CompoundString cs = label;
18             MWLResourceList rl;
19
20             rl.setArg( XmNsubMenuId, pane );
21             rl.setArg( XmNlabelString, (XmString)cs );
22             if( mnemonic )
23                     rl.setArg( XmNmnemonic, (void*)mnemonic );
24
25             //
26             //         Create the CascadeButton
27             //
28             cascade = XmCreateCascadeButton( _main_widget,
                                                label, rl, rl );
29
30             //
31             //         Manage the Button
32             //
33             XtManageChild( cascade );
34
35             return( cascade );
36 }
```

LISTING 11.8. menubar.cxx.

The function, addBar(), creates and manages a cascade button on the menu bar. It assigns to the button's XmNsubMenuId resource the widget ID of the pane it must manage. The client need only provide the label and pane as arguments to the function.

As you must have already noted, addBar() draws upon the services of two other MWL classes: CompoundString and MWLResourceList. Again, we will discuss these classes in Chapter 12, but their basic functionality and usage should be evident from the listing.

11.3.2 *The* MenuPane *Class*

The second part of the menu puzzle is the creation of menu panes. Each pane is essentially an array of pushbuttons, labels, and separators, that pop up whenever the user presses a menu button. The class, MenuPane, creates a pulldown menu. The complete definition appears in Listing 11.9.

```
1      //
2      //              TITLE:         menupane.h
3      //
4      //              FUNCTION:      Menupane Class Definition
5      //
6
7      #ifndef _MENUPANE_H_
8      #define _MENUPANE_H_
9
10     #include "scrn_cmp.h"
11
12     #include <Xm/RowColumn.h>
13     #include <Xm/CascadeB.h>
14     #include <Xm/Separator.h>
15
16     class MenuPane : public ScreenComponent {
17
18     public:
19
20             //
21             //       Constructor
22             //
23             MenuPane( Widget parent, char* name )
                         : ScreenComponent(name)
24             {
25                 //
```

```
26                   //          Create but do not manage a menu pane
27                   //
28                   _main_widget = XmCreatePulldownMenu( parent,
                                    name, NULL, 0 );
29
30                   //
31                   //          Register Destroy Handler
32                   //
33                   registerDestroyCB();
34           }
35
36           //
37           //        Redefine Class name
38           //
39           virtual const char* class_name() const
40           {
41                   return("MenuPane");
42           }
43   };
44
45   #endif
```

LISTING 11.9. menupane.h.

11.3.3 Menu Creation and Usage

The two menu classes simplify the creation of application menus. Listing 11.10 provides an example. Note how the MWL classes simplify menu creation. The program uses both the MenuBar and MenuPane classes, as well as the Label and PushButton classes from earlier in the chapter. It also makes use of the Separator class to separate menu options (see Appendix A for its definition). Figure 11.1 depicts the output of the program.

```
1    //
2    //      Program to Demonstrate the Use of the Menu Classes
3    //
4    #include <stdlib.h>
```

```
5
6     #include <iostream.h>
7
8     #include "pb.h"
9     #include "sep.h"
10    #include "label.h"
11    #include "menubar.h"
12    #include "menupane.h"
13
14    void genericCB (Widget widget, XtPointer client_data,
                      XtPointer call_data)
15    {
16        int data = (int)client_data;
17        cout << "genericCB(): " << data << "\n";
18        if( data == 1 )
19        {
20            exit( 0 );
21        }
22    }
23
24    int main( int ac, char* av[] )
25    {
26        Widget     top;          // Top Level Shell
27        XtAppContext app;        // Application Context
28
29        //
30        //     Initialize the Xt Toolkit
31        //
32        top = XtAppInitialize( &app, "Menutest", NULL, 0,
33             &ac, av, NULL, NULL, 0 );
34
35        //
36        //     Create a MenuBar
37        //
38        MenuBar* menubar = new MenuBar( top, "menu1" );
39
40        //
```

```
41          //      Create a 'File' MenuPane
42          //
43          MenuPane* filepane = new MenuPane(
                              menubar->main_widget(), "filepane" );
44
45          //
46          //      Add 'File' Option to the Menu Bar
47          //
48          (void)menubar->addBar( "FILE", 'F',
                              filepane->main_widget() );
49
50          //
51          //      Create a 'Help' MenuPane
52          //
53          MenuPane* helppane = new MenuPane(
                              menubar->main_widget(), "helppane" );
54
55          //
56          //      A 'Help' Option to the Menu Bar and ...
57          //
58          Widget wtmp = menubar->addBar( "HELP", 'H',
                                  helppane->main_widget() );
59
60          //
61          //      Inform Menu Bar Which Button is 'Help'
62          //
63          menubar->setHelpButton( wtmp );
64
65          //
66          //      Add a Label & Separator to the File Pane
67          //
68          Label* label1 = new Label(
                          filepane->main_widget(), "label1" );
69          label1->setLabelString( "FILE MENU" );
70          label1->manage();
71
72          Separator* sep1 = new Separator(
                          filepane->main_widget(), "sep1" );
```

```
73          sep1->manage();
74
75          //
76          //      Create an 'Exit' Button for the 'File' Pane
77          //
78          PushButton* pb1 = new PushButton(
                                filepane->main_widget(), "pb1" );
79          pb1->setMnemonic( 'E' );
80          pb1->setLabelString( "EXIT" );
81          pb1->setAccelerator( "<CTRL>x", "Ctrl<Key>x" );
82          pb1->addActivateCallback( genericCB, (XtPointer)1 );
83          pb1->manage();
84
85          //
86          //      Add a Label & Separator to the Help Pane
87          //
88          Label* label2 = new Label( helppane->main_widget(),
                                "label2" );
89          label2->setLabelString( "HELP MENU" );
90          label2->manage();
91
92          Separator* sep2 = new Separator( helppane->main_wid-
                                get(), "sep2" );
93          sep2->setType( XmDOUBLE_DASHED_LINE );
94          sep2->manage();
95
96          //
97          //      Create a 'Help' Button for the 'Help' Pane
98          //
99          PushButton* helppb = new PushButton(
                                helppane->main_widget(), "helppb" );
100         helppb->setMnemonic( 'H' );
101         helppb->setLabelString( "HELP ME" );
102         helppb->setAccelerator( "<CTRL>H", "Ctrl<Key>h" );
103         helppb->addActivateCallback( genericCB, (XtPointer)2 );
104         helppb->manage();
105
```

```
106           //
107           //      Manage  the  Menu
108           //
109           menubar->manage();
110
111           //
112           //      Realize  Widgets
113           //
114           XtRealizeWidget( top );
115
116           //
117           //      Enter  Main  Event  Loop
118           //
119           XtAppMainLoop( app );
120     }
```

LISTING 11.10.   menutest.cxx.

11.4 DIALOG BOXES

Dialog boxes are another common feature of GUI-based programs. Obviously, MWL would not be complete without a set of supporting classes. Listing 11.11 contains an abridged presentation of the file dialog.h, which highlights important aspects of the dialog classes.

11.4.1 *The* dialog.h *Header File*

```
10    #include "scrn_cmp.h"
11
12    #include <Xm/MessageB.h>
13
14    //
15    //      Create  basic  dialog  class
16    //
17    class MessageDialog : public ScreenComponent {
18
```

```
19    private:
20
21            XmString dialogTitle;
22            static XtResource dialogResources[];
23
24            //
25            //        Private Function to Set Dialog Resources
26            //
27            void setDialogXmString( char* resource,
                                       char* string )
28            {
29                    XmString xmstring = XmStringCreateLtoR
                                          ( string,
30                      XmSTRING_DEFAULT_CHARSET );
31                    XtVaSetValues( _main_widget, resource,
                                      xmstring, NULL );
32                    XmStringFree( xmstring );
33            }
34
35            //
36            //        Private Function to Unmanage Buttons
37            //
38            void unmanageButton( unsigned char which_button )
39            {
40                    Widget button;
41                    button = XmMessageBoxGetChild(
42                            _main_widget,
43                            which_button
44                    );
45                    XtUnmanageChild( button );
46            }
47
48
49    public:
50
51            MessageDialog( Widget w, char* name,
52                           unsigned char type =
                            XmDIALOG_MESSAGE );
```

```
53
54              ~MessageDialog()
                // Destructor
55              {
56                      XmStringFree( dialogTitle );
57              }
67              //
68              //      Dialog Post Function
69              //
70              void post()
71              {
72                      manage();
73              }
74
75              //
76              //      Convenience Functions to Set Resources
77              //
78              void setOKLabel( char* label )     // OK Label
79              {
80                      setDialogXmString( XmNokLabelString, label );
81              }
82
103             //
104             //      Routines to Register Callbacks
105             //
106             void addOKCallback( XtCallbackProc okFunc,
                                XtPointer client_data )
107             {
108                     XtAddCallback(
109                             _main_widget,    // Widget
110                             XmNokCallback,   // Callback Type
111                             okFunc,          // Callback Func
112                             client_data      // Client Data
113                     );
114             }
136             //
```

```
137                    //          Routines to Unmanage Buttons
138                    //
139                    void unmanageOKButton()   // Unmanage OK Button
140                    {
141                            unmanageButton( XmDIALOG_OK_BUTTON );
142                    }
143
144                    void unmanageHelpButton()   // Unmanage Help Button
145                    {
146                            unmanageButton( XmDIALOG_HELP_BUTTON );
147                    }
148
149                    void unmanageCancelButton()
150                    {
151                            unmanageButton( XmDIALOG_CANCEL_BUTTON );
152                    }
153    };
154
155    //
156    //          Derive Motif-Specific Dialogs
157    //
158
159    class QuestionDialog : public MessageDialog {
160
161    public:
162
163            //
164            //          Redefine Class name
165            //
166            virtual const char* class_name() const
167            {
168                    return("QuestionDialog");
169            }
170
171            //
172            //          Constructor
173            //
```

```
174              QuestionDialog( Widget parent, char* name )
175                 : MessageDialog( parent, name,
                                       XmDIALOG_QUESTION ) {}
176    };
177
```

LISTING 11.11. `dialog.h`

The listing begins by including the now-standard set of header files. Line 17 begins the definition of our basic dialog class called `MassageDialog`. In the `private` section, we declare an `XmString` (for the dialog title) and a resource array (to declare class resources). We use an `XmString` (as opposed to a `CompoundString`) to simplify resource initialization. We also declare two `private` member functions to minimize code duplication in our public signature. The function `setDialogXmString()` sets a resource (passed as its first argument) to the string value contained in its second argument. The `unmanageButton()` routine unmanages one of the dialog's buttons (as specified by its sole argument).

The `public` section begins with line 49. We declare a constructor and define a simple destructor. Following that, we define several convenience routines that address common features of dialog boxes. Beginning with line 155, we redeploy a technique we discussed previously. All dialog boxes based on the `MessageDialog` widget share the same behavior. Thus, we can create new dialog classes by deriving from `MessageDialog`, and passing the appropriate widget class as an argument to the base class constructor. Line 175 highlights the technique with the implementation of `QuestionDialog`. In a similar manner, we can create all of the other basic dialog classes including `WarningDialog`, `ErrorDialog`, `WorkingDialog`, `InformationDialog`, and `Xdialog`.

11.4.2 *The* `dialog.cxx` *Header File*

Listing 11.12 contains the implementation file `dialog.cxx`. It presents definitions for the resource array and the constructor of the MessageDialog class.

```
1    //
2    //         TITLE:      dialog.cxx
3    //
4    //         FUNCTION:   Implementation of dialog classes.
```

```
 5    //
 6
 7    #include "dialog.h"
 8
 9    //
10    //        Class/Component Resources Array Definition
11    //
12    XtResource MessageDialog::dialogResources[] = {
13            {
14                "title",                            // Name
15                "DialogTitle",                      // Class
16                XmRXmString,                        // Type
17                sizeof(XmString),                   // Size
18                XtOffset(MessageDialog*, dialogTitle), // Offset
19                XmRString,                          // Type
20                XtPointer)"MESSAGE DIALOG"          // Value
21            }
22    };
23
24
25    //
26    //        Constructor
27    //
28    MessageDialog::MessageDialog( Widget parent, char* name,
                                  unsigned char type )
29            : ScreenComponent(name)
30    {
31            _main_widget = XmCreateMessageDialog(
32                    parent,                 // Parent
33                    _widget_name,           // Name
34                    NULL,                   // Arg List
35                    0                       // No. of Args
36            );
37
38            //
39            //        Set Master Resources
40            //
```

```
41              XtVaSetValues(
42                  _main_widget,
43                  XmNdialogType, type,
44                  XmNdialogStyle, XmDIALOG_FULL_APPLICATION_MODAL,
45                  NULL
46              );
47
48              //
49              //      Add Destroy CB
50              //
51              registerDestroyCB();
52
53              //
54              //      Query Resource DB
55              //
56              getComponentResources( dialogResources,
57                  XtNumber(dialogResources) );
58      };
```

LISTING 11.12. dialog.cxx

11.4.3 Custom Dialogs

We can take advantage of the class structure presented in Listing 11.12 to create custom dialog boxes. We have several options:

- We can create a new dialog box derived from one of the MWL classes that simply sets resources to appropriate values. For example, we could create a custom version of an InformationDialog that uses a different icon.

- We could derive a new MWL class that adds or subtracts elements such as buttons or labels. Listing 11.13 presents a simple example of a custom dialog box that contains one additional button. Figure 11.2 depicts the program's output. Note that the program contains references to the ApplicationShell class, which we will not discuss until Chapter 12.

- Motif 1.2 contains a Template dialog widget. Its purpose is to support the creation of custom dialog boxes. Obviously, an encapsulation of that widget could serve as a base class for all custom dialog boxes.

```
1      #include <iostream.h>
2
3      #include "pb.h"
4      #include "dialog.h"
5      #include "app_shell.h"
6
7      void externalCB( Widget w, XtPointer c, XtPointer x )
8      {
9              cout << "Button Pressed: " << (int)c << endl;
10     }
11
12     class CustomDialog : public QuestionDialog
13
14     private:
15             PushButton* pb;
16
17     public:
18             CustomDialog( Widget w, String n )
19                     : QuestionDialog(w, n)
20             {
21                     pb = new PushButton( main_widget(), "pb" );
22                     pb->registerCB( XmNactivateCallback, externalCB,
                                        (XtPointer)2 );
23                     pb->setLabelString( "NEW BUTTON" );
24                     pb->manage();
25             }
26
27             ~CustomDialog()
28             {
29                     delete pb;
30             }
31     };
32
33     int main( int ac, char *av[] )
34     {
35             ApplicationShell appShell( &ac, av, "pb" );
36
```

```
37          CustomDialog dialog( appShell.main_widget(),
                                   "CustomDialog" );
38          dialog.manage();
39          dialog.setDialogTitle( "CUSTOM DIALOG EXAMPLE" );
40          dialog.setDialogMessage( "ALL GOOD THINGS COME TO MWL
                                       PROGRAMMERS" );
41
42
43          //
44          // Realize Widgets
45          //
46          appShell.realizeWidget();
47
48          //
49          // Enter Main Event Loop
50          //
51          appShell.appMainLoop();
52      }
```

LISTING 11.13. custom.cxx

11.5 SUMMARY

This chapter has demonstrated the methods and benefits of objectifying Motif widgets. We have presented several examples ranging from labels to dialog boxes. Please note that we could continue our efforts and encapsulate the entire Motif widget set in this manner. Indeed, we could create a library containing one-to-one mapping between C++ classes and Motif widgets. From a pedagogical standpoint, however, we would run the risk of boring you to the point of tears if we were to discuss such an implementation in its entirety.

Nonetheless, there are several important points that we should highlight:

- Consider how much code we have reused: we created PushButton from Label; QuestionDialog from MessageDialog. Moreover, all of the classes inherit basic behavior from ScreenComponent.

- The classes create a higher level of abstraction than Motif widgets in that they truly become screen components. Indeed, theoretically, we could port the classes to another environment (e.g., MS Windows) without modifying application-level code.

- Consider Listing 11.13. How much non-MWL (read that Motif-specific) constructs would you have to know to be able to write that program?

- Motif is a powerful tool. However, it is not unfair to say that programmers can find it tedious to use. As a result, convenience functions, such as `setLabelString()` are really convenient. They minimize and hide implementation details (e.g., what is the name of the resource for the OK label in a dialog boxes?) and perform appropriate data validation and conversion (e.g., what is the data type of the resource for the OK label?) Thus, we as application developers can concentrate more on the application and less on Motif.

- MWL classes shelter programs (and programmers) from changes in Motif. Thus, you can extend the public signature of MWL classes to incorporate Motif extensions, while maintaining backwards compatibility with existing interfaces.

12

THE ANCILLARY CLASSES

Motif provides several ancillary services that support the creation and maintenance of GUIs. These include compound strings, fonts, resources, etc. In this chapter, we will discuss how to create seamless abstractions for these constructs. Our purpose is two-fold. First, we can simplify the lives of application programmers, and second, we can foster code reuse. By objectifying the code, we minimize the tedium and allow programmers to get on with the business of writing applications.

The classes we will create include:

CompoundString   This class encapsulates Motif compound strings. It creates a "string" abstraction that simplifies use.

MWLFont   The MWLFont class simplifies the querying and loading of X fonts.

MWLFontList   A FontList is a widget resource that determines the set of fonts a widget has available to render strings.

`MWLResourceList`   This class simplifies the management of <$iwidget resources.

We will close the chapter by presenting some additional features of the `ScreenComponent` class. So without further ado, let's get on with the discussions.

12.1 THE `CompoundString` CLASS

12.1.1 Introduction

Compound strings allow programmers to render strings (or parts of them) using multiple fonts and multiple character sets. The latter has become increasingly important as more and more applications become multinational.* (Studies have shown that users find programs easier to use when they can read screen prompts in their native tongue—go figure!)

12.1.2 Class Definition

To simplify use, MWL contains a typical string abstraction for the `Compound-String` class. Its definition appears in Listing 12.1.

```
 1    //
 2    //           TITLE:        cs.h
 3    //
 4    //           FUNCTION:     Define CompoundString Class
 5    //
 6
 7    #ifndef _CS_H_
 8    #define _CS_H_
 9
10    #include <string.h>
11
12    #include <Xm/Xm.h>
```

---

* We should point out that release X11R5 contains internationalization features that should minimize some of the burden borne by compound strings to support multinational applications.

```
13
14    class CompoundString {
15
16    private:
17
18            char*            font;              // Font Name
19            XmString         xmstring;          // The XmString
20
21    public:
22
23            //
24            //        Default/String Constructor
25            //
26            CompoundString( char* string = "",
27                    char* f = XmFONTLIST_DEFAULT_TAG )
28            {
29                    font = f;
30                    xmstring = XmStringCreateLtoR( string, f );
31            }
32
33            //
34            //        Copy Constructor
35            //
36            CompoundString( const CompoundString& cs )
37            {
38                    font = cs.font;
39                    xmstring = XmStringCopy( cs.xmstring );
40            }
41
42            //
43            //        Assignment Operator
44            //
45            CompoundString& operator=( const CompoundString& cs )
46            {
47                    if( this != &cs )
48                    {
49                        font = cs.font;
```

```
50                              XmStringFree( xmstring );
51                              xmstring = XmStringCopy( cs.xmstring );
52                      }
53                      return( *this );
54              }
55
56              //
57              //      XmString Constructor
58              //
59              CompoundString( const XmString& xms )
60              {
61                      xmstring = XmStringCopy( xms );
62                      font = XmFONTLIST_DEFAULT_TAG;
63              }
64
65              //
66              //      Destructor
67              //
68              ~CompoundString()
69              {
70                      XmStringFree( xmstring );
71              }
72
73              //
74              //      Cast Operators
75              //
76              operator char*()
77              {
78                      char* cstring;
79
80                      XmStringGetLtoR( xmstring, font, &cstring );
81                      return( cstring );
82              }
83
84              operator XmString()
85              {
86                      return( xmstring );
87              }
```

```
88
89              //
90              //          Concatenation Operator
91              //
92              friend CompoundString operator+( const Compound-
                                                        String&,
93                      const CompoundString& );
94      };
95
96      #endif
```

LISTING 12.1. cs.h

Lines 18–19 contain the declaration of two `private` data members: `xmstring` contains the actual `XmString`, and `font` references the associated font. The class contains three constructors. The first two (lines 26–40), serve as the default constructor and the copy constructor, respectively. For convenience, beginning with line 55, we provide a third constructor, which creates a `CompoundString` from an `XmString`. Line 45 begins the definition of an overloaded assignment operator. (As a rule, whenever a class provides a copy constructor, it should also contain an overloaded assignment operator.) The destructor, line 68, is trivial; it simply frees the object's compound string.

The class provides several cast operators for programming convenience. Line 76 begins the definition of a cast operator that converts the internal `XmString` into a `char*`. Line 84 contains a cast to a `XmString`. The last function is an overloaded version of the addition operator. In this case, it serves as a concatenation operator. Its definition resides in the file `cs.cxx`, which is listed in Appendix A.

Note that, as presented, `CompoundString` does not embody a complete implementation of compound strings. However, we have found that it provides all of the services commonly needed in most business applications. Obviously, the class is extensible and you can add additional features as required.

One other note: there are two implementation problems with our cast operators. These concerns are not all that uncommon. First, for `operator char*()`, we should make it abundantly clear to clients that they are responsible for deleting the storage returned by the function. Second, our implementation of the `operator XmString*()` circumvents encapsulation by returning a pointer to xmstring. We should return a copy of the value, but then we repeat the first problem. There is a third solution wherein we require clients to provide storage (via function arguments) into which we copy internal values. A full discussion of this topic is beyond the scope of this text; please refer to the bibliography for additional references.

12.2 THE MWL FONT CLASSES

12.2.1 *The* MWLFont *Class*

The MWL package provides two classes to simplify font usage. The first, MWL-Font, appears in listing 12.2.

```
 1     //
 2     //              TITLE:   font.h
 3     //
 4     //              FUNCTION:   Definition of MWLFont & MWLFontList
 5     //
 6
 7     #ifndef _FONT_H_
 8     #define _FONT_H_
 9
10     #include <Xm/Xm.h>
11     #include <string.h>
12
13     //
14     //        =======================================================
15     //                           MWLFont
16     //        =======================================================
17     //
18     class MWLFont    {
19
20     private:
21
22             char*          charSet;        // Character Set
23             char*          fontName;       // Font Name
```

```
24
25              Display*       display;              // Display Ptr
26              XFontStruct*   fontStruct;           // X Font Structure
27
28              //
29              //         Private Utility Function
30              //
31              void fontSetup( Display* d, char* fn, char* cs )
32              {
33                      //
34                      //         Save Font Name
35                      //
36                      fontName = new char[ strlen(fn)+1 ];
37                      strcpy( fontName, fn );
38
39                      //
40                      //         Save Character Set Name
41                      //
42                      charSet = new char[ strlen(cs)+1 ];
43                      strcpy( charSet, cs );
44
45                      //
46                      //         Save Display
47                      //
48                      display = d;
49
50                      //
51                      //         Load X Font Structure
52                      //
53                      fontStruct = XLoadQueryFont( d, fontName );
54              }
55
56      public:
57
58              //
59              //         Constructors
60              //
```

```
61              MWLFont( Widget w, char* fontname, char* charset )
62              {
63                      fontSetup( XtDisplay(w), fontname, charset );
64              }
65
66              MWLFont( Display* d, char* fontname, char* charset )
67              {
68                      fontSetup( d, fontname, charset );
69              }
70
71              //
72              //      Destructor
73              //
74              virtual ~MWLFont()
75              {
76                      delete [] charSet;
77                      delete [] fontName;
78                      XFreeFont( display, fontStruct );
79              }
80
81              //
82              //      Cast Operators
83              //
84              operator XFontStruct*() const
85              {
86                      return( fontStruct );
87              }
88
89              operator XmStringCharSet() const
90              {
91                      return( charSet );
92              }
93
94    };
```

LISTING 12.2. font.h (Part 1).

In the `private` section, we define several data elements and one function. The data members include:

fontName A pointer to the name of the font.

charSet This member points to a programmer-defined name or tag used to reference the font.

display The X display on which the font will be used.

fontStruct A pointer to an `XFontStruct` that contains font-specific data.

The `private` function, `fontSetup()`, eliminates redundant code that would otherwise appear in multiple `public` members (see below). The function requires three arguments: a display, a font name, and a tag. After storing all three values, it calls the Xlib function `XLoadQueryFont()` to load the font structure.

The `public` section contains two constructors. Both call `fontSetup()` to actually load the font. The destructor (line 74) relinquishes all resources claimed by the object—including the X font structure. Also, as with the `CompoundString` class, we have included several cast operators.

The following is as an example of `MWLFont` class instantiation.

```
MWLFont font1( obj.main_widget(), "variable", "myfont1" );
```

12.2.2 The `MWLFontList` Class

Every Motif widget that displays text contains a resource called `fontList`. This resource defines the list of fonts available to the widget when rendering strings. The MWL library includes a class called `MWLFontList` that simplifies the creation and manipulation of font lists. The code appears in Listing 12.3.

```
 96    //
 97    //      =================================================
 98    //                      MWLFontList
 99    //      =================================================
100    //
101
```

```
102    class MWLFontList {
103
104    private:
105
106            XmFontList        fontList;
107
108            //
109            //        Declare as Private
110            //
111            MWLFontList( const MWLFontList& );
112            MWLFontList& operator=( const MWLFontList& );
113
114    public:
115
116            //
117            //        Constructors
118            //
119            MWLFontList( const MWLFont& f, char* cs )
120            {
121                    fontList = XmFontListCreate( f, cs );
122            }
123
124            MWLFontList( const MWLFont& f )
125            {
126                    fontList = XmFontListCreate( f, f );
127            }
128
129            //
130            //        Destructor
131            //
132            virtual ~MWLFontList()
133            {
134                    XmFontListFree( fontList );
135            }
136
137            //
138            //        Add Additional Fonts to List
```

```
139                 //
140                 void addFont( const MWLFont& f, char* cs )
141                 {
142                         fontList = XmFontListAdd( fontList, f, cs );
143                 }
144
145                 void addFont( const MWLFont& f )
146                 {
147                         fontList = XmFontListAdd( fontList, f, f );
148                 }
149
150                 //
151                 //        Cast Operators
152                 //
153                 operator long()
154                 {
155                         return( (long)fontList );
156                 }
157
158                 operator XmFontList()
159                 {
160                         return( fontList );
161                 }
162
163         };
164
165     #endif
```

LISTING 12.3. font.h (Part 2)

As you can see, the code is a simple wrapper for several Motif routines, but its simplicity should not belie its power. By creating this class, we allow clients to think in terms of the abstraction, rather than its implementation. Note that the declarations appearing on lines 111 and 112 effectively prevent assignment and initialization among MWLFontList objects. That is, because they are declared private, they are inaccessible to clients. Thus, statements of the form

```
MWLFontList a;

MWLFontList b = a;  // Initialization - Illegal

b = a;              // Assignment - Illegal
```

generate compiler error messages.

12.3 THE MWLResourceList CLASS

Widget resources are another example of a powerful Motif programming construct that can be tedious to use. As should be obvious by now, this is another situation where programmers can benefit from an abstraction. Resources are name/value pairs. As a result, we can use a "map" as the underlying abstraction for the MWLResourceList class. The class will also contain cast operators that provide access to embedded data. The definition appears in Listing 12.4.

```
 1   //
 2   //              FILE:        mwlr.h
 3   //
 4   //              FUNCTION:    MWLResourceList Class Definition
 5   //
 6
 7   #ifndef _MWLR_H_
 8   #define _MWLR_H_
 9
10   #include <Xm/Xm.h>
11
12   class MWLResourceList {
13
14   protected:
15
16           ArgList      argList;   // Pointer to Arg List
17           Cardinal     argCount;  // No. or Args
18
19   public:
20
```

```
21              //
22              //       Default Constructor
23              //
24              MWLResourceList() : argList(NULL), argCount(0) {}
25
26              //
27              //       Copy Constructor
28              //
29              MWLResourceList( const MWLResourceList& );
30
31              //
32              //       Name/Value Pair Constructor
33              //
34              MWLResourceList( String, void* );
35
36              //
37              //       Assignment Operator
38              //
39              MWLResourceList& operator=( const MWLResourceList& r );
40
41              //
42              //       Destructor
43              //
44              ~MWLResourceList();
45
46              //
47              //       Set a Resource Name/Value Pair
48              //
49              void setArg( String resource, void* value );
50              void setArg( String resource, XmString value )
51              {
52                      setArg( resource, (void*)value );
53              }
54
55              //
56              //       Reset to NULL
57              //
58              void zapArgs();
```

```
59
60              //
61              //        Cast Functions
62              //
63              operator ArgList() { return(argList); }
64              operator Cardinal() { return(argCount); }
65      };
66
67      extern const MWLResourceList MWLNoResources;            // NULL
68
69      #endif
```

LISTING 12.4. mwlr.h

The class contains two `protected` data members: `arglist` is an array of Motif resource name/value pairs; `argCount` tracks the number of elements in the array. The public signature begins with the declaration of several constructors and an overloaded assignment operator.

`MWLResourceList` provides several other public members including two overloaded versions of the member `setArg()`. The one that takes a second argument of type `XmString` merely invokes the other using an explicit cast operation. The additional signature eliminates a compiler warning. The function `zapArgs()` deletes all existing resources.

Most Motif functions that use resources (i.e., not the "Va" varieties) require two arguments: a pointer to the argument array and a count of the number of elements. For this reason, the class comes with two cast operators that provide convenient access to those values.

Line 67 contains an `extern` declaration for an "empty" resource object (the definition appears in the class implementation file `mwlr.cxx`.) We can use this declaration whenever we need to refer to a NULL `MWLResourceList` object. For example, you can use it as a default argument value in a member function.

12.4 ScreenComponent EXTENSIONS

In this section, we will discuss some extensions to the basic `ScreenComponent` class that we have found useful in business applications. They include several convenience functions that set and return resources; yet another way

to register callback functions; and additional members functions that support
the ancillary classes.

12.4.1 *Convenience Routines*

Listing 12.5 contains excerpts of the code contained in the extended version of
the ScreenComponent class. Please refer to Appendix A for the complete listing.

```
94              //
95              //          Resource Management Functions
96              //
97              Widget parent_widget()
98              {
99                      return( XtParent(_main_widget) );
100             }
  .
  .
  .
109             //
110             //          Set & Unset Sensitivity
111             //
112             void setSensitive()
113             {
114                     XtSetSensitive( _main_widget, True );
115             }
116             void setInsensitive()
117             {
118                     XtSetSensitive( _main_widget, False );
119             }
120
121             //
122             //          Cast Operator(s)
123             //
124             operator Widget()
125             {
126                     return( _main_widget );
127             }
```

LISTING 12.5. scrn_cmp. h: Selected Sections

These functions provide convenient access to common features of MWL widgets and classes. Despite their simplicity, their inclusion is nonetheless worthwhile for two important reasons: they preserve the abstractions and minimize the amount of Motif-specific code clients must write. Cast operators are particularly useful because clients can use objects in ways that "feel" natural. (However, as with any tool, these cast operators can be abused.)

12.4.2 Resource Management Functions

Listing 12.6 contains examples of some resource manipulation routines. There are two major varieties:

- Conveniences functions that set/get the value of a particular resources

- General-purpose routines that allow clients to set/get the value of any resource

```
141             //
142             //        Generalized Resource Set/Get Functions
143             //
144             void setResource( String name, XtArgVal value )
145             {
146                     XtVaSetValues( _main_widget, name, value,
                                NULL );
147             }
148             void setResource( MWLResourceList res )
149             {
150                     XtSetValues( _main_widget, res, res );
151             }
152             void getResource( String name, void* value )
153             {
154                     XtVaGetValues( _main_widget, name,
                                XtArgVal(value), NULL );
155             }
156
157             //
```

```
158              //         Set & Get User Data Resource
159              //
160              void setUserData( XtPointer val )
161              {
162                      XtVaSetValues( _main_widget, XmNuserData,
                                        val, NULL );
163              }
164              XtPointer getUserData()
165              {
166                  XtPointer       val;
167                  XtVaGetValues( _main_widget, XmNuserData,
                                    &val, NULL );
168                  return( val );
169              }
170
171              void setX( Position x )
172              {
173                      XtVaSetValues( _main_widget, XmNx, x, NULL );
174              }
175              Position getX()
176              {
177                  Position x;
178                  XtVaGetValues( _main_widget, XmNx, &x, NULL );
179                  return( x );
180              }
181                void getX( Position& x )
182              {
183                      XtVaGetValues( _main_widget, XmNx, &x, NULL );
184              }
185
186
187              void setY( Position y )
188              {
189                      XtVaSetValues( _main_widget, XmNy, y, NULL );
190              }
191              Position getY()
192              {
```

```
193                    Position y;
194                    XtVaGetValues( _main_widget, XmNy, &y, NULL );
195                    return( y );
196              }
197         void getY( Position& y )
198         {
199                    XtVaGetValues( _main_widget, XmNy, &y, NULL );
200         }
201
202         void setWidth( Dimension width )
203         {
204                    XtVaSetValues( _main_widget, XmNwidth, width,
                                      NULL );
205         }
206         Dimension getWidth()
207         {
208                    Position width;
209                    XtVaGetValues( _main_widget, XmNwidth,
                       &width, NULL );
210                    return( width );
211         }
212
213         void setHeight( Dimension height )
214         {
215                    XtVaSetValues( _main_widget, XmNheight,
                       height, NULL );
216         }
217         Dimension getHeight()
218         {
219                    Position height;
220                    XtVaGetValues( _main_widget, XmNheight,
                       &height, NULL );
221                    return( height );
222         }
223
224         //
225         //          Set Resource Using MWLResourceLists
```

```
226              //
227              setValues( MWLResourceList rl )
228              {
229                      XtSetValues( _main_widget, rl, rl );
230              }
```

LISTING 12.6. scrn_cmp.h: selected sections

The function setResources() maintains two overloaded signatures. Both allow clients to set the value of any widget resource. The first accepts a name/value pair and invokes its Motif counterpart XtVaSetValues(). Its companion requires a single argument of type MWLResourceList. Their compliment, getResources(), returns the value of a single resource (as indicated by its first argument) and stores it at the location indicated by its second argument.

All Motif widgets support a general resource called XmNuserData. Clients are free to use this resource to store application data. Lines 160 and 164 contain definitions for two convenience functions that get and set the values of the userData resource.

The listing also contains several examples of convenience functions that manipulate a single resource. We would like to call your attention to the two versions of gety(). Both access the value of the widget's *y* coordinates, but one returns it as a value, and the other stores it in a reference argument. This is an example of that old programming adage: when is doubt, add it. Remember, our job as class designers is to make our *client*'s life easier.

12.4.3 *Setting Colors*

Often, we need to alter screen colors to reflect changes in processing state. We have provided two convenience functions that encapsulate all required processing: setForegroundColor() and setBackgroundColor(). Listing 12.7 contains their definitions.

```
139    //
140    //       Routines to Set Foreground & Background Colors
141    //
142    void ScreenComponent::setForegroundColor( char* color )
143    {
```

```
144                 XColor              xcolor[2];
145                 Colormap            colormap;
146
147                 XtVaGetValues( _main_widget, XmNcolormap, |
                                        &colormap, NULL );
148
149                 XAllocNamedColor( XtDisplay(_main_widget),
                                        colormap,
150                         color, &xcolor[0], &xcolor[1] );
151
152                 XtVaSetValues( _main_widget, XmNforeground,
                                        xcolor[0].pixel, NULL );
153     }
154
155     void ScreenComponent::setBackgroundColor( char* color )
156     {
157                 Colormap            colormap;
158                 XColor              xcolor[2];
159                 Pixel               bgColor, topShadow,
160                                     bottomShadow, fgRet, selectColor;
161
162                 XtVaGetValues( _main_widget, XmNcolormap,
                                        &colormap, NULL );
163
164                 XAllocNamedColor( XtDisplay(_main_widget), colormap,
165                         color, &xcolor[0], &xcolor[1] );
166                 bgColor = xcolor[0].pixel;
167
168                 XmGetColors( XtScreen(_main_widget), colormap, bgColor,
169                 &fgRet, &topShadow, &bottomShadow, &selectColor );
170
171                 XtVaSetValues( _main_widget,
172
173                         XmNbackground,              bgColor,
174                         XmNtopShadowColor,          topShadow,
175                         XmNbottomShadowColor,       bottomShadow,
```

```
176                    XmNselectColor,          selectColor,
177                    XmNarmColor,             selectColor,
178                    XmNborderColor,          fgRet,
179
180              NULL  );
181    }
```

LISTING 12.7. scrn_cmp.cxx: selected sections

Both functions call XAllocNamedColor() to convert a color expressed as a string into a pixel value. In setForeground(), we can simply use this pixel value to set the XmNforeground resource. However, setting the background color is somewhat more problematic. Many hues of the background color are used for other color-based resources, such as XmNtopShadowColor and XmN-bottomShadowColor. To simplify our efforts, Motif provides a routine called XmGetColors() that algorithmically calculates these shading differences. We simply provide the appropriate arguments and use the returned values to set the associated resources.

12.5 EXAMPLE PROGRAM

Listing 12.8 contains the code for a simple program called mwltest, which exercises many of the features discussed in this chapter. The program creates and sets resources for a PushButton object. Its output appears in Figure 12.1.

```
1     //
2     //              FILE:        mwltest.cxx
3     //
4     //       FUNCTION:     A Simple Program to Exercise
5     //                     Some of the MWL Utility Classes.
6     //
7
8     #include "mwl.h"          // Includes all MWL Header Files
9
10    int main( int ac, char *av[] )
11    {
12    Widget       top;          // Top Level Shell
```

```
13    XtAppContext app;              // Application Context
14
15    //
16    //      Initialize Xt Toolkit
17    //
18    top = XtAppInitialize( &app, "MWLtest", NULL, 0,
19          &ac, av, NULL, NULL, 0
20    );
21
22    //
23    //      Create the GUI - In this Case a Simple Pushbutton
24    //
25    PushButton *pb = new PushButton( top, "pb" );
26
27    //
28    //      Test Font Classes
29    //
30    MWLFont font( top, "variable", "charset1" );
31    MWLFont font2( top, "cfb-24", "charset2" );
32    MWLFontList fontlist( font );
33    fontlist.addFont( font2 );
34
35    //
36    //      Instantiate a CompoundString
37    //
38    CompoundString cs( "Code Reuse is My Life!", font2 );
39
40    //
41    //      Exercise MWLResourceList Class
42    //
43    MWLResourceList r1( XmNfontList, fontlist );
44    MWLResourceList r2 = r1;
45    MWLResourceList r3;
46    r3 = r1;
47
48    //
49    //      Load Resources into the PushButton Object
```

```
50      //
51      pb->setResource( r3 );
52
53      //
54      //      Set the LabelString Resource
55      //
56      pb->setLabelString( cs );
57
58      //
59      //      Set Colors
60      //
61      pb->setForegroundColor( "magenta" );
62      pb->setBackgroundColor( "yellow" );
63
64      //
65      //      Manage the PushButton
66      //
67      pb->manage();
68
69      //
70      //      Realize Widgets
71      //
72      XtRealizeWidget( top );
73
74      //
75      //      Enter Main Event Loop
76      //
77      XtAppMainLoop( app );
78      }
```

LISTING 12.8. mwltest.cxx

12.6 SUMMARY

In this chapter, we have extended the abstractions we began in Chapters 10 and 11. We created classes for several common Motif features, including compound strings, fonts, font lists, and resources. In addition, we extended the services provided by the ScreenComponent class. Please keep in mind that

`ScreenComponent` serves as the base class for all MWL component classes. As a result, all of the additional features are available in all of the MWL GUI classes. In Chapter 13, we will present additional classes that extend the GUI abstraction even further and complete the application framework.

13

THE APPLICATION FRAMEWORK

Throughout Part 3, we have demonstrated the power of objectifying Motif components. We have created classes for some of the basic GUI components (such as pushbuttons and labels), and some of the ancillary features (such as fonts and compound strings). We have not, however, encapsulated Motif's main application interface. Thus far, the `main()` functions of all the programs we have presented still directly invoke toolkit and Motif routines. We are about to rectify that oversight. In this chapter, we will discuss completing the application framework that we set as our goal earlier in the text.

The goals of this chapter are:

- Most GUI applications share many common coding constructs. We will encapsulate those features in classes.

- We will show how an application framework can enforce a consistent look and feel across applications.

- We can reduce programming effort by encapsulating common, redundant code in framework classes.

- We will take full advantage of the object-oriented paradigm. For example, we can use inheritance to extend or customize the framework classes we will discuss in this chapter.

We will present two versions of framework classes. The first, contained in the ApplicationShell class, takes a direct approach. That is, it creates a model that is essentially a one-to-one correspondence with the Xt/Motif architecture. The second approach takes a different tack. It creates a framework based on the Model-View-Controller (MVC) architecture.

13.1 THE ApplicationShell CLASS

13.1.1 Class Definition

The most direct approach we can take to objectifying the remaining portion of the toolkit is to encapsulate the remainder of the Xt/Motif architecture. This class, which we call ApplicationShell, will perform all required toolkit processing. Listing 13.1 contains its definition.

```
1    //
2    //          TITLE:   app_shell.h
3    //
4    //          FUNCTION:   Definition of the ApplicationShell Class
5    //
6
7    #ifndef _APP_SHELL_H_
8    #define _APP_SHELL_H_
9
10   #include <stdlib.h>                          // exit()
11
12   #include <Xm/AtomMgr.h>
13   #include <Xm/Protocols.h>
14
15   #include "scrn_cmp.h"
16
17   class ApplicationShell : public ScreenComponent {
18
```

```
19    protected:
20
21            XtAppContext       appContext;      // Pgm's AppContext
22
23    public:
24
25          //
26          //        Constructor
27          //
28          ApplicationShell( int* ac, char* av[],
                              char* appName )
29                    : ScreenComponent(appName)
30            {
31                  //
32                  //                 Initialize Xt Toolkit
33                  //
34                  _main_widget = XtAppInitialize(
                              &appContext, appName,
35                      NULL, 0, ac, av, NULL, NULL, 0 );
36
37                  //
38                  //     ==================================
39                  //          Register WM Delete Callback
40                  //     ==================================
41                  //
42                  Atom    deleteWindow;
43
44                  deleteWindow = XmInternAtom(
45                          XtDisplay(_main_widget),
46                          "WM_DELETE_WINDOW",
47                          False
48                  );
49
50                  //
51                  //        Set the Callback Data Structure
52                  //
```

```
53              MemberFunctionCBData* cbd
                        = new MemberFunctionCBData;
54              cbd->theData = NULL;
55              cbd->theFunc = &ScreenComponent::winCloseCB;
56              cbd->theObject = this;
57
58              //
59              //      Register the Callback
60              //
61              XmAddWMProtocolCallback(
62                      _main_widget,      // The Widget
63                      deleteWindow,      // The Atom
64                      activateMemberCB,  // The Function
65                      (XtPointer)cbd     // Client Data
66                  );
67          }
68
69          //
70          //      Redefine Classname
71          //
72          virtual const char* class_name() const
73          {
74                  return("ApplicationShell");
75          }
76
77          //
78          //      Realize Widgets
79          //
80          void realizeWidget()
81          {
82                  XtRealizeWidget( _main_widget );
83          }
84
85          //
86          //      Enter Main Loop
87          //
88          void appMainLoop()
```

```
89                 {
90                         XtAppMainLoop( appContext );
91                 }
92
93                 //
94                 //      Destructor
95                 //
96                 virtual ~ApplicationShell() {}
97      };
98
99      #endif
```

LISTING 13.1. app_shell.h

The definition begins on line 17 where ApplicationShell() inherits behavior from ScreenComponent. On line 21, the class defines one additional protected member: appContext. As its name implies, this variable stores the program's application context. The constructor, beginning with line 28, initializes the toolkit. It requires three arguments: the standard command line parameters (i.e., argc and argv) and an application name. Clients can easily extend the signature so that the function accepts additional arguments that it can pass on to XtAppInitialize().

After the call to XtAppInitialize(), the constructor registers a callback for the MW_DELETE_WINDOW protocol. This callback is sent by the window manager when the client selects the window's Close option. Note that, by default, the clean-up procedure is a member of ScreenComponent. However, this can also be an option or even a separate signature. In any event, all client programs that must relinquish resources should register a function with this callback.

The functions, realizeWidgets() and appMainLoop(), are simply front-end calls for their toolkit counterparts. The class also includes a virtual destructor. We do this because clients are free to instantiate Application-Shell objects as static or external class storage. In such cases— should the program perform a normal exit—the compiler will schedule execution of the destructors. This provides clients another opportunity to clean up after themselves.

13.1.2 ApplicationShell *Class Example*

Listing 13.2 contains a revised version of Listing 12.8. It uses the ApplicationShell class to create a custom, albeit simple, application class. Note the function winCloseCB() (line 24). It provides a custom hook for the window manager callback. To verify that it does get called, execute the program and select the window manager Close option.

```
1    //
2    //               FILE:        mwltest2.cxx
3    //
4    //               FUNCTION:    A Simple Program to Exercise
5    //                            Some of the MWL Utility Classes.
6    //
7
8    #include <iostream.h>
9
10   #include "mwl.h"          // Includes all MWL Header Files
11
12   //
13   //     Derive a Custom Version of ApplicationShell
14   //
15   class MyApplicationShell : public ApplicationShell {
16
17   public:
18         MyApplicationShell( int* ac, char* av[], char* name )
19         : ApplicationShell( ac, av, name ) {}
20
21         //
22         //     New Version of the WM Close Callback
23         //
24         void winCloseCB( Widget, XtPointer, XtPointer )
25         {
26               cout << "New Call Back\n";
27               exit( 0 );
28         }
29   };
30
```

```
31    int main( int ac, char *av[] )
32    {
33    //
34    //      Create an ApplicationShell Instance
35    //
36    MyApplicationShell myShell( &ac, av, "Testpgm2" );
37
38    //
39    // Create the GUI - In this Case a Simple Pushbutton
40    //
41    PushButton *pb = new PushButton( myShell.main_widget(), "pb" );
42
43    //
44    // Test Font Classes
45    //
46    MWLFont font( myShell.main_widget(), "variable", "charset1" );
47    MWLFont font2( myShell.main_widget(), "cfb-24", "charset2" );
48    MWLFontList fontlist( font );
49    fontlist.addFont( font2 );
50
51    //
52    // Instantiate a CompoundString
53    //
54    CompoundString cs( "Code Reuse is My Life, Too!", font2 );
55
56    //
57    //      Exercise MWLResourceList Class
58    //
59    MWLResourceList r1( XmNfontList, fontlist );
60    MWLResourceList r2 = r1;
61    MWLResourceList r3;
62    r3 = r1;
63
64    //
65    // Load Resources into the PushButton Object
66    //
67    pb→setResource( r3 );
```

```
68
69    //
70    // Set the LabelString Resource
71    //
72    pb→setLabelString( cs );
73
74    //
75    // Set Colors
76    //
77    pb→setForegroundColor( "magenta" );
78    pb→setBackgroundColor( "yellow" );
79
80    //
81    // Manage the PushButton
82    //
83    pb→manage();
84
85    //
86    // Realize Widgets
87    //
88    myShell.realizeWidget();
89
90    //
91    // Enter Main Event Loop
92    //
93    myShell.appMainLoop();
94 }
```

LISTING 13.2. mwltest2.h

13.2 THE MVC CLASSES

13.2.1 The Model-View-Controller Architecture

In this section, we will discuss the second approach to constructing an application framework. It is based on the Model-View-Controller (MVC) architecture proposed by A. Goldberg (circa 1983). Under this model, we divide applications into three distinct components. Oddly enough, they are called *models, views,* and *controllers.*

The model is essentially the user's problem domain, an abstraction of the problem we are trying to solve. Views are graphical representations of the underlying information model. For example, we could represent financial data as a report, a pie chart, or a GUI. Controllers manage the application. They allow users, through views, to modify and update the model. Controllers also ensure that when one view updates the model, all other views receive timely and accurate notification. One obvious benefit of the MVC architecture is that it separates *controls* from *views.* That is, it separates interface from implementation. This decouples components of the information model and allows programmers to change one component without affecting others.

In the MWL implementation of this model, views are windows into the application, and controllers are the frameworks. Used in this vein, the term *window* represents a complete screen component that allows users some level of access to the underlying information model. Controllers are one or more classes that support and maintain all the views.

13.2.2 *Implementation Overview*

To implement the MVC architecture, we must obviously design a class structure that supports separate control and view components. In addition, we would like to preserve the benefits of the toolkit abstraction that we developed earlier in the chapter. To accomplish this task, MWL provides two main classes: `MWLAppMgr` and `MWLWindow`.

Objects of type `MWLAppMgr` serve as the main controller for an application. Each process is required to instantiate one, and only one, object of this type. Its job is twofold: it manages the Motif interface and maintains application windows. Applications create MVC windows by creating new classes derived from `MWLWindow`. This class serves as the foundation for application views, and it provides the necessary "hooks" to interface with controllers. (As an aside, note that we did not use class names such as `Controller` or `View`. We felt that the names we selected were more mnemonic for the Motif environment.)

Thus, to create an MVC/MWL application, clients must complete the following steps:

1. Create a class derived from MWLWindow for each view.

2. Provide a definition for a virtual member function declared in MWL-Window. This is where clients create their GUIs.

3. Define an instance of the MWLAppMgr class.

4. Define one or more instances of their application class(es).

Note that we did not include such items as creating a main() or initializing the toolkit. These tasks are performed by the controller.

Enough of this chatter, let's get down to "brass classes."

13.2.3 *The* MWLAppMgr *Class*

13.2.3.1 *Class Definition File*

As mentioned previously, an instance of an MWLAppMgr class will serve as our controller. Listing 13.3 contains its definition.

```
 1    //
 2    //           TITLE:        mwlapp.h
 3    //
 4    //           FUNCTION:     Class definition for MWLAppMgr
 5    //
 6
 7    #ifndef _MWLAPP_H_
 8    #define _MWLAPP_H_
 9
10    #include <Xm/AtomMgr.h>
11    #include <Xm/Protocols.h>
12
13    #include "scrn_cmp.h"
14
15    class MWLWindow;                     // Class declaration
16
17    //
18    //        MWLAppMgr manages application windows
19    //        There is one instance of this class per process
```

```
20    //
21    class MWLAppMgr : public ScreenComponent {
22
23    private:
24
25            //
26            //        Functions to add and remove MWLWindows
27            //
28            void addWindow( MWLWindow* );
29            void delWindow( MWLWindow* );
30
31            //
32            //        State Variables
33            //
34            char*      appClassName;
35
36            //
37            //        Manage MWLWindow List
38            //
39            struct   WinNode {
40                     MWLWindow*      win;
41                     WinNode*        next;
42            };
43            int          numWindows;      // Number of AppWins
44            WinNode*     root;            // Root node for win
45
46    protected:
47
48            Screen*      screen;          // X Screen
49            Display*     display;         // X Display
50            XtAppContext appContext;      // Xt App Context
51
52            virtual void mainLoop();      // Xt Event Loop
53            virtual void mwlAppInit( int*, char** );
54                                          // Called from main()
55    public:
```

```
56
57            //
58            //        Constructor
59            //
60            MWLAppMgr( char* name );
61
62            //
63            //        Destructor
64            //
65            virtual ~MWLAppMgr();
66
67            //
68            //        Redefine MWL Class Name
69            //
70            virtual const char* class_name() const
                        { return( "MWLAppMgr" ); }
71
72            //
73            //        Respond to WM Close
74            //
75            virtual void winMgrClose();
76
77            //
78            //        Convenience Routines
79            //
80            virtual void manage();
81            virtual void iconify();
82            virtual void unmanage();
83
84            Screen* getScreen() const { return(screen); }
85
86            Display* getDisplay() const { return(display); }
87
88            XtAppContext getAppContext() const
                        { return(appContext); }
89
90            const char* getApplicationClass() const
                        { return(appClassName); }
```

```
91
92          //
93          //          Friend declarations
94          //
95          friend MWLWindow;                    // MWLWindow access
96          friend int main( int, char** );  // main() access
97      };
98
99      extern MWLAppMgr* mwlAppMgr;              // Allow external access
100
101     #endif
```

LISTING 13.3. mwlapp.h

The class begins with declarations for two member functions addWinow() and delWindow(). These routines add and remove MWLWindow objects within MWLAppMgr. They are declared private to prohibit direct client access. (As mentioned previously, MWLWindow objects know how to register themselves with the controller.) We lay the foundation for this processing beginning with line 39, where we declare variables that will form the basis of a linked list of registered windows.

The protected section begins with line 46. In it, we declare several X and Xt variables and two virtual functions. The first, mainLoop(), enters Xt's main event loop. The second, mwlAppInit(), initializes the programming environment. As we will see, it is called from MWL's version of main(). We declare both functions virtual for the obvious reason: clients can redefine behavior in subclasses.

In the public sector, we declare a constructor, a destructor, and several convenience routines. We also grant friend status to the MWLWindow class and the function main(). The file closes with an extern declaration of an pointer defined in mwlapp.cxx (see Listing 13.4).

13.2.3.2 *Class Implementation File*
The file mwlapp.cxx contains the implementation of MWLAppMgr. The code appears in Listing 13.4.

```
1     //
2     //      TITLE: mwlapp.h
3     //
4     //      FUNCTION: Definition of the MWLAppMgr member functions
5     //
6
7     #include "mwlapp.h"
8     #include "mwlwin.h"
9
10    //
11    //         Pointer to single instance of the MWLAppMgr class
12    //
13    MWLAppMgr* mwlAppMgr = NULL;
14
15    //
16    //         Constructor
17    //
18    MWLAppMgr::MWLAppMgr( char* appName )
19            : ScreenComponent( "NULL" ), display(NULL),
20              appContext(NULL), root(NULL), screen(NULL)
21    {
22            mwlAppMgr = this;          // Don't rely on client
23
24            appClassName = new char[ strlen(appName)+1 ];
25            strcpy( appClassName, appName );
26    }
27
28    //
29    //         Destructor
30    //
31    MWLAppMgr::~MWLAppMgr()
32    {
33            WinNode* p;
34            WinNode* q;
35
36            delete [] appClassName;
37
```

```
38                    for( p = root; p; p = q )
39                    {
40                            q = p->next;
41                            delete p;
42                    }
43          }
44
45          //
46          //        mainLoop()
47          //
48          void MWLAppMgr::mainLoop()
49          {
50                    //
51                    //        Enter Xt's Main Loop
52                    //
53                    XtAppMainLoop( appContext );
54          }
55
56          //
57          //        mwlAppInit(): called from main()
58          //
59          void MWLAppMgr::mwlAppInit( int* argp, char* argv[] )
60          {
61                    WinNode* p;
62
63                    //
64                    //   Create main application shell & init toolkit
65                    //
66                    MWLResourceList rl( XmNmappedWhenManaged, False );
67                    _main_widget = XtAppInitialize(
68                            &appContext,            // Appl Context
69                            appClassName,           // Appl Class
70                            NULL,                   // Cmd Line
71                            0,                      // No of Options
72                            argp,                   // No of Args
73                            argv,                   // Cmd Line Args
74                            NULL,                   // Fallback Resources
```

```
75                      rl,             // Arg List Resources
76                      rl              // No of Args
77            );
78
79            //
80            //       Save display & screen info
81            //
82            screen = XtScreen( _main_widget );
83            display = XtDisplay( _main_widget );
84
85            //
86            // Destroy handler
87            //
88            registerDestroyCB();
89
90
91            //
92            // Reset widget name to name of appl
93            //
94            delete _widget_name;
95            _widget_name = new char[ strlen(argv[0])+1 ];
96            strcpy( _widget_name, argv[0] );
97
98            //
99            // Realize All Widgets
100           //
101           XtRealizeWidget( _main_widget );
102
103
104           //
105           //       Initialize & manage all MWLWindows
106           //
107           for( p = root; p; p = p->next )
108           {
109                   p->win->winInit();
110                   p->win->manage();
111           }
```

```
112     }
113
114     //
115     //      addWindow(): allows client to register a new window
116     //
117     void MWLAppMgr::addWindow( MWLWindow* w )
118     {
119             int i;
120             WinNode* t = new WinNode;
121
122             t->win = w;
123             t->next = root;
124             root = t;
125             numWindows++;
126     }
127
128     //
129     //      delWindow(): remove a client window
130     //
131     void MWLAppMgr::delWindow( MWLWindow* w )
132     {
133             WinNode* p;
134             WinNode* q;
135
136             for( p = q = root; p; q = p, p = p->next )
137             {
138                     if( p->win == w )
139                     {
140                        if( p == root )
141                                         root = p->next;
142                             else
143                                         q->next = p->next;
144                             delete p;
145                             numWindows-;
146                     }
147             }
148     }
```

```
149
150     //
151     //          manage(): manage all client windows
152     //
153     void MWLAppMgr::manage()
154     {
155             WinNode* t;
156
157             //
158             //          Mananage all MWLWindows
159             //
160             for( t = root; t; t = t->next )
161                     t->win->manage();
162     }
163
164     //
165     //          unmanage(): unmanage all client windows
166     //
167     void MWLAppMgr::unmanage()
168     {
169             WinNode* t;
170
171             //
172             //          Unmananage all MWLWindows
173             //
174             for( t = root; t; t = t->next )
175                     t->win->unmanage();
176     }
177
178     //
179     //          iconify(): iconify all client windows
180     //
181     void MWLAppMgr::iconify()
182     {
183             WinNode* t;
184
185             for( t = root; t; t = t->next )
```

```
186                           t->win->iconify();
187      }
188
189      //
190      //        winMgrClose(): Handle WM Close
191      //
192      void MWLAppMgr::winMgrClose()
193      {
194             WinNode* t;
195
196          //
197          //          Tell each window that WM exit received
198          //
199          for( t = root; t; t = t->next )
200                  t->win->winMgrClose();
201      }
202
203      //
204      //      main(): normal program entry - used to
205      //             initialize environment
206      //
207      int main( int ac, char** av )
208      {
209          if( !mwlAppMgr )
210          {
211              //
212              //      Client must create an instance of
213              //      the AppMgr class
214              //
215              exit( 99 );
216          }
217
218          //
219          //      Initialize the Appl
220          //
221          mwlAppMgr->mwlAppInit( &ac, av );
222
```

```
223          //
224          //      Enter  main  App  loop
225          //
226          mwlAppMgr->mainLoop();
227    }
```

LISTING 13.4. mwlapp.cxx

The file begins with the declaration of the external pointer mwlAppMgr. This pointer provides all MWLWindow objects access to the sole instance of the MWLAppMgr class. The constructor initializes variables, passes values to its base class, and records the application name. Note the assignment statement appearing on line 22. This is where the external pointer becomes initialized.

An important part of the design begins with the definition of the function mwlAppInit() (line 59). Unfortunately, its description depends on other facets of the model, as does theirs on it. We are thus confronted with a classic "chicken-and-egg" dilemma. As a result, we must describe several aspects of the design in parallel.

Before we begin, we should understand the sequence of events involved during program invocation. Due to the high degree of encapsulation, clients programmers do not have access to any start-up routines—including main(). (Take a moment to peruse the last few lines of Listing 13.4.) As a result, the way we construct and execute programs under this model is as follows:

1. Clients declare a single, external instance of an MWLAppMgr object.

2. They then declare one or mode instances of MWLWindow-derived objects. As a result of their inheritance (we will see how in the next section), these objects know how to register themselves with the controller (created in Step 1).

3. The components are then compiled and linked with the MWL library.

4. As usual, program execution begins with the function main(). (In this case, it is the MWL version.) However, as a result of the declarations contained in Steps 1 and 2, all views are registered with the controller.

5. Initialization begins when MWL's main() invokes mwlAppInit(). This leaves us off where we started: discussing the implementation of mwlAppInit().

The function mwlAppInit() initializes both the MWL and the Xt/Motif environments. It performs the following functions:

- It calls XtAppInitialize() with appropriate arguments (line 67). Note that it sets the resource XmNmappedWhenManaged to False. Thus, the shell widget created by the XtAppIntialize() function will never be visible, and all view (MWLWindow) objects must create their own top-level shell widget.

- It records application data values (lines 82–83).

- It registers a destroy handler (line 88).

- Resets its name to the program name (lines 94–96). Keep in mind that this object is instantiated *before* main() executes. As a result, the object does not have access to the program name (argv[0]).

- Realizes all widgets (line 101).

- Invokes the initialize and manage methods of all its registered windows (views). We will see how individual MWLWindow-derived objects initialize and manage themselves later in the chapter.

Lines 117 and 131 begin definitions of the functions that maintain the list of registered windows. As their names imply, addWindow() adds a window to the list, and delWindow() removes a window from the list. The manage() and unmanage() routines manage/unmanage all registered application windows; the iconify() function iconifies all registered windows. The final utility function, winMgrClose(), receives a window manager protocol message and passes it on to all registered windows.

The implementation file closes with a definition of the function main(). The if test ensures that the client has created the one required instance of our control class. After testing for a NULL pointer, main() instructs the controller to initialize all application windows and then enters Xt's main event loop (through the controller). At first glance, it may seem odd that a library provides a definition for main(). However, this design has the advantage of hiding toolkit calls and maintaining the framework abstraction.

13.2.4 *The* MWLWindow *Class*

Let's foucs our attention on the MWLWindow class. Each instance of this class represents a single application window. Although it provides a number of services, it is not meant to be instantiated directly. Rather, its sole purpose is to serve as a base class for derivation.

Clients create custom windows (GUIs) by creating new classes derived from MWLWindow. Derived classes must provide a definition for the pure virtual function mwlMain() (if they are to be instantiated). This is the function that actually creates the user interface.

13.4.1 *Class Definition File*

Listings 13.5 contains the class definition for MWLWindow.

```
1     //
2     //          TITLE:        mwlwin.h
3     //
4     //          FUNCTION:        Class definition for MWLWindow
5     //
6
7     #ifndef _MWLWIN_H_
8     #define _MWLWIN_H_
9
10    #include "scrn_cmp.h"
11    #include "mwlapp.h"
12
13    class MWLWindow : public ScreenComponent {
14
15    private:
16
17            //
18            //      Window Manager Callback
19            //
20            static void winMgrCloseCB( Widget, XtPointer,
                                        XtPointer );
21
22
23    protected:
```

```
24
25              //
26              //          Appl Specific Widget
27              //
28              Widget gui;
29
30              //
31              //          Defined by derived classes
32              //
33              virtual Widget mwlMain( Widget ) = 0;
34
35      public:
36
37              MWLWindow( char* );                 // Constructor
38              virtual ~MWLWindow();               // Destructor
39
40              //
41              //          Convenience Routines
42              //
43              virtual void manage();
44              virtual void iconify();
45              virtual void unmanage();
46
47              //
48              //          Initialize Window
49              //
50              virtual void winInit();
51
52              //
53              //          Set Window Title
54              //
55              virtual void setTitle( char* s )
56              {
57                  XtVaSetValues( _main_widget, XmNtitle, s, NULL );
58              }
59
60              //
```

```
61              //          Default WM Close - client can override
62              //
63              virtual void winMgrClose() {}
64       };
65
66       #endif
```

LISTING 13.5. mwlwin.h

The class provides the basic services required by application windows: manage, unmanage, iconify, etc. Two items are worthy of note. First, line 33 contains the declaration of the pure virtual function mwlMain(). This function must be defined by derived classes. Second, note the declaration of the function winInit() (line 50). As they say, this is where the action is. It is an important function that we will discuss in the next section.

13.2.4.2 Class Implementation File
The definition file for the class <$iMWLWindow> appears in Listing 13.6.

```
 1    //
 2    //          TITLE:          mwlwin.cxx
 3    //
 4    //          FUNCTION:       Definition of MWLWindow functions
 5    //
 6
 7    #include <stdlib.h>
 8
 9    #include "mwlwin.h"
10    #include "mwlapp.h"
11
12    //
13    //        Constructor
14    //
15    MWLWindow::MWLWindow( char* name )
16              : ScreenComponent(name), gui(NULL)
17    {
18              //
```

```
19                 //          Register window w/ AppMgr
20                 //
21                 mwlAppMgr->addWindow( this );
22       }
23
24       //
25       //        Destructor
26       //
27       MWLWindow::~MWLWindow()
28       {
29                 //
30                 //          Unregister window w/ AppMgr
31                 //
32                 mwlAppMgr->delWindow( this );
33       }
34
35       //
36       //        manage(): manage the application window
37       //
38       void MWLWindow::manage()
39       {
40                 XtPopup( _main_widget, XtGrabNone );
41       }
42
43       //
44       //        unmanage(): unmanage the application window
45       //
46       void MWLWindow::unmanage()
47       {
48                 XtPopdown( _main_widget );
49       }
50
51       //
52       //        iconify(): iconify the application window
53       //
54       void MWLWindow::iconify()
55       {
```

```
56                  if( XtIsRealized(_main_widget) )
57                      XIconifyWindow(mwlAppMgr->getDisplay(),
                        XtWindow(_main_widget),0);
58      }
59
60      //
61      //          winInit(): initialze object & window
62      //
63      void MWLWindow::winInit()
64      {
65              //
66              //          Create an Unseen Popup Shell
67              //
68              // Could also use: topLevelShellWidgetClass
69
70              _main_widget = XtVaCreatePopupShell(
71                _widget_name,                 // Name
72                applicationShellWidgetClass,  // Class
73                mwlAppMgr->_main_widget,      // Parent
74                XmNtitle, _widget_name,       // Default Title
75                NULL);
76
77              //
78              //          =========================================
79              //                Handle WinMgr 'Delete' Message
80              //          =========================================
81              //
82
83              Atom deleteWindowAtom;
84
85              //
86              //          Get the Delete Atom
87              //
88              deleteWindowAtom = XmInternAtom (    // Get Atom
89                      mwlAppMgr->getDisplay(),     // X Display
90                      "WM_DELETE_WINDOW",          // Name
91                      False                        // Ignore
```

```
92                 );
93
94             //
95             //          Register WM Callback Routine
96             //
97             XmAddWMProtocolCallback (
98                 _main_widget,               // Widget
99                 deleteWindowAtom,           // Atom Type
100                &MWLWindow::winMgrCloseCB,  // Callback
101                XtPointer)mwlAppMgr         // Client Data
102                );
103
104
105            //
106            //          Register the destroy callback
107            //
108            registerDestroyCB();
109
110            //
111            //          Create the GUI - call derived class'
112            //          implementation of the virtual function
113            //
114            gui = mwlMain( _main_widget );
115
116            //
117            //          If application GUI is not managed,
118            //          manage it
119            //
120            if( ! XtIsManaged(gui) )
121                    XtManageChild( gui );
122     }
123
124 //
125 //          winMgrCloseCB: window manger destroy callback
126 //
127 void MWLWindow::winMgrCloseCB( Widget w, XtPointer c,
                                    XtPointer e )
```

```
128     {
129             MWLAppMgr* theObject = (MWLAppMgr*)c;
130
131             //
132             //      Inform the AppMgr
133             //
134             theObject->winMgrClose();
135     }
```

LISTING 13.6. `mwlwin.cxx`

As you may recall, upon invocation `main()` calls the `mwlAppInit()` member of the controller object. It, in turn, invokes the `winInit()` member of all registered windows. (Remember, `MWLWindow` objects register themselves with the controller in the constructor.) The `winInit()` function performs the following tasks:

- It creates a popup shell to serve as the view's parent
- It registers a protocol callback on the popup shell
- It registers a destroy handler
- It invokes the virtual function `mwlMain()`. The function `winInit()` expects the client to create the window's GUI within the body of `mwlMain()`.
- As a final task, it manages the GUI if the derived class has not done so.

13.2.5 *Example Program*

It's time for an example. Usually, the first attempt in any new arena is some version of the traditional "Hello world" program. As such, we will construct a simple program that displays one pushbutton with the requisite label. When the user presses the button, the program will iconify itself. (I promised simplicity, not excitement.) The code appears in Listing 13.7.

```
1     //
2     //      mwlhello.h: Program to Test MWLApp & MWLWindow
3     //
4
```

```
 5    #include <iostream.h>
 6
 7    #include "mwlwin.h"
 8    #include "pb.h"
 9
10    void pbCB( Widget w, XtPointer c, XtPointer e );
11
12    //
13    //      ========================================================
14    //                       Derived Class Definition
15    //      ========================================================
16    //
17    class Hello : public MWLWindow {
18
19    public:
20
21      Hello( char* name ) : MWLWindow(name) {}   // Constructor
22
23      void winMgrClose();                        // WM Exit
24
25      Widget mwlMain( Widget );                  // GUI for app
26
27      ~Hello() { cout << "~Hello() Called" << endl; }
28    };
29
30    //
31    //      ========================================================
32    //                       Member Function Definitions
33    //      ========================================================
34    //
35
36    //
37    //      Called on WM Exit
38    //
39    void Hello::winMgrClose()
40    {
```

```
41      cout << "This is HELLO Saying GOODBYE" << endl;
42    }
43
44    //
45    // Build Application GUI
46    //
47    Widget Hello::mwlMain( Widget parent )
48    {
49      setTitle( _widget_name );
50
51      PushButton* d = new PushButton( parent, "p1" );
52
53      d→setLabelString( _widget_name );
54      d→addActivateCallback( pbCB, (XtPointer)this );
55
56      d→manage();
57
58      return( d→parent_widget() );
59    }
60
61    //
62    //      ========================================================
63    //                        Instantiate MWL Objects
64    //      ========================================================
65    //
66
67    //
68    //      Create a Controller
69    //
70    MWLAppMgr foo( "Hello" );
71
72    //
73    //      Create a Window
74    //
75    Hello hello( "HELLO WORLD" );
76
77    //
```

```
78   //        ============================================================
79   //                    Define a Simple Pushbutton Callback
80   //        ============================================================
81   //
82   void pbCB( Widget w, XtPointer c, XtPointer e )
83   {
84       Hello* p = (Hello*)c;
85
86       cout << "pbCB(): iconify: " << p->widget_name() << "\n";
87       p->iconify();
88   }
```

LISTING 13.7. mwlhello.cxx

This program is the embodiment of simplicity. We derive a new class from `MWLWindow`, define some member functions, instantiate two objects, and we're off and running. While you peruse this listing, ask yourself the following question: How much X/Xt/Motif must one know to use the MWL classes?

13.3 Calc REVISITED (AGAIN)

For a more complete example, we have provided yet another version of our calculator program. The only class affected by the MVC approach is `Calc`. Instead of existing on its own, it now becomes a derived class of `MWLWindow`. The complete listing appears in Appendix B.

13.4 SUMMARY

In this chapter, we completed our application frameworks and our discussion of objectifying Motif. We demonstrated two methods for encapsulating the remaining pieces of the Xt Toolkit. The first, `MWLApplicationShell`, uses a direct approach. It encapsulates Xt features within its class definition. The second method employs a technique based on the Model-View-Controller architecture. The class `MWLAppMgr` serves as the controller and classes derived from `MWLWindow` act as views.

I would like to add two final notes about the second approach. First, with a little additional effort, we could eliminate the need for clients to instantiate a controller; we could do it for them. Second, through the use of `virtual` functions, clients can customize the behavior of views.

13.5 AFTERWORD

This has been an all-too-brief tour of the world of object-oriented programming and objectifying Motif. There are many ways to extend and enhance the basic features discussed in this text. For example, we could:

- Add additional Motif features
- Add and enforce stylistic features
- Seamlessly embed more X-level features within GUI components
- Create what appear to be new widgets—components that are configured to operate uniquely
- Combine other graphics packages
- Create a portable version of MWL that can serve as a porting base across platforms

At the risk of sounding trite, you are limited only by your imagination. It is my sincere hope that all readers, after reading this book, will feel confident enough to extend the ideas contained herein. As you do, please keep me informed so that I can incorporate your ideas into the basic library. Please contact me via the publisher or by electronic mail at cfb@panix.com.

13.6 MWL AVAILABILTY

The MWL library is available for license. Please contact the author via the publisher, or by electronic mail at cfb@panix.com.

A

THE MWL CLASS LIBRARY

This appendix contains the complete listing of the MWL classes presented and described in this text. Note that many of the classes include additional behavior not otherwise described. The files are listed in alphabetical order by name, with the header file preceding the implementation file (where appropriate).

A.1 FILE: app_shel.h

```
1    //
2    //           TITLE:      app_shell.h
3    //
4    //           FUNCTION:   The ApplicationShell Class
5    //
6
7    #ifndef _APP_SHELL_H_
8    #define _APP_SHELL_H_
9
```

```
10      #include <stdlib.h>                        // exit()
11
12      #include <Xm/AtomMgr.h>
13      #include <Xm/Protocols.h>
14
15      #include "scrn_cmp.h"
16
17      class ApplicationShell : public ScreenComponent {
18
19      protected:
20
21              XtAppContext        appContext;              // AppContext
22
23      public:
24
25              //
26              //          Constructor
27              //
28              ApplicationShell( int* ac, char* av[], char*
                                appName )
29                      : ScreenComponent(appName)
30              {
31                      //
32                      // Initialize Xt Toolkit
33                      //
34                      _main_widget = XtAppInitialize( &appCon-
                            text, appName,
35                          NULL, 0, ac, av, NULL, NULL, 0 );
36
37                      //
38                      //      =============================
39                      //         Register WM Delete Callback
40                      //      =============================
41                      //
42                      Atom    deleteWindow;
43
44                      deleteWindow = XmInternAtom( // The Atom
45                          XtDisplay(_main_widget), // Display
```

```
46                              "WM_DELETE_WINDOW",     // Protocol
47                              False                   // Ignore
48                  );
49
50                  //
51                  //      Set the Callback Data Structure
52                  //
53                  MemberFunctionCBData* cbd =
                            new MemberFunctionCBData;
54                  cbd->theData = NULL;
55                  cbd->theFunc =
                            &ScreenComponent::winCloseCB;
56                  cbd->theObject = this;
57
58                  //
59                  //      Register the Callback
60                  //
61                  XmAddWMProtocolCallback(
62                      _main_widget,           // The Widget
63                      deleteWindow,           // The Atom
64                      activateMemberCB,       // The Function
65                      (XtPointer)cbd          // Client Data
66                  );
67          }
68
69          //
70          //      Redefine Classname
71          //
72          virtual const char* class_name() const
73          {
74                  return("ApplicationShell");
75          }
76
77          //
78          //      Realize Widgets
79          //
80          void realizeWidget()
```

```
81                {
82                        XtRealizeWidget( _main_widget );
83                }
84
85                //
86                //      Enter Main Loop
87                //
88                void appMainLoop()
89                {
90                        XtAppMainLoop( appContext );
91                }
92
93                //
94                //      Destructor
95                //
96                virtual ~ApplicationShell() {}
97      };
98
99      #endif
```

A.2 FILE: cs.h

```
1       //
2       //              TITLE:        cs.h
3       //
4       //              FUNCTION:     Define CompoundString Class
5       //
6
7       #ifndef _CS_H_
8       #define _CS_H_
9
10      #include <string.h>
11
12      #include <Xm/Xm.h>
13
```

```
14    class CompoundString {

15

16    private:

17

18            char*          font;              // Font Name

19            XmString       xmstring;          // The XmString

20

21    public:

22

23            //

24            //          Default/String Constructor

25            //

26            CompoundString( char* string = "",

27                char* f = XmFONTLIST_DEFAULT_TAG )

28            {

29                font = f;

30                xmstring = XmStringCreateLtoR( string, f );

31            }

32

33            //

34            //          Copy Constructor

35            //

36            CompoundString( const CompoundString& cs )

37            {

38                    font = cs.font;

39                    xmstring = XmStringCopy( cs.xmstring );

40            }

41

42            //

43            //          Assignment Operator

44            //

45        CompoundString& operator=( const CompoundString& cs )

46            {

47                    if( this != &cs )

48                    {

49                        font = cs.font;

50                        XmStringFree( xmstring );
```

```
51                                    xmstring = XmStringCopy( cs.xmstring );
52                            }
53                            return( *this );
54                    }
55
56              //
57              //      XmString Constructor
58              //
59              CompoundString( const XmString& xms )
60              {
61                            xmstring = XmStringCopy( xms );
62                            font = XmFONTLIST_DEFAULT_TAG;
63              }
64
65              //
66              //      Destructor
67              //
68              ~CompoundString()
69              {
70                            XmStringFree( xmstring );
71              }
72
73              //
74              //      Cast Operators
75              //
76              operator char*()
77              {
78                      char* cstring;
79
80                      XmStringGetLtoR( xmstring, font, &cstring );
81                      return( cstring );
82              }
83
84              operator XmString()
85              {
86                            return( xmstring );
87              }
```

```
88
89          //
90          //          Concatenation Operator
91          //
92          friend CompoundString operator+( const CompoundString&,
93                      const CompoundString& );
94     };
95
96     #endif
```

A.3 FILE: cs.cxx

```
 1     //
 2     //          TITLE:      cs.cxx
 3     //
 4     //          FUNCTION:      Define CompoundString Class Functions
 5     //
 6
 7     #include "cs.h"
 8
 9     //
10     //          Concatenation Operator
11     //
12     CompoundString operator+(const CompoundString& l, const
                            CompoundString& r)
13     {
14              char* cstr1;
15              char* cstr2;
16
17              XmStringGetLtoR( l.xmstring, XmFONTLIST_DEFAULT_TAG,
                        &cstr1 );
18              XmStringGetLtoR( r.xmstring, XmFONTLIST_DEFAULT_TAG,
                        &cstr2 );
19
20              char* buf = new char[ strlen(cstr1) +
                        strlen(cstr2) + 1 ];
```

```
21          strcpy( buf, cstr1 );
22          strcat( buf, cstr2 );
23
24          CompoundString t = buf;
25          delete [] buf;
26
27          return( t );
28    }
```

A.4 FILE: dialog.h

```
1    //
2    //          TITLE:          dialog.h
3    //
4    //          FUNCTION:       Define classes that create and
                                 manage dialogs.
5    //
6
7    #ifndef _DIALOG_H_
8    #define _DIALOG_H_
9
10   #include "scrn_cmp.h"
11
12   #include <Xm/MessageB.h>
13
14   //
15   //       Create basic dialog class
16   //
17   class MessageDialog : public ScreenComponent {
18
19   private:
20
21          XmString dialogTitle;
22          static XtResource dialogResources[];
23
24          //
```

```
25              //        Private Function to Set Dialog Resources
26              //
27              void setDialogXmString( char* resource, char*
                                       string )
28              {
29                      XmString xmstring = XmStringCreateLtoR(
30                          string, XmSTRING_DEFAULT_CHARSET );
31                      XtVaSetValues( _main_widget, resource,
                            xmstring, NULL );
32                      XmStringFree( xmstring );
33              }
34
35          //
36          //        Private Function to Unmanage Buttons
37          //
38          void unmanageButton( unsigned char which_button )
39          {
40            Widget button;
41            button = XmMessageBoxGetChild(
42                    _main_widget,            // Dialog
43                    which_button             // Button
44                    );
45            XtUnmanageChild( button );
46          }
47
48
49   public:
50
51        MessageDialog( Widget w, char* name,
52                unsigned char type = XmDIALOG_MESSAGE );
53
54        ~MessageDialog(                        // Destructor
55        {
56                XmStringFree( dialogTitle );
57        }
58
59          //
```

```
60              //          Redefine Classname
61              //
62              virtual const char* class_name() const
63              {
64                      return("MessageDialog");
65              }
66
67              //
68              //          Dialog Post Function
69              //
70              void post()
71              {
72                      manage();
73              }
74
75              //
76              //          Convenience Functions to Set Resources
77              //
78              void setOKLabel( char* label )          // OK
79              {
80                      setDialogXmString( XmNokLabelString,
                                    label );
81              }
82
83              void setHelpLabel( char* label )        // Help
84              {
85                setDialogXmString( XmNhelpLabelString, label );
86              }
87
88              void setCancelLabel( char* label )      // Cancel
89              {
90                      setDialogXmString( XmNcancelLabelString,
                                    label );
91              }
92
93              void setDialogTitle( char* title )      // Title
94              {
```

```
95                          setDialogXmString( XmNdialogTitle, title );
96              }
97
98          void setDialogMessage( char* message )
99          {
100             setDialogXmString( XmNmessageString, message );
101         }
102
103         //
104         //          Routines to Register Callbacks
105         //
106         void addOKCallback(XtCallbackProc okFunc, XtPointer
                                client_data)
107         {
108             XtAddCallback(
109                 _main_widget,              // Widget
110                 XmNokCallback,             // Callback Type
111                 okFunc,                    // Callback Func
112                 client_data                // Client Data
113             );
114         }
115
116         void addHelpCallback( XtCallbackProc helpFunc,
117                 XtPointer client_data )
118         {
119             XtAddCallback(
120                 _main_widget,                  // Widget
121                 XmNhelpCallback,               //   Type
122                 helpFunc,                      //   Func
123                 client_data                    //   Data
124             );
125         }
126
127         void addCancelCallback( XtCallbackProc cancelFunc,
128                             XtPointer client_data )
                {
                    XtAddCallback(
```

```
129                                    _main_widget,        // Widget
130                                    XmNcancelCallback,   // Type
131                                    cancelFunc,          // Func
132                                    client_data          // Data
133                                 );
134                }
135
136               //
137               //        Routines to Unmanage Buttons
138               //
139               void unmanageOKButton()         // Unmanage OK
140               {
141                        unmanageButton( XmDIALOG_OK_BUTTON );
142               }
143
144               void unmanageHelpButton()
145               {
146                        unmanageButton( XmDIALOG_HELP_BUTTON );
147               }
148
149               void unmanageCancelButton()    // Unmanage Canc
150               {
151                        unmanageButton( XmDIALOG_CANCEL_BUTTON );
152               }
153     };
154
155     //
156     //        Derive MOTIF-Specific Dialogs
157     //
158
159     class QuestionDialog : public MessageDialog {
160
161     public:
162
163               //
164               //        Redefine Classname
165               //
```

```
166             virtual const char* class_name() const
167             {
168                     return("QuestionDialog");
169             }
170
171             //
172             //      Constructor
173             //
174             QuestionDialog( Widget parent, char* name )
175                     : MessageDialog( parent, name, <$iXmDIA-
                        LOG_QUESTION ) {}
176      };
177
178      class WarningDialog : public MessageDialog {
179
180      public:
181
182             //
183             //      Redefine Classname
184             //
185             virtual const char* class_name() const
186             {
187                     return("WarningDialog");
188             }
189
190             //
191             //      Constructor
192             //
193             WarningDialog( Widget parent, char* name )
194                     : MessageDialog( parent, name,
                        XmDIALOG_WARNING ) {}
195      };
196
197      class ErrorDialog : public MessageDialog {
198
199      public:
200
```

```
201               //
202               //        Redefine Classname
203               //
204               virtual const char* class_name() const
205               {
206                       return("ErrorDialog");
207               }
208
209               //
210               //        Constructor
211               //
212               ErrorDialog( Widget parent, char* name )
213                       : MessageDialog( parent, name,
                          XmDIALOG_ERROR ) {}
214       };
215
216       class WorkingDialog : public MessageDialog {
217
218       public:
219
220               //
221               //        Redefine Classname
222               //
223               virtual const char* class_name() const
224               {
225                       return("WorkingDialog");
226               }
227
228               //
229               //        Constructor
230               //
231               WorkingDialog( Widget parent, char* name )
232                       : MessageDialog( parent, name,
                          XmDIALOG_WORKING ) {}
233       };
234
```

```
235    class InformationDialog : public MessageDialog {
236
237    public:
238
239            //
240            //          Redefine Classname
241            //
242            virtual const char* class_name() const
243            {
244                     return("InformationDialog");
245            }
246
247            //
248            //          Constructor
249            //
250            InformationDialog( Widget parent, char* name )
251                      : MessageDialog( parent, name,
                          XmDIALOG_INFORMATION ) {}
252    };
253
254    #endif
```

A.5 FILE: dialog.cxx

```
1    //
2    //      TITLE: dialog.cxx
3    //
4    //      FUNCTION:   Dianlog Classes.
5    //
6
7    #include "dialog.h"
8
9    //
10   //          Class/Component Resources Array Definition
11   //
12   XtResource MessageDialog::dialogResources[] = {
```

```
13              {
14                  "title",                    // Resource Name
15                  "DialogTitle",              // Class
16                  XmRXmString,                // Data Type
17                  sizeof(XmString),           // Size
18                  XtOffset(MessageDialog*, dialogTitle),   // Offset
19                  XmRString,                  // Default Type
20                  (XtPointer)"MESSAGE DIALOG" // Default Value
21              }
22      };
23
24
25      //
26      //          Constructor
27      //
28      MessageDialog::MessageDialog( Widget parent, char* name,
                                unsigned char type )
29              : ScreenComponent(name)
30      {
31          _main_widget = XmCreateMessageDialog(
32              parent,                         // Parent
33              _widget_name,                   // Name
34              NULL,                           // Arg List
35              0                               // No. of Args
36          );
37
38              //
39              //          Set Master Resources
40              //
41          XtVaSetValues(
42                  _main_widget,
43                  XmNdialogType, type,
44                  XmNdialogStyle,
                    XmDIALOG_FULL_APPLICATION_MODAL,
45                  NULL
46              );
47
```

```
48                //
49                //          Add  Destroy  CB
50                //
51             registerDestroyCB();
52
53                //
54                //          Query  Resource  DB
55                //
56             getComponentResources( dialogResources,
57                    XtNumber(dialogResources) );
58      };
```

A.6 FILE: font.h

```
1     //
2     //              TITLE:        font.h
3     //
4     //              FUNCTION:     MWLFont & MWLFontList Classes
5     //
6
7     #ifndef _FONT_H_
8     #define _FONT_H_
9
10    #include <Xm/Xm.h>
11    #include <string.h>
12
13    //
14    //        ==================================================
15    //                        MWLFont
16    //        ==================================================
17    //
18    class MWLFont    {
19
20    private:
21
22             char*         charSet;        // Character Set
```

```
23              char*            fontName;        // Font Name
24
25              Display*         display;         // Display Ptr
26              XFontStruct*     fontStruct;      // X Font Struct
27
28                  //
29                  //          Private Utility Function
30                  //
31              void fontSetup( Display* d, char* fn, char* cs )
32                  {
33                      //
34                      //          Save Font Name
35                      //
36                      fontName = new char[ strlen(fn)+1 ];
37                      strcpy( fontName, fn );
38
39                      //
40                      //          Save Character Set Name
41                      //
42                      charSet = new char[ strlen(cs)+1 ];
43                      strcpy( charSet, cs );
44
45                      //
46                      //          Save Display
47                      //
48                      display = d;
49
50                      //
51                      //          Load X Font Structure
52                      //
53                      fontStruct = XLoadQueryFont( d, fontName );
54                  }
55
56      public:
57
58                  //
59                  //          Constructors
```

```
60              //
61              MWLFont( Widget w, char* fontname, char* charset )
62              {
63                      fontSetup( XtDisplay(w), fontname, charset );
64              }
65
66              MWLFont( Display* d, char* fontname, char*
                        charset )
67              {
68                      fontSetup( d, fontname, charset );
69              }
70
71              //
72              //       Destructor
73              //
74              virtual ~MWLFont()
75              {
76                      delete [] charSet;
77                      delete [] fontName;
78                      XFreeFont( display, fontStruct );
79              }
80
81              //
82              //       Cast Operators
83              //
84              operator XFontStruct*() const
85              {
86                      return( fontStruct );
87              }
88
89              operator XmStringCharSet() const
90              {
91                      return( charSet );
92              }
93
94      };
95
```

```
96      //
97      //          ================================================
98      //                          MWLFontList
99      //          ================================================
100     //
101
102     class MWLFontList {
103
104     private:
105
106             XmFontList          fontList;
107
108             //
109             //     Private Copy Construct & Assignment of
110             //
111             MWLFontList( const MWLFontList& );
112             MWLFontList& operator=( const MWLFontList& );
113
114     public:
115
116             //
117             //          Constructors
118             //
119             MWLFontList( const MWLFont& f,  char* cs  )
120             {
121                     fontList  =  XmFontListCreate( f,  cs  );
122             }
123
124             MWLFontList( const MWLFont& f  )
125             {
126                     fontList  =  XmFontListCreate( f,  f  );
127             }
128
129             //
130             //          Destructor
131             //
132             virtual  ~MWLFontList()
```

```
133                 {
134                         XmFontListFree( fontList );
135                 }
136
137             //
138             //          Add  Additional  Fonts  to  List
139             //
140             void addFont( const MWLFont& f, char* cs )
141             {
142                 fontList = XmFontListAdd( fontList, f, cs );
143             }
144
145             void addFont( const MWLFont& f )
146             {
147                     fontList = XmFontListAdd( fontList, f, f );
148             }
149
150             //
151             //          Cast  Operators
152             //
153             operator long()
154             {
155                     return( (long)fontList );
156             }
157
158             operator XmFontList()
159             {
160                     return( fontList );
161             }
162
163     };
164
165     #endif
```

A.7 FILE: label.h

```
1      //
2      //              TITLE:        Label.h
3      //
4      //              FUNCTION:     Label Class Definition
5      //
6
7      #ifndef _LABEL_H_
8      #define _LABEL_H_
9
10     #include "scrn_cmp.h"
11     #include "mwlr.h"
12     #include "cs.h"
13
14     #include <Xm/Label.h>
15
16     class Label : public ScreenComponent {
17
18     private:
19
20             static XtResource LabelResources[];
21
22     protected:
23
24             XmString my_label;
25
26     public:
27             //
28             //       Constructors
29             //
30             Label( Widget parent, char* name,
31                     WidgetClass wclass = xmLabelWidgetClass,
32                     MWLResourceList res = MWLNoResources );
33
34             Label( Widget parent, char* name,
                       MWLResourceList res )
```

```
35                        : ScreenComponent(name),  my_label(NULL)
36              {
37
38                      _main_widget = XmCreateLabel( parent,
                                    name,  res,  res  );
39
40                      //
41                      //        Register Destroy Handler
42                      //
43                      registerDestroyCB();
44              }
45
46              //
47              //        Destructor
48              //
49              ~Label()
50              {
51                      XmStringFree( my_label );
52              }
53
54              //
55              //        Redefine Classname
56              //
57       virtual const char* class_name() const
58              {
59                      return("Label");
60              }
61
62              //
63              //        Set Label String (char*)
64              //
65       void setLabelString( char* str )
66              {
67                      CompoundString cs = str;
68                      XtVaSetValues( _main_widget,
69                              XmNlabelString, (XmString)cs,
70                      NULL );
71              }
```

```
72
73              //
74              //          Set  Label  String  (XmString)
75              //
76              void setLabelString( XmString xmstring )
77              {
78                      XtVaSetValues( _main_widget, XmNlabelString,
                                        xmstring,  NULL );
79              }
80
81              //
82              //          Set  Label  String  (CompoundString)
83              //
84              void setLabelString( CompoundString cs )
85              {
86                          XtVaSetValues(_main_widget,XmNlabelString,
                                        XmString(cs),NULL);
87              }
88      };
89
90      #endif
```

A.8 FILE: label.cxx

```
1     //
2     //      TITLE:       label.cxx
3     //
4     //  FUNCTION:        Label class member function definitions
5     //
6
7     #include "label.h"
8
9     //
10    //       Label Class/Component Resources
11    //
12    XtResource Label::LabelResources[] = {
```

```
13              {
14                  "LabelString",              // Resource Name
15                  "labelString",              // Resource Class
16                  XmRXmString,                // Data Type
17                  sizeof(XmString),           // Size
18                  XtOffset(Label*, my_label), // Offset
19                  XmRString,                  // Default Type
20                  (XtPointer)""               // Default Value
21              }
22      };
23
24      //
25      //          Label Constructor
26      //
27      Label::Label( Widget parent, char* name, WidgetClass wclass,
28                  MWLResourceList res )
29                  :  ScreenComponent(name)
30      {
31          MWLResourceList rl;
32
33          _main_widget = XtCreateWidget( name, wclass,
34                                         parent, res, res );
34
35          //
36          //          Register Destroy Handler
37          //
38          registerDestroyCB();
39
40          //
41          //          Query Resource DB
42          //
43          LabelResources[0].default_addr =
44                      (XtPointer)_widget_name;
44          getComponentResources(LabelResources,
45                      XtNumber(LabelResources));
45
46          //
```

```
47              //        Use Class Resources to Change/Set Label
48              //
49              rl.setArg( XmNlabelString, my_label );
50              setValues( rl );
51      }
```

A.9 FILE: mainwin.h

```
1    //
2    //              TITLE:          mainwin.h
3    //
4    //              FUNCTION:       Definition of the MainWindow Class
5    //
6
7    #ifndef _MW_H_
8    #define _MW_H_
9
10   #include "scrn_cmp.h"
11
12   #include "Xm/MainW.h"
13
14   class MainWindow : public ScreenComponent {
15
16   private:
17
18           //
19           //        Main Window Areas
20           //
21           Widget menuBar;
22           Widget workArea;
23           Widget messageArea;
24           Widget commandArea;
25
26
27   public:
28
```

```
29              MainWindow( Widget, char* );        // Constructor
30
31              ~MainWindow()                       // Destructor
32              {
33                      XtDestroyWidget( menuBar );
34                      XtDestroyWidget( workArea );
35                      XtDestroyWidget( messageArea );
36                      XtDestroyWidget( commandArea );
37              }
38
39              //
40              //      Redefine Classname
41              //
42              virtual const char* class_name() const
43              {
44                      return("MainWindow");
45              }
46
47              //
48              //      Convenience Routines
49              //
50              void setMenuBar( Widget w )
51              {
52                  menuBar = w;
53                  XtVaSetValues( _main_widget, XmNmenuBar,
                                    w, NULL );
54              }
55              Widget getMenuBar() { return( menuBar ); }
56
57              void setWorkArea( Widget w )
58              {
59                  workArea = w;
60                  XtVaSetValues( _main_widget, XmNworkWindow,
                                    w, NULL );
61              }
62              Widget getWorkArea() { return( workArea ); }
63
```

```
64              void setMessageArea( Widget w )
65              {
66                  messageArea = w;
67                  XtVaSetValues(_main_widget,
                              XmNmessageWindow, w, NULL);
68              }
69              Widget getMessageArea() { return( messageArea ); }
70
71              void setCommandArea( Widget w )
72              {
73                  commandArea = w;
74                  XtVaSetValues( _main_widget, XmNcommandWindow,
                              w, NULL );
75              }
76              Widget getCommandArea() { return( commandArea ); }
77
78              void setSeparators( Boolean v = False )
79              {
80                  XtVaSetValues( _main_widget, XmNshowSeparator, v );
81              }
82      };
83
84      #endif
```

A.10 FILE: mainwin.cxx

```
1      //
2      //          TITLE:          mainwin.cxx
3      //
4      //          FUNCTION:       Definition of the MainWindow
5      //
6
7      #include "mainwin.h"
8
9      //
10     //          Constructor
```

```
11    //
12    MainWindow::MainWindow( Widget parent, char* name )
13            : ScreenComponent( name )
14    {
15            //
16            //      Create a MainWindow
17            //
18            _main_widget = XtVaCreateWidget(
19                    name,                       // Name
20                    xmMainWindowWidgetClass  // Widget Class
21                    parent,                     // Parent Widget ID
22
23                    XmNscrollBarDisplayPolicy,      XmAS_NEEDED,
24                    XmNscrollingPolicy,             XmAUTOMATIC,
25
26                    NULL );
27
28            //
29            //      Register Destroy Handler
30            //
31            registerDestroyCB();
32    }
```

A.11 FILE: menubar.h

```
1     //
2     //          TITLE:        menubar.h
3     //
4     //          FUNCTION:     MenuBar Class Definition
5     //
6
7     #ifndef _MENUBAR_H_
8     #define _MENUBAR_H_
9
10    #include "scrn_cmp.h"
11
```

```
12      #include <Xm/RowColumn.h>
13      #include <Xm/CascadeB.h>
14      #include <Xm/Separator.h>
15
16      class MenuBar : public ScreenComponent {
17
18      private:
19
20      public:
21
22              //
23              // Constructor
24              //
25              MenuBar( Widget parent, char* name )
                        : ScreenComponent(name)
26              {
27                      _main_widget = XmCreateMenuBar( parent,
                                        name, NULL, 0 );
28
29                      //
30                      //      Register Destroy Handler
31                      //
32                      registerDestroyCB();
33              }
34
35              //
36              //      Redefine Classname
37              //
38              virtual const char* class_name() const
39              {
40                      return("MenuBar");
41              }
42
43              //
44              //      Identify the 'Help' Button
45              //
46              void setHelpButton( Widget w )
```

```
47              {
48                  XtVaSetValues(_main_widget, XmNmenuHelpWidget, w,
                        NULL);
49              }
50
51              //
52              //        Add a CascadeButton to Menu Bar
53              //
54              Widget addBar( char* label, char mnem,
                        Widget pane );
55      };
56
57      #endif
```

A.12 FILE: menubar.cxx

```
1       //
2       //            TITLE:       menubar.cxx
3       //
4       //            FUNCTION:        MenuBar Member Function Definitions
5       //
6
7       #include "cs.h"
8       #include "mwlr.h"
9       #include "menubar.h"
10
11      //
12      //        Add option to MenuBar
13      //
14      Widget MenuBar::addBar( char* label, char mnemonic,
                        Widget pane )
15      {
16              Widget cascade;
17              CompoundString cs = label;
18              MWLResourceList rl;
19
```

```
20              rl.setArg( XmNsubMenuId, pane );
21              rl.setArg( XmNlabelString, (XmString)cs );
22              if( mnemonic )
23                    rl.setArg( XmNmnemonic, (void*)mnemonic );
24
25              //
26              //      Create the CascadeButton
27              //
28              cascade = XmCreateCascadeButton( _main_widget,
                                            label, rl, rl );
29
30              //
31              //      Manage the Button
32              //
33              XtManageChild( cascade );
34
35              return( cascade );
36    }
```

A.13 FILE: menupane.h

```
 1    //
 2    //            TITLE:        menupane.h
 3    //
 4    //            FUNCTION:        Menupane Class Definition
 5    //
 6
 7    #ifndef _MENUPANE_H_
 8    #define _MENUPANE_H_
 9
10    #include "scrn_cmp.h"
11
12    #include <Xm/RowColumn.h>
13    #include <Xm/CascadeB.h>
14    #include <Xm/Separator.h>
15
```

```
16      class MenuPane : public ScreenComponent {
17
18      public:
19
20              //
21              //          Constructor
22              //
23              MenuPane( Widget parent, char* name ) :
                        ScreenComponent(name)
24              {
25                      //
26                      //          Create but do not manage
27                      //
28                      _main_widget = XmCreatePulldownMenu
                                (parent,name,NULL,0);
29
30                      //
31                      //          Register Destroy Handler
32                      //
33                      registerDestroyCB();
34              }
35
36              //
37              //          Redefine Classname
38              //
39              virtual const char* class_name() const
40              {
41                      return("MenuPane");
42              }
43      };
44
45      #endif
```

A.14 FILE: mwl.h

```
1    //
2    //              FILE:        mwl.h
3    //
4    //              FUNCTION:        Include all MWL header files
5    //
6
7    #ifndef _MWL_H_
8    #define _MWL_H_
9
10   #include "scrn_cmp.h"
11
12   #include "cs.h"
13   #include "pb.h"
14   #include "font.h"
15   #include "mwlr.h"
16   #include "label.h"
17   #include "dialog.h"
18   #include "mwlapp.h"
19   #include "mwlwin.h"
20   #include "mainwin.h"
21   #include "menubar.h"
22   #include "menupane.h"
23   #include "app_shell.h"
24
25   #endif
```

A.15 FILE: mwlapp.h

```
1    //
2    //              TITLE:        mwlapp.h
3    //
4    //              FUNCTION:        Class defintion for MWLAppMgr
5    //
6
7    #ifndef _MWLAPP_H_
```

```
 8     #define _MWLAPP_H_
 9
10     #include <Xm/AtomMgr.h>
11     #include <Xm/Protocols.h>
12
13     #include "scrn_cmp.h"
14
15     class MWLWindow;                      // Class declaration
16
17     //
18     //       MWLAppMgr manages application windows
19     //       There is one instance of this class per process
20     //
21     class MWLAppMgr : public ScreenComponent {
22
23     private:
24
25             //
26             //       Functions to add and remove MWLWindows
27             //
28             void addWindow( MWLWindow* );
29             void delWindow( MWLWindow* );
30
31             //
32             //       State Variables
33             //
34             char*    appClassName;        // For XtAppInit()
35
36             //
37             //       Manage MWLWindow List
38             //
39             struct  WinNode {
40                     MWLWindow*      win;
41                     WinNode*        next;
42             };
43             int          numWindows;      // Numb of AppWins
44             WinNode*     root;            // Root for win list
```

```
45
46    protected:
47
48            Screen*         screen;         // X Screen
49            Display*        display;        // X Display
50            XtAppContext    appContext;     // App Context
51
52            virtual void mainLoop();        // Event Loop
53            virtual void mwlAppInit( int*, char** );
54
55    public:
56
57            //
58            //          Constructor
59            //
60            MWLAppMgr( char* name );
61
62            //
63            //          Destructor
64            //
65            virtual ~MWLAppMgr();
66
67            //
68            //          Redefine MWL Class Name
69            //
70            virtual const char* class_name() const
                         {return( "MWLAppMgr" );}
71
72            //
73            //          Respond to WM Close
74            //
75            virtual void winMgrClose();
76
77            //
78            //          Convenience Routines
79            //
```

```
80              virtual void manage();
81              virtual void iconify();
82              virtual void unmanage();
83
84              Screen* getScreen() const { return(screen); }
85
86              Display* getDisplay() const { return(display); }
87
88              XtAppContext getAppContext() const
                            { return(appContext); }
89
90              const char* getApplicationClass() const
                            {return(appClassName);}
91
92          //
93          //       Friend declarations
94          //
95              friend MWLWindow;
96              friend int main( int, char** );
97      };
98
99      extern MWLAppMgr* mwlAppMgr;           // External access
100
101     #endif
```

A.16 FILE: mwlapp.cxx

```
1       //
2       //          TITLE:       mwlapp.h
3       //
4       //          FUNCTION:       Definition of MWLAppMgr
5       //
6
7       #include "mwlapp.h"
8       #include "mwlwin.h"
9
```

```
10      //
11      //       Pointer to single instance of the MWLAppMgr class
12      //
13      MWLAppMgr* mwlAppMgr = NULL;
14
15      //
16      //       Constructor
17      //
18      MWLAppMgr::MWLAppMgr( char* appName )
19               : ScreenComponent( "NULL" ), display(NULL),
20                 appContext(NULL), root(NULL), screen(NULL)
21      {
22              mwlAppMgr = this;        // Don't rely on client
23
24              appClassName = new char[ strlen(appName)+1 ];
25              strcpy( appClassName, appName );
26      }
27
28      //
29      //       Destructor
30      //
31      MWLAppMgr::~MWLAppMgr()
32      {
33              WinNode* p;
34              WinNode* q;
35
36              delete [] appClassName;
37
38              for( p = root; p; p = q )
39              {
40                      q = p->next;
41                      delete p;
42              }
43      }
44
45      //
46      //       mainLoop()
```

```
47      //
48      void MWLAppMgr::mainLoop()
49      {
50              //
51              //          Enter Xt's Main Loop
52              //
53              XtAppMainLoop( appContext );
54      }
55
56      //
57      //          mwlAppInit(): called from main()
58      //
59      void MWLAppMgr::mwlAppInit( int* argp, char* argv[] )
60      {
61              WinNode* p;
62
63              //
64              //      Create main applicaion shell & init toolkit
65              //
66              MWLResourceList rl( XmNmappedWhenManaged, False );
67              _main_widget = XtAppInitialize(
68                      &appContext,            // Appl Context
69                      appClassName,           // Appl Class
70                      NULL,                   // Cmd Line Options
71                      0,                      // No of Options
72                      argp,                   // No of Args
73                      argv,                   // Cmd Line Args
74                      NULL,                   // Fallback Resources
75                      rl,                     // Resources
76                      rl                      // No of Args
77              );
78
79              //
80              //          Save display & screen info
81              //
82              screen = XtScreen( _main_widget );
83              display = XtDisplay( _main_widget );
```

```
 84
 85              //
 86              //        Destroy handler
 87              //
 88              registerDestroyCB();
 89
 90
 91              //
 92              //      Reset widget name (in ScreenComponent)
 93              //
 94              delete _widget_name;
 95              _widget_name = new char[ strlen(argv[0])+1 ];
 96              strcpy( _widget_name, argv[0] );
 97
 98              //
 99              //        Realize All Widgets
100              //
101              XtRealizeWidget( _main_widget );
102
103
104              //
105              //        Initialize & manage all MWLWindows
106              //
107              for( p = root; p; p = p->next )
108              {
109                      p->win->winInit();
110                      p->win->manage();
111              }
112      }
113
114      //
115      //        addWindow(): Register a new window
116      //
117      void MWLAppMgr::addWindow( MWLWindow* w )
118      {
119              int i;
120              WinNode* t = new WinNode;
```

```
121
122                t->win = w;
123                t->next = root;
124                root = t;
125                numWindows++;
126      }
127
128      //
129      //        delWindow(): remove a cient window
130      //
131      void MWLAppMgr::delWindow( MWLWindow* w )
132      {
133                WinNode* p;
134                WinNode* q;
135
136                for( p = q = root; p; q = p, p = p->next )
137                {
138                        if( p->win == w )
139                        {
140                                if( p == root )  // 1st element
141                                        root = p->next;
142                                else
143                                        q->next = p->next;
144                                delete p;
145                                numWindows-;
146                        }
147                }
148      }
149
150      //
151      //        manage(): manage all client windows
152      //
153      void MWLAppMgr::manage()
154      {
155                WinNode* t;
156
157                //
```

```
158                    //          Mananage all MWLWindows
159                    //
160                    for( t = root; t; t = t->next )
161                            t->win->manage();
162     }
163
164     //
165     //          unmanage(): unmanage all client windows
166     //
167     void MWLAppMgr::unmanage()
168     {
169                    WinNode* t;
170
171                    //
172                    //          Unmananage all MWLWindows
173                    //
174                    for( t = root; t; t = t->next )
175                            t->win->unmanage();
176     }
177
178     //
179     //          iconify(): iconify all client windows
180     //
181     void MWLAppMgr::iconify()
182     {
183                    WinNode* t;
184
185                    for( t = root; t; t = t->next )
186                            t->win->iconify();
187     }
188
189     //
190     //          winMgrClose(): Handle WM Close
191     //
192     void MWLAppMgr::winMgrClose()
193     {
194                    WinNode* t;
```

```
195
196             //
197             //          Tell each window that WM exit received
198             //
199             for( t = root;  t;  t = t->next )
200                     t->win->winMgrClose();
201     }
202
203     //
204     //          main(): normal program entry - used to
205     //                   initialize environment
206     //
207     int main( int ac, char** av )
208     {
209             if( !mwlAppMgr )
210             {
211                //
212                //     Client must create an instance of
213                //     the AppMgr class.
214                //
215                exit( 99 );
216             }
217
218             //
219             //          Initialize the Appl
220             //
221             mwlAppMgr->mwlAppInit( &ac, av );
222
223             //
224             //          Enter main App loop
225             //
226             mwlAppMgr->mainLoop();
227     }
```

A.17 FILE: mwlr.h

```
1      //
2      //      FILE:  mwlr.h
3      //
4      //      FUNCTION:     MWLResourceList Class Definition
5      //
6
7      #ifndef _MWLR_H_
8      #define _MWLR_H_
9
10     #include <Xm/Xm.h>
11
12     class MWLResourceList {
13
14     protected:
15
16             ArgList       argList;        // Arg List
17             Cardinal      argCount;       // No. or Args
18
19     public:
20
21             //
22             //      Default Constructor
23             //
24             MWLResourceList() : argList(NULL), argCount(0) {}
25
26             //
27             //      Copy Constructor
28             //
29             MWLResourceList( const MWLResourceList& );
30
31             //
32             //      Name/Value Pair Constructor
33             //
34             MWLResourceList( String, void* );
35
```

```
36              //
37              //          Assignment Operator
38              //
39              MWLResourceList& operator=( const MWLResourceList& r );
40
41              //
42              //          Destructor
43              //
44              ~MWLResourceList();
45
46              //
47              //          Set a Resource Name/Value Pair
48              //
49              void setArg( String resource, void* value );
50              void setArg( String resource, XmString value )
51              {
52                      setArg( resource, (void*)value );
53              }
54
55              //
56              //          Reset to NULL
57              //
58              void zapArgs();
59
60              //
61              //          Cast Functions
62              //
63              operator ArgList() { return(argList); }
64              operator Cardinal() { return(argCount); }
65      };
66
67      extern const MWLResourceList MWLNoResources;           // NULL
68
69      #endif
```

A.18 FILE: mwlr.cxx

```
1      //
2      //                FILE:         mwlr.cxx
3      //
4      //                FUNCTION:     MWLResourceList Member Functions
5      //
6
7      #include "mwlr.h"
8
9      //
10     //        Copy Constructor
11     //
12     MWLResourceList::MWLResourceList( const MWLResourceList& r )
13     {
14             int      i;
15
16             //
17             //        Create  Arg Array
18             //
19             argCount = r.argCount;
20             argList = new Arg[ argCount ];
21
22             //
23             //        Copy Old Values into New Object
24             //
25             for( i = 0; i < argCount; i++ )
26             {
27                     argList[i].value = r.argList[i].value;
28
29                     argList[i].name = new char[strlen
                                        (r.argList[i].name)+1];
30                     strcpy( argList[i].name, r.argList[i].name );
31             }
32     }
33
```

```
34      //
35      //          Name/Value Pair Constructor
36      //
37      MWLResourceList::MWLResourceList( String resourceName, void*
                                          resourceValue )
38      {
39              //
40              //          Create Arg Array
41              //
42              argCount = 1;
43              argList = new Arg;
44
45              //
46              //          Store the Name/Value Pair
47              //
48              argList->value = (XtArgVal)resourceValue;
49              argList->name = new char[ strlen(resourceName)+1 ];
50              strcpy( argList->name, resourceName );
51      }
52
53      //
54      //          Destructor
55      //
56      MWLResourceList::~MWLResourceList()
57      {
58              int     i;
59
60              for( i = 0; i < argCount; i++ )
61                      delete argList[i].name;
62
63              delete argList;
64      }
65
66      //
67      //          Assignment Operator
68      //
```

```
69      MWLResourceList& MWLResourceList::operator=(
                                   const MWLResourceList& r )
70      {
71              int     i;
72
73              if( this != &r )
74              {
75
76                      //
77                      //      Delete the Old
78                      //
79                      for( i = 0; i < argCount; i++ )
80                              delete argList[i].name;
81                      delete argList;
82
83                      //
84                      //      Copy the New
85                      //
86                      argCount = r.argCount;
87                      argList = new Arg[ argCount ];
88
89                      for( i = 0; i < argCount; i++ )
90                      {
91                        argList[i].value = r.argList[i].value;
92
93                        argList[i].name = new char[strlen
                                           (r.argList[i].name)+1];
94                        strcpy( argList[i].name,
                           r.argList[i].name );
95                      }
96              }
97
98              return( *this );
99      }
100
101     //
102     //      Set a Name/Value Pair
```

```
103     //
104     void MWLResourceList::setArg( String resourceName, void*
                                      resourceValue )
105     {
106             int     i;
107             ArgList tmp;
108
109             //
110             //      Create New, Larger Arg Array
111             //
112             tmp = new Arg[ argCount+1 ];
113
114             //
115             //      Copy Old Values into New Array
116             //
117             for( i = 0; i < argCount; i++ )
118             {
119                     tmp[i].name = argList[i].name;
120                     tmp[i].value = argList[i].value;
121             }
122
123             //
124             //      Store the New Name/Value Pair
125             //
126             tmp[ argCount ].value = (XtArgVal)resourceValue;
127             tmp[ argCount ].name = new
                                      char[ strlen(resourceName)+1 ];
128             strcpy( tmp[ argCount ].name, resourceName );
129
130             //
131             //      Wrap Up
132             //
133             argCount++;
134             delete argList;
135             argList = tmp;
136     }
137
```

```
138     //
139     //          Reset to NULL
140     //
141     void MWLResourceList::zapArgs()
142     {
143             int     i;
144
145             //
146             //          Delete Old Args
147             //
148             for( i = 0; i < argCount; i++ )
149                     delete argList[i].name;
150             delete argList;
151
152             argCount = 0;
153             argList = NULL;
154     }
155
156     //
157     //          NULL Constant
158     //
159     const MWLResourceList MWLNoResources;
```

A.19 FILE: mwlwin.h

```
1       //
2       //          TITLE:          mwlwin.h
3       //
4       //          FUNCTION:       Class definition for MWLWindow
5       //
6
7       #ifndef _MWLWIN_H_
8       #define _MWLWIN_H_
9
10      #include "scrn_cmp.h"
11      #include "mwlapp.h"
```

```
12
13     class MWLWindow : public ScreenComponent {
14
15   private:
16
17           //
18           //         Window Manager Callback
19           //
20           static void winMgrCloseCB( Widget, XtPointer,
                                          XtPointer );
21
22
23   protected:
24
25           //
26           //         Appl Specific Widget
27           //
28           Widget gui;
29
30           //
31           //         Must be supplied by the app
32           //
33           virtual Widget mwlMain( Widget ) = 0;
34
35   public:
36
37           MWLWindow( char* );              // Constructor
38           virtual ~MWLWindow();            // Destructor
39
40           //
41           //         Convenience Routines
42           //
43           virtual void manage();
44           virtual void iconify();
45           virtual void unmanage();
46
47           //
```

```
48                //         Initialize Window
49                //
50                virtual void winInit();
51
52                //
53                //         Set Window Title
54                //
55                virtual void setTitle( char* s )
56                {
57                  XtVaSetValues( _main_widget, XmNtitle, s, NULL );
58                }
59
60                //
61                //         Default WM Close - client can override
62                //
63                virtual void winMgrClose() {}
64        };
65
66      #endif
```

A.20 FILE: mwlwin.cxx

```
1       //
2       //          TITLE:          mwlwin.cxx
3       //
4       //          FUNCTION:       Defintion of MWLWindow
5       //
6
7       #include <stdlib.h>
8
9       #include "mwlwin.h"
10      #include "mwlapp.h"
11
12      //
13      //          Constructor
14      //
```

```
15    MWLWindow::MWLWindow( char* name )
16              : ScreenComponent(name), gui(NULL)
17    {
18              //
19              //        Register window w/ AppMgr
20              //
21              mwlAppMgr->addWindow( this );
22    }
23
24    //
25    //        Destructor
26    //
27    MWLWindow::~MWLWindow()
28    {
29              //
30              //        Unregister window w/ AppMgr
31              //
32              mwlAppMgr->delWindow( this );
33    }
34
35    //
36    //        manage(): manage the application window
37    //
38    void MWLWindow::manage()
39    {
40              XtPopup( _main_widget, XtGrabNone );
41    }
42
43    //
44    //        unmanage(): unmanage the application window
45    //
46    void MWLWindow::unmanage()
47    {
48              XtPopdown( _main_widget );
49    }
50
51    //
```

```
52      //          iconify(): iconify the application window
53      //
54      void MWLWindow::iconify()
55      {
56              if( XtIsRealized(_main_widget) )
57                  XIconifyWindow(mwlAppMgr->getDisplay(),
                                   XtWindow(_main_widget),0);
58      }
59
60      //
61      //          winInit(): initialze object & window
62      //
63      void MWLWindow::winInit()
64      {
65              //
66              //          Create an Unseen Popup Shell
67              //
68              // Could also use: topLevelShellWidgetClass
69
70              _main_widget = XtVaCreatePopupShell(
71                  _widget_name,                   // Name
72                  applicationShellWidgetClass,    // Class
73                  mwlAppMgr->_main_widget,        // Parent
74                  XmNtitle, _widget_name,         // Default Title
75                  NULL);
76
77              //
78              //          ========================================
79              //              Handle WinMgr 'Delete' Message
80              //          ========================================
81              //
82
83              Atom deleteWindowAtom;               // Delete Window
84
85              //
86              //          Get the Delete Atom
```

```
87              //
88              deleteWindowAtom = XmInternAtom (   // Get Atom
89                  mwlAppMgr->getDisplay(),  // X Display
90                  "WM_DELETE_WINDOW",       // Name
91                  False                     // Ignore
92              );
93
94              //
95              //          Register WM Callback Routine
96              //
97              XmAddWMProtocolCallback (
98                  _main_widget,             // Widget
99                  deleteWindowAtom,         // Atom Type
100                 &MWLWindow::winMgrCloseCB, // Callback Routine
101                 (XtPointer)mwlAppMgr      // Client Data
102             );
103
104
105             //
106             //          Register the destroy callback
107             //
108             registerDestroyCB();
109
110             //
111             //          Create the GUI - call derived class'
112             //          implementation of the virtual function
113             //
114             gui = mwlMain( _main_widget );
115
116             //
117             //          If application GUI is not managed,
118             //          manage it
119             //
120             if( ! XtIsManaged(gui) )
121                     XtManageChild( gui );
122     }
123
```

```
124     //
125     //        winMgrCloseCB: window manger destroy callback
126     //
127     void MWLWindow::winMgrCloseCB( Widget w, XtPointer c,
                                       XtPointer e )
128     {
129             MWLAppMgr* theObject = (MWLAppMgr*)c;
130
131             //
132             //        Inform the AppMgr
133             //
134             theObject->winMgrClose();
135     }
```

A.21 FILE: pb.h

```
1      //
2      //      TITLE: pb.h
3      //
4      //      FUNCTION:    PushButton class definition
5      //
6
7      #ifndef _PUSHBUTTON_H_
8      #define _PUSHBUTTON_H_
9
10     #include "label.h"
11     #include "mwlr.h"
12
13     #include <Xm/PushB.h>
14
15     //
16     //      Pushbutton class definition
17     //
18     class PushButton : public Label {
19
20     private:
```

```
21
22              static XtResource PushButtonResources[];
23
24   public:
25
26              //
27              //       Constructor
28              //
29              PushButton( Widget, char*,
                           MWLResourceList = MWLNoResources );
30
31
32              //
33              //       Destructor
34              //
35              ~PushButton()
36              {
37                      XmStringFree( my_label );
38              }
39
40              //
41              //       Redefine Classname
42              //
43              virtual const char* class_name() const
44              {
45                      return("PushButton");
46              }
47
48              //
49              //       Set Accellerator
50              //
51              void setAccelerator( char* acc_label, char*
                                     acc_key );
52
53              //
54              //       Add an Activate Callback
55              //
```

```
56                void addActivateCallback( XtCallbackProc proc,
                                           XtPointer data )
57                {
58                    XtAddCallback(_main_widget,
                                   XmNactivateCallback,proc,data);
59                }
60
61                //
62                //         Set Button Mnemonic
63                //
64                void setMnemonic( char mnem )
65                {
66                    XtVaSetValues( _main_widget,
                                   XmNmnemonic, mnem, NULL );
67                }
68        };
69
70    #endif
```

A.22 FILE: pb. cxx

```
 1    //
 2    //            TITLE:       pb.cxx
 3    //
 4    //            FUNCTION:       PushButton class definitions
 5    //
 6
 7    #include "pb.h"
 8
 9    //
10    //       PB Class/Component Resources
11    //
12    XtResource PushButton::PushButtonResources[] = {
13            {
14                "pushbuttonLabel",             // Name
15                "PushbuttonLabel",             // Class
```

```
16                     XmRXmString,                        // Type
17                     sizeof(XmString),                   // Size
18                     XtOffset(PushButton*, my_label),// Offset
19                     XmRString,                          // Type
20                     (XtPointer)""                       // Value
21              }
22      };
23
24      //
25      //        PB Constructor
26      //
27      PushButton::PushButton( Widget parent, char* name,
                            MWLResourceList res )
28          : Label( parent, name, xmPushButtonWidgetClass, res )
29      {
30          //
31          //        No need to register destroy callback -
32          //        done in Label
33          //
34
35          //
36          // Query Resource DB
37          //
38          PushButtonResources[0].default_addr =
                                  (XtPointer) _widget_name;
39          getComponentResources( PushButtonResources,
40                  XtNumber(PushButtonResources) );
41
42          //
43          // Use Class Resources to Change/Set Label
44          //
45          res.setArg( XmNlabelString, my_label );
46          XtSetValues( _main_widget, res, res );
47      }
48
49      //
50      //        Set PB Accellerator
```

```
51      //
52      void PushButton::setAccelerator( char* acc_label, char*
                                          acc_key )
53      {
54              MWLResourceList res;
55              CompoundString acceleratorText = acc_label;
56
57              res.setArg( XmNaccelerator, acc_key );
58              res.setArg( XmNacceleratorText, acceleratorText );
59              XtSetValues( _main_widget, res, res );
60      }
```

A.23 FILE: scrn_cmp.h

```
1       //
2       //              TITLE:          scrn_cmp.h
3       //
4       //              FUNCTION:       ScreenComponent Class Definition
5       //
6
7       #ifndef _SCREEN_COMPONENT_H_
8       #define _SCREEN_COMPONENT_H_
9
10      #include <stdlib.h>                      // For exit() ...
11      #include <string.h>                      // For strcpy() ...
12
13      #include "mwlr.h"                         // MWLResource Class
14
15      #include <Xm/Xm.h>                        // MOTIF header file
16
17      //
18      //              Convenience typedefs
19      //
20
21      class ScreenComponent;
22
```

```
23     typedef void (*MCBF)( ScreenComponent*, Widget, XtPointer,
                          XtPointer );
24     typedef void (ScreenComponent::*MWLCallbackProc)
                      (Widget,XtPointer,XtPointer);
25
26     class ScreenComponent {
27
28     protected:
29
30             //
31             //          Protected data to allow derived classes
32             //          direct access
33             //
34             char*   _widget_name;   // Name for resource DB
35             Widget  _main_widget;   // Main "parent" widget
36
37             //
38             //          Protected constructor: we do not want
39             //          this class to be instantiated - only
40             //          derived from.
41             //
42             ScreenComponent( char* name );
43
44             //
45             //          Supply a default WM Protocol Callback
46             //
47             virtual void winCloseCB( Widget, XtPointer,
                                    XtPointer )
48             {
49                     exit( 0 );
50             }
51
52     public:
53
54             //
55             //          Basic Features
56             //
```

```
57              virtual ~ScreenComponent();    // Destructor
58
59              Widget main_widget()           // Return "parent"
60              {
61                      return( _main_widget );
62              }
63
64              char* widget_name()            // Return name
65              {
66                char *t = new char[ strlen(_widget_name)+1 ];
67                  strcpy( t, _widget_name );
68
69                      //
70                      // N.B.: Client must "free" storage
71                      //
72                      return( t );
73              }
74
75      //
76      //      Virtual Functions
77      //
78      virtual void manage();      // Manage
79      virtual void unmanage();    // Unmanage
80
81      //
82      //      =======================================
83      //                Additional Features
84      //      =======================================
85      //
86
87      //
88      //      Widget Destruction
89      //
90      void registerDestroyCB();
91      virtual void destroyWidget();
92      static void destroyCB( Widget, XtPointer,
                               XtPointer );
```

```
 93
 94              //
 95              //         Resource Management Functions
 96              //
 97              Widget parent_widget()
 98              {
 99                      return( XtParent(_main_widget) );
100              }
101
102              virtual const char* class_name() const
103              {
104                      return("ScreenComponent");
105              }
106
107              void getComponentResources( const XtResourceList,
                                             const int );
108
109              //
110              //         Set & Unset Sensitivity
111              //
112              void setSensitive()
113              {
114                      XtSetSensitive( _main_widget, True );
115              }
116              void setInsensitive()
117              {
118                      XtSetSensitive( _main_widget, False );
119              }
120
121              //
122              //         Cast Operator(s)
123              //
124              operator Widget()
125              {
126                      return( _main_widget );
127              }
128
```

```
129          //
130          //         ========================================
131          //                     Utility Routines
132          //         ========================================
133          //
134
135          //
136          //       Set Colors
137          //
138          void setForegroundColor( char* color );
139          void setBackgroundColor( char* color );
140
141          //
142          //       Generalized Resource Set/Get Functions
143          //
144          void setResource( String name, XtArgVal value )
145          {
146                  XtVaSetValues( _main_widget, name, value,
                                     NULL );
147          }
148          void setResource( MWLResourceList res )
149          {
150                  XtSetValues( _main_widget, res, res );
151          }
152          void getResource( String name, void* value )
153          {
154              XtVaGetValues( _main_widget, name,
                             XtArgVal(value), NULL );
155          }
156
157          //
158          //       Set & Get User Data Resource
159          //
160          void setUserData( XtPointer val )
161          {
162                  XtVaSetValues( _main_widget, XmNuserData,
                                     val, NULL );
163          }
```

```
164              XtPointer getUserData()
165              {
166                  XtPointer        val;
167                  XtVaGetValues( _main_widget, XmNuserData,
                              &val, NULL );
168                  return( val );
169              }
170
171              void setX( Position x )
172              {
173                XtVaSetValues( _main_widget, XmNx, x, NULL );
174              }
175              Position getX()
176              {
177                Position x;
178                XtVaGetValues( _main_widget, XmNx, &x, NULL );
179                return( x );
180              }
181              void getX( Position& x )              // Alt Sig
182              {
183                  XtVaGetValues( _main_widget, XmNx, &x, NULL );
184              }
185
186
187              void setY( Position y )
188              {
189                  XtVaSetValues( _main_widget, XmNy, y, NULL );
190              }
191              Position getY()
192              {
193                Position y;
194                XtVaGetValues( _main_widget, XmNy, &y, NULL );
195                return( y );
196              }
197              void getY( Position& y )              // Alt Sig
198              {
199                  XtVaGetValues( _main_widget, XmNy, &y, NULL );
200              }
```

```
201
202            void setWidth( Dimension width )
203            {
204                XtVaSetValues( _main_widget, XmNwidth, width,
                                    NULL );
205            }
206            Dimension getWidth()
207            {
208                Position width;
209                XtVaGetValues( _main_widget, XmNwidth, &width,
                                    NULL );
210                return( width );
211            }
212
213            void setHeight( Dimension height )
214            {
215                XtVaSetValues( _main_widget, XmNheight, height,
                                    NULL );
216            }
217            Dimension getHeight()
218            {
219                Position height;
220                XtVaGetValues( _main_widget, XmNheight,
                                    &height, NULL );
221                return( height );
222            }
223
224            //
225            //      Set Resource Using MWLResourceLists
226            //
227            setValues( MWLResourceList rl )
228            {
229                    XtSetValues( _main_widget, rl, rl );
230            }
231
232            //
```

```
233          //          ========================================
234          //                    Generalized Callback Functions
235          //          ========================================
236          //
237
238
239          //
240          //          Callback Data Structure
241          //
242          struct CallbackData {
243                  XtPointer           theData;
244                  void*               theFunc;
245                  ScreenComponent*    theObject;
246          };
247
248
249          //
250          //          Respond to any Callback
251          //
252          static void activateCB( Widget w, XtPointer c,
                                      XtPointer x )
253          {
254                  CallbackData* cbd = (CallbackData*)c;
255
256                  //
257                  //          Extract Data Elements
258                  //
259                  XtPointer data = cbd->theData;
260                  ScreenComponent* theObject =
                                      cbd->theObject;
261
262                  //
263                  //          Pass on Callback
264                  //
265                  if( theObject )
266                  {
267                          //
```

```
268                              //         Pass Object Ptr
269                              //
270                              MCBF func = (MCBF)cbd->theFunc;
271                              func( theObject, w, data, x );
272                      } else {
273                              //
274                              //      External Class Function
275                              //
276                              XtCallbackProc func =
                                (XtCallbackProc)cbd->theFunc;
277                              func( w, data, x );
278                      }
279              }
280
281      //
282      //      Register a Callback
283      //
284      void registerCB( String cb, XtCallbackProc func,
                        XtPointer data )
285      {
286              CallbackData* cbd = new CallbackData;
287
288              cbd->theData = data;        // Data
289              cbd->theFunc = func;        // Function
290              cbd->theObject = NULL;      // NO OBJECT
291
292              //
293              //      Register the Callback
294              //
295              XtAddCallback( _main_widget, cb,
                        activateCB, (XtPointer)cbd );
296      }
297
298      //
299      //      Register a Member Callback Function
300      //
```

```
301            void registerCB( String cb, void* func,
                        XtPointer data )
302            {
303                    CallbackData* cbd = new CallbackData;
304
305                    cbd->theData = data;          // Data
306                    cbd->theFunc = func;          // CB Func
307                    cbd->theObject = this;        // Object
308
309                    //
310                    //       Register the Callback
311                    //
312                    XtAddCallback( _main_widget, cb,
                                activateCB, (XtPointer)cbd );
313            }
314
315            //
316            //     =========================================
317            //                Member Callback Functions
318            //     =========================================
319            //
320
321            //
322            //     Callback Data Structure
323            //
324            struct MemberFunctionCBData {
325                    XtPointer          theData;
326                    MWLCallbackProc    theFunc;
327                    ScreenComponent*   theObject;
328            };
329
330
331            //
332            //     Respond to any Callback
333            //
334            static void activateMemberCB( Widget w,
                        XtPointer c, XtPointer x )
```

```
335             {
336                 MemberFunctionCBData* cbd =
                                (MemberFunctionCBData*)c;
337
338                 //
339                 //         Extract Data Elements
340                 //
341                 XtPointer data = cbd->theData;
342                 MWLCallbackProc theFunc = cbd->theFunc;
343                 ScreenComponent* theObject =
                                cbd->theObject;
344
345                 //
346                 //         Pass on the Callback
347                 //
348                 (theObject->*theFunc)( w, data, x );
349             }
350
351             //
352             //         Register a Member Function Callback
353             //         Must be Derived from ScreenComponent
354             //
355             void registerCB( String cb, MWLCallbackProc func,
                            XtPointer data,
356                 ScreenComponent* theObject = NULL )
357             {
358                 CallbackData* cbd = new CallbackData;
359
360                 cbd->theData = data;      // Client Data
361                 cbd->theFunc = func;      // Callback Func
362                 cbd->theObject = theObject ? theObject :
                                this;   // The Object
363
364                 //
365                 //         Register the Callback
366                 //
367                 XtAddCallback( _main_widget, cb,
                            activateMemberCB,
```

```
368                              (XtPointer)cbd );
369                    }
370
371     };
372
373     #endif
```

A.24 FILE: scrn_cmp.cxx

```
1     //
2     //           TITLE:        scrn_cmp.cxx
3     //
4     //           FUNCTION:     Final version of the ScreenCompo-
                                 nent class
5     //
6
7     #include "scrn_cmp.h"
8
9     //
10    //        Constructor
11    //
12    ScreenComponent::ScreenComponent( char* name )
13    {
14        _main_widget = (Widget)NULL;   // No interface built
15
16            _widget_name = new char[ strlen(name)+1 ];
17            strcpy( _widget_name, name );
18    }
19
20    //
21    //        Destructor
22    //
23    virtual ScreenComponent::~ScreenComponent()
24    {
25            if( _main_widget != (Widget)NULL )
26            {
27                    //
```

```
28                          // Remove Destroy Callback
29                          //
30                          XtRemoveCallback(
31                                  _main_widget,
32                                  XmNdestroyCallback,
33                                  &ScreenComponent::destroyCB,
34                                  (XtPointer)this
35                          );
36                  }
37
38          //
39          // Relinquish dynamic memory
40          //
41          delete [] _widget_name;
42  }
43
44  //
45  //          Manage the Component
46  //
47  virtual void ScreenComponent::manage()
48  {
49          //
50          //          Only manage if we have a widget
51          //
52          if( _main_widget != (Widget)NULL )
53          {
54                  XtManageChild( _main_widget );
55
56                  //
57                  // Verify destroy handler
58                  // if not - register it now
59                  //
60                  // This is not foolproof - as this
61                  // routine is virtual
                     // and can be redefined in a derived
                     // class
62                  //
```

```
63                              if( XtHasCallbacks(_main_widget,
                                        XmNdestroyCallback)
64                                      != XtCallbackHasSome  )
65                              {
66                                      registerDestroyCB();
67                              }
68                      }
69      }
70
71      //
72      //          Unmanage  the  Component
73      //
74      virtual  void  ScreenComponent::unmanage()
75      {
76              //
77              //          Only  unmanage  if  we  have  a  widget
78              //
79              if( _main_widget != (Widget)NULL )
80                      XtUnmanageChild( _main_widget );
81      }
82
83      //
84      // Routines  to  manage  widget  destruction
85      //
86      void ScreenComponent::registerDestroyCB()
87      {
88              //
89              // Convenience  routine  to  register  a
                // XmNdestroyCallback
90              // for class
91              //
92              if( _main_widget != (Widget)NULL )
93                      XtAddCallback(
94                              _main_widget,
95                              XmNdestroyCallback,
96                              &ScreenComponent::destroyCB,
97                              (XtPointer)this
98                      );
```

```
99      }
100
101     virtual void ScreenComponent::destroyWidget()
102     {
103             //
104             // Record that the widget has been destroyed
105             //
106             _main_widget = (Widget)NULL;
107     }
108
109     void ScreenComponent::destroyCB( Widget w,
110             XtPointer client, XtPointer call )
111     {
112             //
113             // Pass on callback to appropriate object
114             //
115             ScreenComponent* theObject =
116                             (ScreenComponent*) client;
117             theObject->destroyWidget();
118     }
119
120     //
121     // Routine to Get Component Resources
122     // Called from Derived Classes
123     //
124     void ScreenComponent::getComponentResources(
125             const XtResourceList res, const int cnt )
126     {
127             XtGetSubresources(
128                     parent_widget(),    // Parent Widget
129                     (XtPointer)this,    // Data Structure
130                     _widget_name,       // Instance Name
131                     class_name(),       // Class Name
132                     res,                // Resource Array
133                     cnt,                // Number of Resources
134                     NULL,               // Arg Array
```

```
135                          0                      // Number of Args
136                  );
137     }
138
139     //
140     //        Routines to Set Foreground & Background Colors
141     //
142     void ScreenComponent::setForegroundColor( char* color )
143     {
144              XColor           xcolor[2];
145              Colormap         colormap;
146
147              XtVaGetValues( _main_widget, XmNcolormap,
                                  &colormap, NULL );
148
149              XAllocNamedColor( XtDisplay(_main_widget),
150                      colormap, color, &xcolor[0], &xcolor[1] );
151
152              XtVaSetValues( _main_widget, XmNforeground,
                                  xcolor[0].pixel, NULL );
153     }
154
155     void ScreenComponent::setBackgroundColor( char* color )
156     {
157              Colormap         colormap;
158              XColor           xcolor[2];
159              Pixel            bgColor, topShadow,
160                               bottomShadow, fgRet,
                                  selectColor;
161
162              XtVaGetValues( _main_widget, XmNcolormap,
                                  &colormap, NULL );
163
164              XAllocNamedColor( XtDisplay(_main_widget),
165                      colormap, color, &xcolor[0], &xcolor[1] );
166              bgColor = xcolor[0].pixel;
```

```
167
168             XmGetColors( XtScreen(_main_widget), colormap,
169                     bgColor, &fgRet, &topShadow, &bottomShadow,
                        &selectColor );
170
171             XtVaSetValues( _main_widget,
172
173                     XmNbackground,          bgColor,
174                     XmNtopShadowColor,      topShadow,
175                     XmNbottomShadowColor,   bottomShadow,
176                     XmNselectColor,         selectColor,
177                     XmNarmColor,            selectColor,
178                     XmNborderColor,         fgRet,
179
180             NULL );
181     }
```

A.25 FILE: sep.h

```
1   //
2   //          TITLE:      sep.h
3   //
4   //          FUNCTION:       Separator Class Definition
5   //
6
7   #ifndef _SEPARATOR_H_
8   #define _SEPARATOR_H_
9
10  #include "mwlr.h"
11  #include "scrn_cmp.h"
12
13  #include "Xm/Separator.h"
14
15  class Separator : public ScreenComponent {
16
17  public:
18
```

```
19                  //
20                  //          Constructor
21                  //
22                  Separator( Widget parent, char* name,
23                          MWLResourceList res = MWLNoResources )
24                          :  ScreenComponent(name)
25                  {
26
27                          //
28                          //          Create the Widget
29                          //
30                          _main_widget = XmCreateSeparator
                                    ( parent, name, res, res );
31
32                          //
33                          //          Register Destroy Handler
34                          //
35                          registerDestroyCB();
36                  }
37
38                  //
39                  //          Convenience Routines
40                  //
41                  void setOrientation( unsigned char orient )
42                  {
43                          XtVaSetValues( _main_widget,
                                    XmNorientation, orient, NULL );
44                  }
45
46                  void setType( unsigned char type )
47                  {
48                          XtVaSetValues( _main_widget,
                                    XmNseparatorType, type, NULL );
49                  }
50
51                  void setMargin( Dimension d )
```

```
52              {
53                      XtVaSetValues( _main_widget, XmNmargin,
                                d, NULL );
54              }
55
56              //
57              //      Redefine Classname
58              //
59      virtual const char* class_name() const
60              {
61                      return("Separator");
62              }
63      };
64
65      #endif
```

B

MWL
CALCULATOR

This appendix contains the complete listing for the MWL/MVC version of the calculator program.

B.1 FILE: Calc

```
!
!      Resource File for Calulator Program
!
*background:                                        tan
*display.columns:                                   30
*keypad.y:                                          35
Calc.Calc.initDisplay:                              WELCOME
Calc.Calculator1.calcform.display.foreground:       red
Calc.Calculator2.calcform.display.foreground:       brown
Calc.Calculator1.calcform.keypad.C.foreground:      green
Calc.Calculator2.calcform.keypad.C.foreground:      yellow
```

B.2 FILE: `calc.cxx`

```
//
//                    TITLE:        CALC.CXX
//
//                    FUNCTION:     Member function definitions for
//                                  the Calc class.
//

#include "calc.h"


//
// Calc Class Resources
//
XtResource Calc::Calc_resources[] = {
     {
               "initDisplay",               // Resource Name
               "InitDisplay",               // Resource Class
               XmRString,                   // Data Type
               sizeof(String),              // Size of Resource
               XtOffset(Calc*, label),      // Offset of Resource
               XmRString,                   // Default Type
               (XtPointer)"0.00"            // Default Value
     }
};

Widget Calc::mwlMain( Widget parent )
{
     Widget w;

     //
     //     Set Window Title
     //
     setTitle( _widget_name );

     //
     //     Create Form Widget
     //
```

```
w = XmCreateForm( parent, "calcform", NULL, 0 );

//
// Add Destroy CB
//
registerDestroyCB();

//
// Query Resource DB
//
getComponentResources( Calc_resources,
      XtNumber(Calc_resources) );

//
//     Create CalcDisplay Object
//
display = new CalcDisplay( w, "display" );

//
//     Create Engine Object
//
engine  = new CalcEngine( disp, (void *)this );

//
//     Create Keypad
//
keypad = new Keypad( w, "keypad", engine );

//
//     Manage Sub-components
//
keypad->manage();
display->manage();

//
// Use a "Class" resource to initialize display
//
display->SetDisplay( label );
```

```
//
//      Return Widget to AppMgr
//
    return( w );
}

Calc::~Calc( Widget p )
{
//
//      Clean-up
//
    delete display;
    delete engine;
    delete keypad;
}
```

B.3 FILE: calc.h

```
//
//                  TITLE:      CALC.H
//
//                  FUNCTION:   Class definition for Calc -
//                              controlling class
//                              for the calcualtor program.
//

#ifndef _CALC_H_
#define _CALC_H_

#include <stdlib.h>
#include <string.h>

#include <Xm/Form.h>
#include <Xm/Text.h>
#include <Xm/TextF.h>
#include <Xm/RowColumn.h>
```

```
#include "mwlapp.h"
#include "mwlwin.h"
#include "pb.h"

#include "keypad.h"
#include "display.h"
#include "calc_eng.h"


class Calc : public MWLWindow {

private:

        Keypad      *keypad;        // Pointer to Keypad Object
        CalcEngine  *engine;        // Pointer to Engine Object
        CalcDisplay *display;       // Pointer to Display Object

        //
        //      Resource Array for Class Resources
        //
        char*  label;
        static XtResource Calc_resources[];

        //
        // DISP():
        //      "Callback" Routine used as an
        //      interface to the Engine class.
        //
        //      disp() is called form a calculator
        //      and the call us passed on to a
        //      display object. The "callback" is
        //      "registered" in the constructor (Calc()).
        //
        static void disp( char *str, void *obj )
        {
                ((Calc *)obj)->display->SetDisplay( str );
        }
```

```
public:

    virtual ~Calc();                                        // Destructor

    Calc( char* name ) : MWLWindow(name) {};          // Constructor

    //
    //      Redefine Classname
    //
    virtual const char* class_name() const { return( "Calc" ); }

    //
    //      Build GUI
    //
    virtual Widget mwlMain( Widget );
};

#endif
```

B.4 FILE: calc_eng.cxx

```
//
//                       TITLE:      CALC_ENG.CXX
//
//                       FUNCTION:   This file implements the CalcEngine
//                                   class as a state machine.
//

#include "calc_eng.h"

//
// DIGIT():
//      Received a new digit from the keypad
//
void CalcEngine::digit( int d )
{
    char buf[ 256 ];
```

```
            sprintf( buf, "%1d", d );

            switch( state )
            {

            case INIT:
                    strcpy( str, buf );
                    display();
                    state = LEFT;
                    break;

            case LEFT:
                    strcat( str, buf );
                    display();
                    state = LEFT;
                    break;

            case OPERATOR:
                    strcpy( str, buf );
                    display();
                    state = LEFT;
                    break;

            case RIGHT:
                    strcat( str, buf );
                    display();
                    state = RIGHT;
                    break;
            }
}

//
// DECIMAL_POINT():
//     User entered a decimal point - only
//     allow 1 as part of a number.
//
void CalcEngine::decimal_point()
```

```
{
      switch( state )
      {

      case OPERATOR:
            strcpy( str, "." );
            display();
            state = RIGHT;
            break;

      case INIT:
            strcat( str, "." );
            display();
            state = RIGHT;
            break;

      case LEFT:
            strcat( str, "." );
            display();
            state = RIGHT;
            break;
      }
}

//
// CALC():
//    Perform indicated operation.
//
void CalcEngine::calc()
{
      double ans, operand1, operand2;

      switch( oper )
      {

      case ADD:
            if( s.pop(&operand2) != Stack::OK )
                  _error( "ADD: Missing Operand2" );
```

```
            if( s.pop(&operand1) != Stack::OK )
                    _error( "ADD: Missing Operand1" );
            ans = operand1 + operand2;
            s.push( ans );
            sprintf( str, "%f", ans );
            break;

    case SUB:
            if( s.pop(&operand2) != Stack::OK )
                    _error( "SUB: Missing Operand2" );
            if( s.pop(&operand1) != Stack::OK )
                    _error( "SUB: Missing Operand1" );
            ans = operand1 - operand2;
            s.push( ans );
            sprintf( str, "%f", ans );
            break;

    case MUL:
            if( s.pop(&operand2) != Stack::OK )
                    _error( "MUL: Missing Operand2" );
            if( s.pop(&operand1) != Stack::OK )
                    _error( "MUL: Missing Operand1" );
            ans = operand1 * operand2;
            s.push( ans );
            sprintf( str, "%f", ans );
            break;

    case DIV:
            if( s.pop(&operand2) != Stack::OK )
                    _error( "DIV: Missing Operand2" );
            if( s.pop(&operand1) != Stack::OK )
                    _error( "DIV: Missing Operand1" );
            if( operand2 == 0.0 )
                    _error( "DIV: Division by Zero" );
            ans = operand1 / operand2;
            s.push( ans );
            sprintf( str, "%f", ans );
            break;
    }
```

```
        display();
}


//
// ADD():
//      Add top two numbers on the stack - push answer
//
void CalcEngine::add()
{

        switch( state )
        {

        case LEFT:
        case RIGHT:
                s.push( atof(str) );
                calc();
                oper = ADD;
                state = OPERATOR;
                break;

        case OPERATOR:
                oper = ADD;
                break;
        }
}


//
// SUB():
//      Subtract top two numbers on the stack - push answer
//
void CalcEngine::sub()
{

        switch( state )
        {

        case LEFT:
```

```
        case RIGHT:
                s.push( atof(str) );
                calc();
                oper = SUB;
                state = OPERATOR;
                break;

        case OPERATOR:
                oper = SUB;
                break;
        }
}


//
// MUL():
//      Multiply top two numbers on the stack - push answer
//
void CalcEngine::mul()
{

        switch( state )
        {

        case LEFT:
        case RIGHT:
                s.push( atof(str) );
                calc();
                oper = MUL;
                state = OPERATOR;
                break;

        case OPERATOR:
                oper = MUL;
                break;
        }
}
```

```
//
// DIV():
//     Divide top two numbers on the stack - push answer
//     Ensure proper order of operands and check fo
//     division by zero.
//
void CalcEngine::div()
{

      switch( state )
      {

      case LEFT:
      case RIGHT:
            s.push( atof(str) );
            calc();
            oper = DIV;
            state = OPERATOR;
            break;

      case OPERATOR:
            oper = DIV;
            break;
      }
}


//
// EQUAL():
//     Perform indicated operation and display result
//
void CalcEngine::equal()
{
      switch( state )
      {

      case LEFT:
      case RIGHT:
            s.push( atof(str) );
```

```
                    calc();
                    oper  = EQUAL;
                    state = OPERATOR;
                    break;
            }
    }
```

B.5 FILE: calc_eng.h

```
//
//                  TITLE:      CALC_ENG.H
//
//                  FUNCTION:   Class definition for the "engine"
//                              portion of the calculator program.
//
//                              This class is implelmented as
//                              a "State Machine".
//

#ifndef _CalcEngine_H_
#define _CalcEngine_H_

#include <string.h>
#include <stdlib.h>

#include <iostream.h>              // For 'CERR'

#include "stack.h"

class CalcEngine {

private:

        //
        //      Internal State
        //
        enum State { INIT, LEFT, RIGHT, OPERATOR };
```

```
//
//      Operations
//
enum Operation { ADD, SUB, MUL, DIV, EQUAL, CLEAR };

Stack s;              // The calcualtor stack
State state;          // Master "state" variable
Operation oper;       // Operation flag
char str[ 100 ];      // Operand (display) value

//
//      These next two variables implement a kind
//      of "callback" mechinism for displaying
//      values computed by an engine.
//
void *cd;                         // Pointer to "client_data"
void (*display_function)( char *, void * );

//
// DISPLAY():
//      Display a new value. Implemented as a "callback"
//      so that Engine class is not tightly coupled to
//      some other class (e.g., CalcDisplay).
//
void display()
{
        //
        // If "callback" is registered, call routine
        // with display string and client data
        //
        if( display_function )            // (In)Sanity Check
              display_function( str, cd );
}



//
// CALC():
//      Calcualtion Routine: this performs all the basic
```

```
//        operations of the calculator (add, sub, ...)
//
void calc();

//
// RESET():
//        Reset the engine to the INIT state.
//
void reset()
{
        s.reset();
        oper = CLEAR;
        state = INIT;
        strcpy( str, "0.00" );
}


//
// ERROR():
//        Error handler. Should use Exceptions.
//
void _error( char *arg )
{
        cerr << "CalcEngine: **ERROR: " << arg << "\n";
        exit( -1 );
}


public:
    //
    // Constructor:
    //        Objects require two arguments: a display function
    //        to invoke and optional client data.
    //
    CalcEngine( void (*f)(char*, void*), void *client_data )
    {
            //
            // Save callback info
            //
```

```
                cd = client_data;
                display_function = f;

                //
                // Reset engine.
                //
                reset();
                display();
        }

        //
        // CLEAR():
        //      Clear engine.  Invoked when user press
        //      the "C" key on the keypad.
        //
        void clear()
        {
                reset();
                display();
        }

        //
        // Delcarations for "event" functions.
        //
        void add();
        void sub();
        void mul();
        void div();
        void equal();
        void digit( int );
        void decimal_point();
};

#endif
```

B.6 FILE: display.h

```
//
//              TITLE:  DISPLAY.H
//
//           FUNCTION:  Definition of the CalcDisplay Class.
//                      This version is derived from ScreenComponent.
//

#ifndef _CALC_DSIPLAY_H_
#define _CALC_DSIPLAY_H_

#include <Xm/Text.h>
#include <Xm/TextF.h>

#include "scrn_cmp.h"

class CalcDisplay : public ScreenComponent
{

public:

        //
        //      Constructor
        //
        CalcDisplay( Widget parent, char* name )
                : ScreenComponent(name)
        {
                //
                //      Create TextField Widget for Calulator Display
                //
                _main_widget = XtVaCreateWidget( name,

                        xmTextFieldWidgetClass,     parent,

                        XmNeditable,                False,
                        XmNcursorPositionVisible,   False,
                        XmNtraversalOn,             False,
```

```
        NULL );

        //
        // Add Destroy CB
        //
        registerDestroyCB();
}


//
// Redefine Classname
//
virtual const char* class_name() const
{
        return( "CalcDisplay" );
}


//
//      Displays string
//
void SetDisplay( char *str )
{
        register        i;
        short           cols;
        Arg             args[ 50 ];
        char            buf[ 256 ];

        //
        //      Determine Number of Columns
        //
        i = 0;
        XtSetArg( args[i], XmNcolumns, &cols ); i++;
        XtGetValues( _main_widget, args, i );

        //
        //      Format Buffer
        //
        sprintf( buf, "%*.*s", cols, cols, str );
```

```
                //
                //      Update Display
                //
                XmTextSetString( _main_widget, buf );
        }
};


#endif
```

B.7 FILE: keypad. cxx

```
//
//      TITLE:      KEYPAD.CXX
//
//      FUNCTION:   Functions to process keystrokes for the
//                  MWL calc program.
//


#include "cs.h"

#include "keypad.h"
#include "calc_eng.h"


//
//      Button Structure - Serves as "client data"
//      in callbacks.
//
struct button_struct {
        char        label;
        Keypad*     object;
        Widget      widget;
};


//
//      Button Labels
//
static char *cb[] =
```

```
{
     "1",   "2",   "3",   "/",
     "4",   "5",   "6",   "*",
     "7",   "8",   "9",   "-",
     "C",   "0",   "=",   "+"
};

//
//     Constructor
//
Keypad::Keypad( Widget parent, char* name, CalcEngine* e )
     : ScreenComponent(name)
{
     int           index, row, col;
     button_struct *buttons;

     //
     //     Save pointer to CalcEngine object
     //
     engine = e;

     //
     //     Create Form to Hold Calculator Buttons
     //
     _main_widget = XtVaCreateWidget( name,

          xmFormWidgetClass,   parent,

          XmNfractionBase,     4,

          XmNlength,           200,
          XmNwidth,            200,

          NULL );

     //
     // Add Destroy CB
     //
```

```
    registerDestroyCB();

    //
    //      Allocate storage for button callback structs
    //
    buttons = new button_struct[ max_rows * max_cols ];

    //
    //      Create Calculator Buttons
    //
    PushButton*       pb;
    CompoundString cs;
    for( row = 0; row < max_rows; row++ )
    {
            for( col = 0; col < max_cols; col++ )
            {
                    index = (row * max_cols) + col;


                    //
                    //      Create Button
                    //
                    pb = new PushButton( _main_widget, cb[index] );

                    //
                    //      Save state info in callback struct
                    //
                    buttons[index].object = this;
                    buttons[index].label = cb[index][0];
                    buttons[index].widget = pb->main_widget();

                    //
                    //      Set Constraints on button
                    //
                    cs = cb[index];                           // Label
                    XtVaSetValues( pb->main_widget(),

                            XmNlabelString,              (XmString)cs,
```

```
                        XmNtopAttachment,    XmATTACH_POSITION,
                        XmNtopPosition,      row,

                        XmNbottomAttachment, XmATTACH_POSITION,
                        XmNbottomPosition,   row+1,

                        XmNleftAttachment,   XmATTACH_POSITION,
                        XmNleftPosition,     col,

                        XmNrightAttachment,  XmATTACH_POSITION,
                        XmNrightPosition,    col+1,

                NULL );

                //
                //      Register Callback
                //
                pb->addActivateCallback( ButtonPressedCB,
                        (XtPointer)&buttons[index] );
                pb->manage();
            }
        }
}


//
//      Static Callback Function
//
void Keypad::ButtonPressedCB( Widget widget,
        XtPointer client_data, XtPointer call_data )
{
        button_struct *b = (button_struct *)client_data;

        Keypad *obj = (Keypad *)b->object;

        //
        //      Pass on callback to actuall object
        //
        obj->ButtonCB( b->widget, (XtPointer)b->label,
```

```
                (XtPointer)call_data );
}


//
//      Pushbutton Callback Routine
//
void Keypad::ButtonCB( Widget widget,
      XtPointer client_data, XtPointer call_data )
{
        char which_button = (char)client_data;


        switch( which_button )
        {
                case '0':
                case '1':
                case '2':
                case '3':
                case '4':
                case '5':
                case '6':
                case '7':
                case '8':
                case '9':
                    //
                    // Pass on digit to engine
                    //
                    engine->digit( which_button-'0' );
                    break;

                case 'C':
                    //
                    // Clear button pressed
                    //
                    engine->clear();
                    break;

                case '+':
```

```
                //
                // Add operation
                //
                engine->add();
                break;

        case '-':
                //
                // Subtraction operation
                //
                engine->sub();
                break;

        case '*':
                //
                // Multiply operation
                //
                engine->mul();
                break;

        case '/':
                //
                // Division operation
                //
                engine->div();
                break;

        case '=':
                //
                // Compute & display result
                //
                engine->equal();
                break;
        }
}
```

B.8 FILE: keypad.h

```
//
//          TITLE:      KEYPAD.H
//
//      FUNCTION:      Definition for the class Keypad.
//                     This version derived from the
//                     ScreenComponent class.
//

#ifndef _Keypad_H_
#define _Keypad_H_

#include <stdlib.h>
#include <string.h>

#include <Xm/Form.h>
#include <Xm/RowColumn.h>

#include "scrn_cmp.h"
#include "pb.h"

class CalcEngine;           // Declare Engine Class

//
//     Constants (for button alignment)
//
const int max_rows = 4;
const int max_cols = 4;

//
//     Class Definiton
//
class Keypad : public ScreenComponent {

private:

    CalcEngine *engine;       // Pointer to Engine Object
```

```
public:

        Keypad( Widget, char*, CalcEngine* );

        //
        //      Callback Functions
        //
        static void ButtonPressedCB( Widget, XtPointer, XtPointer );
        virtual void ButtonCB( Widget, XtPointer, XtPointer );

        //
        // Redefine Classname
        //
        virtual const char* class_name() const
        {
                return( "Keypad" );
        }
};

#endif
```

B.9 FILE: main.cxx

```
//
//                      TITLE: MAIN.CXX
//
//                      FUNCTION: Driving module for the MWL calc program
//


#include "calc.h"

MWLAppMgr calcMgr( "Calc" );

Calc calc1( "Calculator1" );
Calc calc2( "Calculator2" );
```

B.10 FILE: makefile

```
#
#
#=====================================================================
#                    MWL  Version  of  the  Calc  Program
#=====================================================================
#
          C++      =  g++
       C++ARGS     =  -c  -I../mwl/inc
          LD       =  g++
        LDARGS     =
       XWINLIBS    =  -lXm  -lXt  -lX11
        MWLLIB     =  ../mwl/lib/libMWL.a


        SOURCE     =  calc.cxx  calc_eng.cxx  keypad.cxx  main.cxx
       HEADERS     =  calc.h  calc_eng.h  display.h  keypad.h  stack.h
      RESOURCE     =  Calc
     MISCFILES     =  Makefile


          COPY     =  cp
         FILES     =  $(SOURCE)  $(HEADERS)  $(RESOURCE)  $(MISCFILES)
    TARGET_DIR     =  /c:/wrk/books/sig/src/linux/mwlcalc
        FLOPPY     =  /floppy/mwlcalc
       SAVEDIR     =  ./SAVE
       CFBHOME     =  /home/cfb


      CALCOBJS     =  main.o  calc_eng.o  keypad.o  calc.o

c:      calc
        calc


#
#       MWL  Verison  of  the  Calc  Program
#
main.o:         main.cxx  calc.h
        $(C++)  $(C++ARGS)  main.cxx
```

```
calc_eng.o:   calc_eng.cxx calc.h stack.h
        $(C++) $(C++ARGS) calc_eng.cxx

keypad.o:     keypad.cxx keypad.h
        $(C++) $(C++ARGS) keypad.cxx

calc.o:       calc.cxx calc.h
        $(C++) $(C++ARGS) calc.cxx

calc: $(CALCOBJS)
        $(LD) $(LDARGS) -o calc $(CALCOBJS) $(MWLLIB) $(XWINLIBS)
```

B.11 FILE: stack.h

```
//
//        TITLE:    STACK.H
//
//    FUNCTION:    Quick and dirty implementation of
//                 a Stack - for used as a part of
//                 the Engine class.
//

#ifndef _Stack_H_
#define _Stack_H_

#include <stdio.h>
#include <string.h>
#include <stdlib.h>

class Stack {

private:

        const int max_stack;      // Stack Size
        double *stack;            // The Stack
        int top;                  // Top of Stack
```

```
public:

    //
    //      Return Codes
    //
    enum StackVal { EMPTY, OVERFLOW, UNDERFLOW, OK, FAIL };

    //
    // Constructor:
    //      Initialize Stack
    //
    Stack( int stk_size = 200 )
    :       max_stack(stk_size)
    {
            stack = new double[ max_stack ];
            top = -1;
    }


    //
    // PUSH():
    //      Push a new value on the stack.
    //
    StackVal push( double v )
    {
            if( max_stack - top > 1 )
            {
                    stack[ ++top ] = v;
                    return( OK );
            } else {
                    return( OVERFLOW );
            }
    }


    //
    // POP():
    //      remove the top value from the stack.
    //
    StackVal pop( double *v )
```

```
        {
                if( top == -1 )
                        return( EMPTY );
                *v = stack[ top- ];
                return( OK );
        }


        //
        // PEEK():
        //      Return (w/o removing) top value.
        //
        StackVal peek( double *v )
        {
                if( top == -1 )
                        return( EMPTY );
                *v = stack[ top ];
                return( OK );
        }


        //
        // RESET():
        //      Reset stack to initial state.
        //
        StackVal reset()
        {
                top = -1;
                return( OK );
        }
};

#endif
```

BIBLIOGRAPHY

Adelson-Velskii, G.M., and Landis, E.M. "An Algorithm for the Organization of Information," *Dokl. Akad. Nauk SSSR, Mat,* 146(2):263–66, 1962.

Aho, A., and Ullman, J. *Principles of Compiler Design,* Reading, Mass.: Addison-Wesley, 1977.

Amble, O., and Knuth, D.E. "Ordered Hash Tables," *Comp. J.,* 18:135–42, 1975.

Augenstein, M., and Tenenbaum, A. "A Lesson in Recursion and Structured Programming," *SIGCSE Bulletin,* 8(1):17–23, February 1976.

Augenstein, M., and Tenenbaum, A. "Approaches to Based Storage in PL/I," *SIGCSE Bulletin,* 9(1):145–50, February 1977.

Auslander, M.A., and Strong, H.R. "Systematic Recursin Removal," *Communications of ACM,* 21(2), February 1978.

Bellman, R. *Dynamic Programming,* Princeton, N.J.: Princeton University Press, 1957.

Bender, E., Praeger, C., and Wormald, N. "Optimal Worst Case Trees," *Acta Informatica,* 24(4):475–89, August 1987.

Bentley, J. "Programming Pearls," *Communications of the ACM*, August 1983.

Bentley, J. "Programming Pearls: Thanks Heaps," *Communications of the ACM*, 28(3):245–50, March 1985.

Bentley, J. "Programming Pearls: How to Sort," *Communications of the ACM*, 27(4):287–91, April 1984.

Bentley, J. *Writing Efficient Programs,* Englewood Cliffs, N.J.: Prentice-Hall, 1982.

Berry, R., and Meekings, B. "A Style Analysis of C Programs," *Communications of the ACM,* 28(1):80–88, January 1988.

Berztiss, A.T. Data Structures, *Theory and Practice (2d ed.),* New York: Academy, 1977.

Bird, R.S. "Improving Programs by the Introduction of Recursion," *Communications of the ACM,* 20(11), November 1977.

Boothroyd, J. "Algorithm 201 (Shellsort)," *Communications of the ACM,* 6:445, 1963.

Borodin, A., and Munro, I. *Computational Complexity of Algebraic and Numeric Problems,* New York: American Elsevier, 1975.

Bowman, C.F. "Backtracking," *Dr. Dobbs Journal of Software Tools,* August 1987.

Bowman, C.F. "Backtracking," *Dr. Dobbs Journal of Software Tools,* August 1987.

Bowman, C.F. "Pattern Matching Using Finite State Machines," *Dr. Dobbs Journal of Software Tools,* October 1987.

Bowman, C.F. "On Selecting a Relational Database Management System," *White Paper, Hewlett-Packard,* May 1992.

Bowman, C.F. "Introduction to Object-Oriented Databases," *The Relational Journal—A Codd & Date Publication,* October 1992.

Bowman, C.F. "Introduction to Object-Oriented Databases—Part II," *The Relational Journal—A Codd & Date Publication,* December 1992.

Bowman, C.F. "So You Want to Go Object-Oriented," *Object Magazine,* May/June 1993.

Bowman, C.F. "Open Systems: Aspiring to Mediocrity?" *Object Magazine,* September/October 1993.

Bowman, C.F. "Objectifying X-Classes, Widgets, and Objects." *Object Magazine,* July/August 1993.

Bowman, C.F. "Why We Need Object-Oriented Systems," *Database Programming and Design,* February 1994.

Bowman, C.F. "Yes, We Do Windows," *The X Journal,* November/December 1994.

Bowman, C.F. "Hello World—X-Style," *The X Journal,* January/February 1995.

Bowman, C.F. "Quick on the Draw," *The X Journal,* March/April 1995.

Bowman, C.F. "Stretching a Point," *The X Journal,* May/June 1995.

Bowman, C.F. *Algorithms and Data Structure, An Approach in C,* New York: Harcourt Brace & Co., 1994

Boyer, R.S., and Moore, J.S. "A Fast String Searching Algorithm, *Communications of the ACM,* 20(10):762–72, 1977.

Brainerd, W.S., and Landweber, L.H. *Theory of Computation,* New York: Wiley, 1974.

Brown, P.J., "Programming and Documenting Software Projects," *ACM Comp. Surv.,* 6(4), December 1974.

Bruno, J., and Coffman, E.G., "Nearly Optimal Binary Search Trees," *Proc. IFIP Cong.* 71, North-Holland, Amsterdam, 1972, pp. 99–103.

Chang, H., and Iyengar, S. "Efficient Algorithms to Globally Balance a Binary Search Tree," *Communications of the ACM,* 27(7):695–702, July 1984.

Cheriton, D., and Tarjan, R. "Finding Minimum Spanning Trees," *SIAM Journal on Computing,* 5(4):724–42, December 1976.

Cichelli, R., "Minimal Perfect Hash Functions Made Simple," *Communications of the ACM,* 23(1):17–19, January 1980.

Cook, S.A., and Reckhow, R.A., "Time-Bounded Random Access Machines," *Journal of Computer and System Sciences,* 7:354–75, 1973.

Cranston, B., and Thomas, R. "A Simplified Recombination Scheme for the Fibonacci Buddy System," *Communications fo the ACM,* 18(6), June 1975.

Deo, N. *Graph Theory with Applications to Engineering and Computer Science,* Englewood Cliffs, N.J.: Prentice-Hall, 1974.

Dijkstra, E. "Notes on Structured Programming," in *Structured Programming*, New York, Academic, 1972.

Dobosiewicz, W. "Optimal Binary Search Trees," *International Journal of Computer Mathematics*, 19(2):135–51, 1986.

Earley, J. "Toward an Understanding of Data Structures," *Communications of the ACM*, 14(10):617–27, October 1971.

Elson, M. *Data Structures*, Palo Alto, Calif.: Science Research, 1975.

Elspas, B., Levitt, K.N., Waldinger, R.J., and Waksman, A. "An assessment of techniques for proving program correctness," *ACM Computing Surveys*, 4(2):97–147, 1972.

Er, M. "Efficient Generation of Binary Trees from Inorder-Postorder Sequences," *Information Sciences*, 40(2):175–81, 1986.

Even, S. *Graph Algorithms*, Potomac, Md., Computer Science, 1978.

Ferguson, P.M. *Motif Reference Manual*, O'Reilly & Associates, 1993.

Fischer, M.J. "Efficiency of Equivalence Algorithms." In R.E. Miller and J.W. Thatcher (eds.), *Complexity of Computer Computations*, pp. 153–67. New York, Plenum Press, 1972.

Fishman, G.S. *Concepts and Methods in Discrete Event Digital Simulation*, New York: Wiley, 1973.

Flajolet, P., and Prodinger, H. "Level Number Sequences for Trees," *Discrete Mathematics*, 65(2):149–56, June 1987.

Flores, I. *Computer Sorting*, Englewood Cliffs, N.J.: Prentice-Hall, 1969.

Flores, I. *Data Structure and Management*, Englewood Cliffs, N.J.: Prentice-Hall, 1970.

Floyd, R., and Rivest, R.L. "Algorithm 489 (Select)," *Communications of the ACM*, 18(3):173, March 1975.

Floyd R., and Rivest, R.L. "Expected Time Bounds for Selection," *Communications of the ACM*, 18(3), March 1975.

Ford, L.R., and Fulkerson, D.R. *Flows in Networks*, Princeton, N.J.: Princeton University Press, 1972.

Frederickson, G. "Data Structures for On-Line Updating of Minimum Spanning Trees, with Applications," *SIAM Journal on Computing*, 14(4):781–98, November 1985.

Frederickson, G. "Fast Algorithms for Shortest Paths in Planar Graphs with Applications," *SIAM Journal on Computing*, 16(6):1004–22, December 1987.

Frederickson, G. "Implicit Data Structures for Weighted Elements," *Information and Control*, 66(1–2):61–82, July–August 1985.

Gajewska, H., and Tarjan, R. "Deques with Heap Order," *Information Processing Letters*, 22(4):197–200, April 1986.

Gabow, H.N. "Two Algorithms for Generating Weighted Spanning Trees in Order," *SIAM Journal on Computing*, 6(1):139–150, 1977.

Galil, Z. "Real-time algorithms for string-matching and palindrome recognition," *Proceedings of the Fourth Annual ACM Symposium on Theory of Computing*, pp. 143–150, 1972.

Garey, M.R., Graham, R.L., and Ullman, J.D. "Worst-case analysis of memory allocation algorithms," *Proceedings of the Fourth Annual ACM Symposium on Theory of Computing*, pp. 143–150, 1972.

Gotlieb, C., and Gotlieb, I. *Data Types and Structures*, Englewood Cliffs, N.J.: Prentice-Hall, 1978.

Graham, R.L. "Bounds on multiprocessing timing anomalies," *SIAM Journal of Applied Math*, 17(2):416–29, 1969.

Gries, D. *Compiler Construction for Digital Computers*, New York: WIley, 1971.

Hancock, L., and Krieger, M. *The C Primer*, New York: McGraw-Hill, 1982.

Hantler, S.L., and King, J.C. "An Introduction to Proving the Correctness of Programs," *ACM Computing Surveys*, 8(3):331–53.

Harary, F. *Graph Theory*, Reading, Mass.: Addison-Wesley, 1969.

Harrisoin, M.C. *Data Structures and Programming*, Glenview, Ill.: Scott Foresman, 1973.

Heller, D., and Ferguson, P.M. *Motif Programming Manual (2d ed.)*, O'Reilly & Associates, 1994.

Hirschberg, D.S. "A Class of Dynamic Memory Allocation Algorithms," *Communications of the ACM,* 16(10):615–18, October 1973.

Hirschberg, D.S. "An Insertion Technique for One-Sided Height-Balanced Trees," *Communications of the ACM,* 19(8):August 1976.

Hoare, C.A.R. "Quicksort," *Comput. J.,* 5:10–15, 1962.

Hopcroft, J.E., and Tarjan, R.E. "Dividing a graph into triconnected components,"*SIAM Journal on Computing,* 2(3):135–57, 1973.

Hopcroft, J.E., and Ullman, J.D. *Formal Languages and Their Relations to Automata,* Reading, Mass.: Addison-Wesley, 1969.

Hopcroft, J.E., and Ullman, J.D. "Set merging algorithms," *SIAM Journal on Computing,* 2(4):294–303, 1973.

Horowitz, E., and Sahni, S. "Computing partitions with applications to the knapsack problem," *Journal of the ACM,* 21(2):277–92, 1974.

Horowitz, E., and Sahni, S. Fundamentals of Data Structures, Woodland Hills, Calif.: *Computer Science Press,* 1976.

Horowitz, E., and Sahni, S. Algorithms: Design and Analysis, Potomac, Md.: *Computer Science,* 1977.

Huang, J.C. "An Approach to Program Testing," *ACM Comput. Surv.,* 7(3), September 1975.

Huffman, D. "A Method for the Construction of Minimum Redundancy Codes," *Proc. IRE,* 40, 1952.

Jalote, P. "Synthesizing Implementations of Abstract Data Types from Axiomatic Specifications," *Software Practice and Experience,* 17(11):847–58, November 1987.

Johnson, D.S. "Fast allocation algorithms," *Proceedings of the Thirteenth Annual Symposium on Switching and Automata Theory,* pp. 144–54, 1972.

Johnson, D.S. "Worst-case behavior of graph coloring algorithms," *Proceedings of the Fifth Southeastern Conference on Combinatories, Graph Theory, and Computing,* pp. 513–28. Winnipeg, Canada: Utilitas Mathematica Publishing, 1974.

Jones, O. *Introduction to the X Window System,* Englewood Cliffs, N.J.: Prentice-Hall, 1989.

Kelley, A., and Pohl, I. *A Book on C (2d ed.)*, Benjamin Cummings, 1990.

Kernighan, B., and Ritchie, D. *The C Programming Language (2nd ed.)*, Englewood Cliffs, N.J.: Prentice-Hall, 1988.

Kernighan, B., and Plauger, R. *Software Tools*, Reading, Mass., Addison-Wesley, 1976.

Kernighan, B., and Plauger, P.J. *The Elements of Programming Style*, New York, McGraw-Hill, 1970.

Kernighan, B., and Plauger, R. *The Elements of Programming Style (2d ed.)*, New York, McGraw-Hill, 1978.

Kernighan, B., and Ritchie, D. *The C Programming Language (2d ed.)*, Englewood Cliffs, N.J., Prentice-Hall Software Series, 1988.

Knowlton, K. "A Fast Storage Allocator," *Communications of the ACM*, 8(10), October 1965.

Knuth, D. "Optimum Binary Search Trees," *Acta Informatica*, 1:14–25, 1971.

Knuth, D. *The Art of Computer Programming, Volume III: Sorting and Searching*. Reading, Mass., Addison-Wesley, 1973.

Knuth, D. "Structured Programming with Goto Statements," *ACM Comput. Sur.*, 6(4):261, December 1974.

Knuth, D. *Fundamental Algorithms (2d ed.)*, Reading, Mass.: Addison-Wesley, 1973.

Knuth, D. *Sorting and Searching*, Reading, Mass.: Addison-Wesley, 1973.

Knuth, D. "Big Omicron and Big Omega and Big Theta." *SIGACT News*, 8(2):18–24, 1976.

Knuth, D. "The Complexity of Songs," *SIGACT News*, 9(2):17–24, 1977.

Kosaraju, S.R. "Insertions and Deletions in One-Sided Height Balanced Trees," *Communications of the ACM*, 21(3), March 1978.

Kruse, R. *Data Structures and Program Design (2d ed.)*, Englewood Cliffs, N.J.: Prentice-Hall, 1987.

Larson, P. "Dynamic Hash Tables," *Communications of the ACM*, 31(4):446–57, April 1988.

Ledgard, H., with Tauer,J. *C with Excellence*, Indianapolis, Ind.: Hayden Books, 1987.

Lewis, T.G., and Smith, M.Z. *Applying Data Structures*, Boston: Houghton Mifflin, 1976.

Lockyer, K.G. *An Introduction to Critical Data Analysis*, London: Pitman, 1964.

Lockyer, K.G. *Critical Path Analysis: Problems and Solutions*, Londong, Pitman, 1966.

Lodi, E., and Luccio, F. "Split Sequence Hash Search," *Infomration Processing Letters*, 20(3):131–36, April 1985.

Lum, U.Y. "General Performance Analysis of Key-to-Address Transformation Methods using an Abstract File Concept," *Communications of the ACM*, 16(10):603, October 1973.

Lum, U.Y., and Yuen, P.S.T., and Dodd, M. "Kety-to-Address Transform Techniques: A Fundamental Performance Study on Large Existing Formatted Files," *Communications of the ACM*, 14:228, 1971.

Maekinen, E. "On the Rotation Distance of Binary Tresst," *Information Processing Letters*, 26(5):271–72, January 1988.

Manna, Z., and Shamir, A. "The Optimal Approach to Recursive Programs," *Communications of the ACM*, 20(11), November 1977.

Martin, J. *Data Types and Data Structures*, Englewood Cliffs, N.J.: Prentice-Hall 1986.

Maurer, H.A., and Williams, M.R. *A Collection of Programming Problems and Techniques*, Englewood Cliffs, N.J.: Prentice-Hall 1972.

Merritt, S. "An Inverted Taxonomy of Sorting Algorithms," *Communications of the ACM*, 28(1):96–99, January 1985.

Millspaugh, A. *Business Programming in C*, The Dryden Press, 1993.

Morgan, C. "Data Refinement by Miracles," *Information Processing Letters*, 26(5)243–46, January 1988.

Morris, R. "Scatter Storage Techniques," *Communications of the ACM*, 11(1):38–44, January 1968.

Morris, J.H., Jr., and Pratt, V.R. "A Linear Pattern-Matching Algorithm," *Tech. Rep.,* 40. University of California, Berkeley, 1970.

Nye, A., and O'Reilly, T. *X Toolkit Intrinsics Programming Manual,* O'Reilly & Associates, 1990.

Nye, A. *Xlib Programming Manual,* O'Reilly & Associates, 1992.

Nye, A. *Xlib Reference Manual (3d ed.),* O'Reilly & Associates, 1992.

Nye, A., and O'Reilly, T. *X Toolkit Intrinsics Programming Manual (2d ed.),* O'Reilly & Associates, 1992.

Quericia, V. and O'Reilly, T. *X Window System User's Guide,* O'Reilly & Associates, 1993.

Tarjan, R.E. "Depth-First Search and Linear Graph Algorithms," *SIAM Journal on Computing,* 1(2):146–60, 1972.

Tarjan, R.E. "On the Efficiency of a Good but Not Linear Set Union Algorithm," *Journal of the ACM,* 22(2):215–25, 1975.

Tarjan, R.E. *Data Structures and Network Algorithms,* SIAM, 1983.

Tarjan, R.E. "Algorithm Design," *Communications of the ACM,* 30(3):204–12, March 1987.

Tenenbaum, A. "Simulations of Dynamic Sequential Search Algorithms," *Communications of the ACM,* 21(9), September 1978.

Tenenbaum, A., and Widder, E. "A Comparison of First-Fit Allocation Strategies," *Proc. ACM 78,* December 1978.

Tenenbaum, A., and Augenstein, M. *Data Structures Using Pascal (2nd ed.),* Englewood Cliffs, N.J.: Prentice-Hall, 1976.

Tsakalidis, A. "AVL Trees for Localized Search," *Informations and Control.* 67(1–3):173–94, October–December 1985.

Tucker, A. *Applied Combinatories.* New York: Wiley, 1980.

Van Emden, M.H. "Increasing Efficiency of Quicksort," *Communications of the ACM,* 13:563–67, 1970.

Van Tassel, D. *Program Style, Design, Debugging, and Testing (2nd ed.).* Englewood Cliffs, N.J.: Prentice-Hall, 1978.

Vuillemin, J. "A Unifying Look at Data Structures," *Communications of the ACM,* 23(4):229–39, April 1980.

Wegner,P. "Modifications of Aho and Ullman's correctness proof of Warshaw's algorithm," *SIGACT News,* 6(1):32–35, 1974.

Weinberg, G. *The Psychology of Computer Programming.* New York: Van Nostrand, 1971.

Williams, J. "Algorithm 232 (Heapsort)," *Communications of the ACM,* 7(6)34–48, June 1964.

Wirth, N., "Program Development by Stepwise Refinement," *Communications of the ACM,* 14(4):221–27, April 1971.

Wirth, N. *Systematic Programming: An Introduction.* Englewood Cliffs, N.J.: Prentice-Hall 1973.

Wirth, N. "On the Composition of Well-Structured Programs," *ACM Comm. Surv.,* 6(4), December 1974.

Wirth, N. *Algorithms + Data Structures = Programs.* Englewood Cliffs, N.J.: Prentice-Hall 1976.

Wood, D. "The Towers of Brahma and Hanoi Revisited," *Journal of Recreational Mathematics,* 14:17–24, (1981–2).

Yao, A.C. "On the average behavior of set merging algorithms," *Proceedings of the Eighth Annual ACM Symposium on Theory of Computing,* pp. 192–95, 1976.

Young, D.A. *The X Window System.* Englewood Cliffs, N.J.: Prentice-Hall, 1990.

Yourdon, E. *Techniques of Program Structure and Design.* Englewood Cliffs, N.J.: Prentice-Hall, 1975.

INDEX